PENGUI

THE PENGUIN DICTIC

James Cochrane was born in Edinburgh and educated there and at Cambridge. He joined Penguin Books as an editor in 1961 and has worked in publishing ever since. His own publications include *The Penguin Book of American Short Stories*, *Rudyard Kipling: Selected Verse*, *The Great British Song Book* (with Kingsley Amis) and *Stipple, Wink and Gusset*.

JAMES COCHRANE

———————

THE PENGUIN
DICTIONARY GAME
DICTIONARY

PENGUIN BOOKS

PENGUIN BOOKS

Published by the Penguin Group
Penguin Books Ltd, 27 Wrights Lane, London W8 5TZ, England
Penguin Books USA Inc., 375 Hudson Street, New York, New York 10014, USA
Penguin Books Australia Ltd, Ringwood, Victoria, Australia
Penguin Books Canada Ltd, 10 Alcorn Avenue, Toronto, Ontario, Canada M4V 3B2
Penguin Books (NZ) Ltd, 182–190 Wairau Road, Auckland 10, New Zealand

Penguin Books Ltd, Registered Offices: Harmondsworth, Middlesex, England

First published by W. and R. Chambers Ltd 1988
Published in Penguin Books 1992
1 3 5 7 9 10 8 6 4 2

Preface

The Penguin Dictionary Game Dictionary is a collection of odd, curious and unfamiliar words culled from *Chambers English Dictionary,* the favourite source of such words for players of the Dictionary Game. Readers of this preface who are unfamiliar with the Dictionary Game will find its very simple rules explained below. Those who are already experienced players may well agree that the one unsatisfactory thing about this most satisfying of word games is the time spent looking through a conventional dictionary for suitable words. The purpose underlying this dictionary is to reduce that time considerably, and thus allow more rounds of the game itself to be played in the course of an evening.

The words included here are given with pronunciation guides and, in most cases, with their etymologies. Although such information is not, strictly speaking, relevant to the game it was felt that players are likely to be lovers of curious words as well as of the mischief and deception which give the game its special flavour. Again, definitions are given in full for the same reason, and players may want to exercise reasonable discretion in occasionally shortening and simplifying them.

How to play the Dictionary Game

Materials required: a stock of paper and pens or pencils for each player and one copy of the Dictionary Game Dictionary or of any good dictionary.

Number of players: three or more.

One player is designated scorer.

Decide by whatever means you prefer which player is to be first Dictionary Holder (henceforth referred to as the Holder).

The Holder takes the Dictionary, selects a word and reads it out to the other players.

The players then write invented definitions for the word selected on their pieces of paper and pass them, folded, to the Holder.

The Holder writes the correct definition on his paper (ignoring information given in italics and in brackets which, as explained above, is included for reasons extraneous to the game).

If only a few players are available a possible variant is that the Holder writes his own invented definition as well as the correct one. In such a case he scores as a player as well as a Holder (see 'How to score' below).

When all the definitions have been handed to the Holder he reads out all the definitions, including the correct one, in random order.

Starting with the player on the Holder's left, and proceeding clockwise, the players then state which definition they believe is the correct one.

The Holder then announces the correct definition, the hand is scored, and the Dictionary is passed to the player on the Holder's left, who becomes the next Holder.

How to score

Scoring systems vary. The one given here has the advantage of simplicity but is also designed to favour the skilful deceiver:

for each other player deceived by a player's invented definition the inventor receives 2 points a player who recognises the correct definition when the definitions are read out by the Holder receives 1 point

if no player recognises the correct definition when they are read out the Holder receives 1 point

(If, as described above, the Holder has also written his own invented definition, he also receives 2 points for every player deceived by it).

Some hints on play

Develop a 'dictionary style' for your invented definitions, especially one that mimics the style of the dictionary you are using.

Memorise a few technical – e.g. geological or botanical – terms and drop them into your definitions.

Vary the style of your definitions – e.g. between short and long, simple and technical – so that your 'handwriting' is not too easily recognised by other players.

As a cunning ploy, occasionally choose your own invented definition when the definitions are read out, especially if you are close to the Holder's left. By doing so you will of course lose one point, but you may gain several more by deceiving other players.

Always remember: the true definitions you will find in Chambers Dictionary Game Dictionary are often more extraordinary than anything you can invent.

The Reverse Dictionary Game

As an occasional change from the Dictionary Game try playing in reverse.

In the Reverse Game the Holder reads out a definition from the Dictionary and writes down the word to which it corresponds, while the players produce their invented words and pass them to the Holder. Play then proceeds and the game is scored in exactly the same way as for the Dictionary Game.

After a few rounds of the Reverse Game players may well agree that it is surprisingly difficult to invent words and that by comparison composing definitions is an easy and relaxing business.

A final word

The compiler of Chambers Dictionary Game Dictionary has been playing the Dictionary Game ever since he was first introduced to it in the 1950s and has met enthusiasts for it in many parts of Great Britain and the USA. He has however found practically no references to the game in print, from which he concludes that its origins are unknown and that it has become as widely known as it now is purely as the result of word-of-mouth transmission. He would like to make it clear that the rules of play given here are simply the ones he is familiar with and are not intended to represent an orthodoxy either in procedure or in scoring.

Both the compiler and the publishers hope that publication of the Dictionary will widen knowledge of a game which combines bluff, deception, inventiveness and love of words in a unique way, as well as bringing to existing players the convenience of a dedicated source of words to play with.

A

aasvogel

äs′fōōl (S.Afr.), *äs′fō-gəl,* n.

a South African vulture.

[Du. *aas*, carrion, *vogel*, bird.]

aba, abba

a′bə, or **abaya** *a-bā′yə,* ns.

a Syrian cloth, of goat's or camel's hair, usually striped: an outer garment made of it.

[Ar. ʽ*abā,* ʽ*abāya.*]

abaca

ä-bä-kä′, n.

a plantain grown in the Philippine Islands: its fibre, called Manila hemp.

[Tagálog.]

abactor

ab-ak′tər, n.

a cattle thief.

[L.L.]

abature

ab′ə-chər, n.

the trail through underwood beaten down by a stag.

[Fr.]

abb

ab, n.

properly woof- or weft-yarn, but sometimes warp-yarn.

[O.E. *āb, āweb* — pfx, *ā,* out, *webb,* web.]

abele

ə-bēl′, ā′bl, n.

the white poplar-tree.

[Du. *abeel* — O.Fr. *abel, aubel* — L.L. *albellus* — L. *albus,* white.]

aberdevine

ab-ər-di-vīn′, n.

a bird-fancier's name for the siskin.

[Ety. uncertain.]

aboideau, aboiteau

ä-bwä-dō, -tō, ns.

a tide-gate.

[Canadian Fr.]

abolla

ab-ol′ä, n.

a Roman military cloak.

[L.]

abomasum

ab-ō-mā′səm, n.

the fourth or true stomach of ruminants, lying close to the omasum. — Also **abomā′sus**.

[L. *ab*, away from, *omāsum*, tripe, paunch (a Gallic word).]

absquatulate

ab-skwot′ū-lāt, (*facet.*; *U.S.*) v.i.

to decamp: to squat.

abthane

ab′thān, n.

a monastic territory of the Columban church.

[L.L. *abthania* — Gael. *abdhaine*, abbacy.]

abuna

ä-bōō′nə, n.

an Ethiopian patriarch.

[Ethiopian, — Ar., our father.]

acajou

ak′ə-zhōō, -zhōō′, n.

the cashew tree or its fruit or gum: a kind of mahogany.

acapnia

ə-kap′ni-ə, n.

deficiency of carbon dioxide.

[Gr. *a-*, priv., *kapnos*, smoke.]

acates

ə-kāts′, (*obs.*) n.pl.

bought provisions.

n. **acāt′er, -our** (*obs.*) an officer who bought provisions, a caterer.

[O.Fr. *acat* — L.L. *accaptāre*, to acquire — L. *ad*, to, *captāre*, to seize.]

accinge

ak-sinj′, (*fig.*) v.t.

to gird.

[L. *ad*, to, *cingĕre*, to gird.]

accipitrine

ak-sip′i-trīn, -trin, adj.

pertaining to hawks.

[L. *accipiter*, a hawk.]

accloy

ə-kloi′, (*obs.*) v.t.

to prick or lame with a horseshoe nail: to clog, choke or encumber (*Spens.*): to sate, cloy (*Spens.*).

achkan

äch′kən, n.

in India, a knee-length coat with a high collar, buttoned all the way down.

[Hind. *ackan*.]

acoemeti

a-sem′i-tī, n.pl.

an Eastern order of monks (5th–6th cent.), who by

2

alternating choirs kept divine service going on day and night. [Latinised pl. of Gr. *akoimētos*, sleepless — *a-*, priv., and *koimaein*, to put to sleep.]

acouchy

ə-koo'shē, n.
a kind of agouti.
[Tupí *acuchy*.]

acroamatic, -al

ak-rō-ə-mat'ik, -əl, adjs.
oral (not published): esoteric.
[Gr. *akroāmatikos* — *akroāma*, anything to be listened to — *akroaesthai*, to listen.]

acronychal

ə-kron'ik-əl, adj.
at nightfall (of the rising or setting of stars).
adv. **acron'ychally.**
[Gr. *akronychos*, at nightfall — *akron*, point, *nychos, -eos*, night.]

acrospire

ak'rō-spīr, (*bot.*) n.
the first leaf that sprouts from a germinating seed.
[M.E. *akerspire* — O.E. *æhher*), ear.]

acrotism

ak'rot-izm, (*med.*) n.
absence of pulsation.
[Gr. *a-*, priv., *krotos*, sound made by striking.]

acton

ak'tən, **ha(c)queton** *hak'(i)tən*, ns.
a stuffed jacket worn under a coat of mail.
[O.Fr. *auqueton* — Sp. — Ar. *al qūtun*, the cotton.]

addax

ad'aks, n.
a large African antelope with long slightly twisted horns.
[L., from an African word.]

adelantado

a-de-lan-tä'dō, n.
a grandee: a provincial governor: — pl. **adelanta'dos.**
[Sp.]

adespota

ad-es'pot-a, n.pl.
anonymous works.
[Gr. *a-*, priv., and *despotēs*, master.]

adharma

ə-där'mä, ə-dûr'mə, n.
unrighteousness — opposite of **dharma.**
[Sans.]

adiabatic

ad-i-ə-bat'ik, adj.
without transference of heat.
adv. **adiabat'ically.**
[Gr. *a-*, priv., *dia*, through, *batos*, passable.]

adiaphoron

ad-i-af'ə-ron, n.

in theology and ethics, a thing indifferent — any tenet or usage considered non-essential: — pl. **adiaph'ora**.
ns. **adiaph'orism** tolerance or indifference in regard to non-essential points in theology: latitudinarianism;
adiaph'orist.
adj. **adiaph'orous**.
[Gr., from *a-*, priv., *diaphoros*, differing — *dia*, apart, *pherein*, to carry.]

aerenchyma

ā-(ə)r-eng'ki-mə, (bot.) n.
respiratory tissue.
adj. **aerenchymatous** (*-kī'*).
[Gr. *āēr*, air, *en*, in, *chyma*, that which is poured.]

aethrioscope

ē'thri-ō-skōp, n.
an instrument for measuring the minute variations of temperature due to the condition of the sky.
[Gr. *aithriā*, the open sky, *skopeein*, to look at.]

affenpinscher

af'en-pinsh-ər, n.
a small dog related to the Brussels griffon, having tufts of hair on the face.
[Ger., — *Affe*, monkey, *Pinscher*, terrier.]

affreightment

ə-frāt'mənt, n.
the hiring of a vessel.
[Fr. *affrétement* (*affrètement*), remodelled upon *freight.*]

afrit, afreet

ä-frēt', af'rēt, n.
an evil demon in Arabian mythology.
[Ar.'*ifrīt*, a demon.]

agalloch

ə-gal'ək, n.
eaglewood.
[Gr. *agallochon*, a word of Eastern origin.]

agalmatolite

ag-al-mat'ə-līt, n.
material of various kinds (steatite, pyrophyllite, etc.) from which the Chinese cut figures.
[Gr. *agalma, -atos*, a statue (of a god), *lithos*, stone.]

agami

ag'ə-mi, n.
the golden-breasted trumpeter, a crane-like bird of South America.
[Carib name.]

aggri, aggry

ag'ri, adj.
applied to ancient West African variegated glass beads.
[Origin unknown.]

agila

ag'i-lä, n.

eaglewood.

[Port. *águila,* eaglewood, or Sp. *águila,* eagle .]

agist

ə-jist', v.t.

to take in to graze for payment: to charge with a public burden. ns. **agist'ment** the action of agisting: the price paid for cattle pasturing on the land: a burden or tax; **agist'or, agist'er** an officer in charge of cattle agisted.

[O.Fr. *agister* — *à* (L. *ad*) to, *giste,* resting-place — *gésir,* from a freq. of. L. *jacēre,* to lie.]

agonothetes

ə-gō-nə-thē'tēz,
a-gō'no-thet-ās, (Gr.) n.

a judge or director of public games.

agraffe

ə-graf', n.

a hooked clasp.

[Fr. *agrafe* — *à,* to, *grappe* — L.L. *grappa* — O.H.G. *chrapfo* (Ger. *krappen*), hook.]

aguacate

ä-gwä-kä'tä, n.

the avocado pear.

[Sp., — Nahuatl *ahuacatl.*]

ahimsa

ə-him'sə, n.

duty of sparing animal life: non-violence.

[Sans. *ahiṁsā.*]

aidos,

ī'dōs, (Gr.) n.

shame, modesty.

aikido

ī-kē'dō, n.

a Japanese combative sport using locks and pressure against joints.

[Jap., — *ai,* harmonise, *ki,* breath, spirit, *dō,* way, doctrine.]

ailanto

ā-lan'tō, n.

the tree of heaven (genus *Ailantus;* family *Simarubaceae*), a lofty and beautiful Asiatic tree: — pl. **-s.** — Also **ailan'thus.**

[Amboyna (Moluccas) name *aylanto,* tree of the gods.]

ajowan

aj'ō-wən, or **ajwan** *aj'wən,* ns.

a plant of the caraway genus yielding ajowan oil and thymol.

[Origin uncertain.]

alalagmos

a-la-lag'mos, (Gr.) n.

a war-cry, cry of *alalai*.

alameda

a-la-mā'dä, n.

a public walk, esp. between rows of poplars.

[Sp. *álamo*, poplar.]

alastrim

ə-las'trim, n.

a mild form of smallpox or a similar disease.

[Port.]

albacore

al'bə-kōr, -kör, n.

a large tunny: a species of mackerel (*S.Afr.*). — Also written **al'bicore.**

[Port. *albacor* — Ar. *al*, the, *bukr*, young camel.]

albarello

al-bə-rel'ō, al-bar-el'lō, n.

a majolica jar used for dry drugs: — pl. **albarell'os, albarel'li** (*-lē*).

[It.]

albata

al-bā'tə, n.

a variety of German silver.

[L. *albāta* (*fem.*), whitened — *albus*, white.]

albespyne, albespine

al'bə-spīn, (*arch.*) n.

hawthorn.

[O.Fr. *albespine* (Fr. *aubépine*) — L. *alba spīna*, white thorn.]

albricias

al-brē-thē'as, (Sp.) n.

a reward to the bearer of good news.

alcarraza

al-ka-ra'tha, (Sp.) n.

a porous vessel for cooling water.

alcatras

al'kə-tras, n.

a name applied to several large water birds, as the pelican, gannet, frigate bird, albatross.

[Sp. *alcatraz*, pelican.]

alcorza

al-kör'tha, (Sp.) n.

a kind of sweetmeat: icing.

aldea

al-dā'a, (Sp.) n.

a village, hamlet.

alectryon

a-lek'tri-ōn, (Gr.) n.

a cock.

alegar

al' or *āl'i-gər,* n.

sour ale, or vinegar made from it.

[**ale,** with termination as **vinegar.**]

alepine

al'i-pēn, n.

a mixed fabric of wool and silk or mohair and cotton.

[Perh. *Aleppo.*]

alerion, allerion

a-lē'ri-ən (*her.*) n.

an eagle displayed, without feet or beak.

[Fr.]

aleurone

a-lū'rōn, n.

a protein found in some seeds. — Also **aleu'ron** (*-on, -ən*).

[Gr. *aleuron,* flour.]

alevin

al'i-vin, n.

a young fish, esp. a salmonid.

[Fr., — O.Fr. *alever,* to rear — L. *ad,* to, *levāre,* to raise.]

alfaquí

al-fa-kē', (Sp.) n.

a Muslim expounder of the law.

alférez

al-fā'rāth, (Sp.) n.

a standard-bearer.

alforja

al-för'hha, (Sp.) n.

a saddle-bag: a baboon's cheek-pouch.

algarroba

al-ga-rō'bə, n.

the carob: the mesquite: the fruit of either. — Also **algarō'ba, algarrō'bŏ** (pl. **-os**).

[Sp. *algarroba, -o.* — Ar. *al kharrūbah.*]

algolagnia

al-gō-lag'ni-ə, n.

sexual pleasure got from inflicting or suffering pain.

[Gr. *algos,* pain, *lagneiā,* lust.]

alguazil

al-gwa-zil', **alguacil** *äl-gwä-thēl',* n.

in Spain, an officer who makes arrests, etc.

[Sp. (now) *alguacil* — Ar. *al-wazīr.]*

algum

al'gəm, (B.) n.

a wood imported into ancient Palestine, prob. red sandalwood. — Also **al'mug.**

[Heb. *algūm.*]

alkahest, alcahest
al'kə-hest, n.
the universal solvent of the
alchemists.
[App. a sham Ar. coinage of
Paracelsus.]

allenarly
al-en'ər-li (*obs.* except in Scots
law) adv.
solely, only.

alliaceous
al-i-ā'shəs, adj.
garlic-like.
[L. *allium,* garlic.]

allice, allis
al'is, n.
a species of shad. — Also **allis
shad.**
[L. *alōsa, alausa,* shad.]

allonge
al-ōzh, n.
a piece of paper attached to a
bill of exchange for further
endorsement.
[Fr.]

almirah
al-mīr'ə, n.
a cupboard, wardrobe, cabinet.
[Hindi *almārī* — Port. *almario* —
L. *armārium.*]

alnage
öl'nij, n.
measurement by the ell:
inspection of cloth.
n. **al'nager** an official
inspector of cloth.
[O.Fr. *aulnage* — *aulne,* ell.]

alpargata
äl-pär-gä'tä, n.
a light sandal with rope or hemp
sole.
[Sp.]

alpeen
al'pēn, n.
a cudgel.
[Ir. *ailpín.*]

alsike
al'sik, n.
a white or pink-flowered clover.
[From *Alsike,* near Uppsala, a
habitat.]

althorn
alt'hörn, n.
a tenor saxhorn.

altrices
al-trī'sēz, n.pl.
birds whose young are hatched
very immature and have to be
fed in the nest by the parents.
adj. **altricial** (*-trish'l*).
[L. *altrīcēs* (pl. of *altrix*),
feeders, nurses.]

aludel

al'ōō-dəl, -ū-, n.

a pear-shaped pot used in sublimation.

[Sp., — Ar. *al-uthāl.*]

alure

al'yər, (*obs.*) n.

a walk behind battlements: a gallery: a passage.

[O.Fr. *aleure* — *aller*, to go.]

alvine

al'vīn, adj.

of the belly.

[L. *alvīnus* — *alvus*, belly.]

amadavat

am-ə-də-vat', n.

an Indian songbird akin to the weaver-birds. — Now usu. **avadavat'.**

[From *Ahmadabad,* whence they were sent to Europe.]

amaracus

ə-mar'ə-kəs, n.

marjoram.

[L. *amāracus* — Gr. *amārakos.*]

amaurosis

am-ö-rō'sis, n.

blindness without outward change in the eye.

adj. **amaurotic** (*-rot'ik*).

[Gr. *amaurōsis* — *amauros*, dark.]

amban

am'ban, n.

a Chinese resident official in a dependency.

[Manchu, minister.]

ambatch

am'bach, n.

a pith-tree.

[Apparently native name.]

ambitty

am-bit'i, adj.

devitrified.

[Fr. *ambité*, of obscure origin.]

ambo

am'bō, n.

an early Christian raised reading-desk or pulpit: — pl. **am'bōs, ambō'nes** (*-nēz*).

[L.L. *ambō* — Gr. *ambōn, -ōnos*, crest of a hill, pulpit.]

ambry, aumbry, almery,

Scot. **awmry, awmrie** *am', öm'(b)ri*, ns.

a recess for church vessels: a cupboard: a pantry: a dresser: a safe.

[O.Fr. *almerie* — L. *armārium*, a chest, safe — *arma*, arms, tools.]

amildar

am'il-där, n.

a factor or manager in India: a collector of revenue amongst the Mahrattas.

[Hind. '*amaldār* — Ar. '*amal*, work, Pers. *dār*, holder.]

amorce

ə-mörs', n.

a percussion cap for a toy pistol.

[Fr., priming.]

amphigory

am'fi-gə-ri, n.

nonsense verse.

[Fr. *amphigouri*: origin unknown.]

amrit

am'rət, n.

a sacred sweetened water used in the Sikh baptismal ceremony: the ceremony itself.

[Punjabi, — Sans. *amr̤ta*, immortal.]

amrita

am-rē'tä, n.

the drink of the Hindu gods. n. **amritattva** (*am-rē-tät'vä*) immortality.

[Sans. *amr̤ta*, immortal; cf. Gr. *ambrotos*.]

anadem

an'ə-dem, n.

a fillet, chaplet, or wreath.

[Gr. *anadēma* — *ana*, up, and *deein*, to bind.]

anadiplosis

an-ə-di-plō'sis, n.

rhetorical repetition of an important word (or sometimes phrase).

[Gr. *anadiplōsis* — *ana*, back, *diploein*, to double.]

ananke

a-nangk'ē, (Gr. *anankē*) n.

necessity.

anaplerosis

an-ə-plē-rō'sis, n.

the filling up of a deficiency. adj. **anaplerŏt'ic.**

[Gr. *anaplērōsis* — *ana*, up, and *plēroein*, to fill.]

ancome

an'kəm, (*obs.* or *dial.*) n.

a sudden inflammation: a whitlow.

[Cf. **oncome, income.**]

anele

ə-nēl', v.t.

to anoint (*arch.*): to administer extreme unction to.

[O.E. *an*, on, *ele*, oil .]

anetic

a-net'ik, (med.) adj.
soothing.
[L. *aneticus* — Gr. *anetikos,*
abating sickness.]

angary

ang'gər-i, n.
a belligerent's right to seize and
use neutral or other property
(subject to compensation).
[Gr. *angareiā,* forced service —
angaros, a courier — a Persian
word — Assyrian *agarru,* hired
labourer.]

angek(k)ok

ang'gi-kok, n.
an Eskimo sorcerer or shaman.
[Eskimo.]

angwantibo

ang-wän'ti-bō, n.
a small W. African lemur: — pl.
angwan'tibos.
[W. African word.]

anicut, annicut

an'i-kut, n.
a dam.
[Tamil *anaikattu.*]

anil

an'il, n.
indigo, plant or dye.
[Port. *anil* — Ar. *an-nil,* the
indigo plant — Sans. *nīlī,*
indigo.]

anker

angk'ər, n.
an old measure for wines and
spirits used in Northern Europe,
varying considerably — that of
Rotterdam $8\frac{1}{2}$ imperial gallons.
[Du.]

ankh

angk, n.
an ansate cross — T-shaped
with a loop above the horizontal
bar — the symbol of life.
[Egypt., life.]

anlace, anelace

an'las, -ləs, n.
a short two-edged tapering
dagger.
[Ety. unknown.]

annat

an'ət, n., **annates** *an'āts,* n.pl.,
the first-fruits, or one year's
income of a benefice, paid to
the Pope (in England from 1535
to the crown, from 1703 to
Queen Anne's bounty;
extinguished or made
redeemable 1926): **annat** or
ann (*Scots law*) from 1672 to
1925 the half-year's stipend
payable after a parish minister's
death to his widow or next of
kin.
[L.L. *annāta* — L. *annus,* a
year.]

an(n)atto

a- or *ə-nat′ō,* **an(n)atta** *-ə,*
arnotto *ār-not′ō,* ns.

a bright orange colouring matter
got from the fruit pulp of a
tropical American tree, *Bixa
orellana* (fam. *Bixaceae*): — pl.
-s.

[Supposed to be of Carib
origin.]

anoa

a-nō′ə, n.

the sapi-utan, or wild ox of
Celebes, like a small buffalo.

[Native name.]

anosmia

an-oz′mi-ə, n.

the loss of sense of smell.

[Gr. *an-,* priv., *osmē,* smell, *-ia.*]

ansate, -d

an′sāt, -id, adjs.

having a handle.

ansate cross see **ankh.**

[L. *ansātus — ansa,* handle.]

anta

an′tə, n.

a square pilaster at either side
of a doorway or the corner of a
flank wall: — pl. **an′tae** *(-tē).*

[L.]

antefix

an′ti-fiks, n. (usu. in pl.)

an ornament concealing the
ends of roofing tiles: — pl.
an′tefixes, antefix′a (L.).
adj. **antefix′al.**

[L. *ante,* before, in front, and
figĕre, fixum, to fix.]

antiaditis

an-ti-ə-dī′tis, n.

tonsillitis.

[Gr. *antias, -ados,* tonsil.]

antiar

an′chär, an′ti-är, n.

the upas-tree: its poisonous
latex.

[Jav. *antjar.*]

antigropelo(e)s

an-ti-grop′ə-lōz, (*old*) n.pl.

waterproof leggings.

[Said to be from Gr. *anti,*
against, *hygros,* wet, and *pēlos,*
mud.]

antiscian

an-tish′i-ən, n.

a dweller on the same meridian
on the other side of the equator,
whose shadow at noon falls in
the opposite direction. — Also
adj.

[Pfx. **anti-,** Gr. *skiā,* shadow.]

antithalian

an-ti-thə-lī'ən, adj.

opposed to mirth.

[Pfx. **anti-**, Gr. *Thaleia*, the comic muse.]

antrorse

an-trörs', adj.

turned up or forward.

[From *anterus*, hypothetical positive of L. *anterior*, front, and L. *versus*, turned.]

anziani

ant-sē-än'ē, (It.) n.pl.

councillors, senators.

aoudad

ä'ōō-dad, n.

a North African wild sheep.

[Native name in French spelling.]

aphanite

af'ə-nīt, n.

any rock of such close texture that separate minerals contained within cannot be distinguished by the naked eye.

[Gr. *aphanes*, invisible.]

aplustre

a-plus'tər, n.

the stern ornament of an ancient ship.

[L. *āplustre, ăplustre* — Gr. *aphlaston*.]

apopemptic

ap-ə-pemp'tik, adj.

valedictory.

[Gr. *apopemptikos* — *apo*, away from, *pempein*, to send.]

apophyge

a-pof'i-jē, n.

the curve where a column merges in its base or capital.

[Gr. *apophygē*, escape.]

apositia

ap-ō-sish'i-ə, n.

an aversion to food.

[Gr. *apo*, away from, *sītos*, bread, food.]

apozem

ap'ə-zem, n.

a decoction.

[Gr. *apozema* — *apo*, off, and *zeein*, to boil.]

appalto

a-päl'tō, (It.) n.

a contract or monopoly: — pl. **appal'ti** (*-tē*).

appleringie

ap-əl-ring'i, (*Scot.*) n.

southernwood (*Artemisia abrotanum*).

[Anglo-Fr. *averoine* — L. *abrotanum* — Gr. *abrotanon*.]

13

apricate

ap′ri-kāt, v.i.

to bask in the sun.

v.t. to expose to sunlight.

n. **aprica′tion.**

[L. *aprīcārī,* to bask in the sun, *aprīcus,* open to the sun.]

aptote

ap′tōt, n.

an indeclinable noun.

adj. **aptotic** (*-tot′ik*) uninflected.

[Gr. *aptōtos* — a-, priv., *ptōsis,* case.]

aquamanile

ak-wə-mə-nī′lē, -nē′lā,
aquamanale *-nā′lē,* ns.

a mediaeval ewer: a basin in which the priest washes his hands during the celebration of mass.

[Through L.L. — L. *aquae,* of water, *mānālis,* flowing, or *manus,* hand.]

araba

är-ä′bä, n.

a heavy screened wagon used by the Tatars and others. — Also **ar′ba, arō′ba.**

[Ar. and Pers. *'arābah.*]

arapunga

ar-ə-pung′gə, **araponga**
-pong′gə, ns.

the campanero or South American bell-bird.

[Tupí *araponga.*]

arar

är′är, n.

the sandarac tree.

[Moroccan name.]

archil

är′chil, -kil, n.

a red or violet dye made from various lichens: a lichen yielding it.

[O.Fr. *orchel, orseil* (Fr. *orseille*) — It. *orcello,* origin undetermined.]

archilowe

är′hhi-lō, (*obs. Scot.*) n.

a treat in return.

[Origin unknown.]

arctophile

ärk′tə-fīl, n.

a lover or collector of teddy-bears (also **arc′tophil**).

ns. **arctoph′ilist;
arctophil′ia; arctoph′ily.**

[Gr. *arktos,* bear, and **-phile.**]

ardeb

är′deb, n.

an Egyptian dry measure of $5\frac{1}{2}$ bushels.

[Ar. *irdab.*]

argala

är′gə-lə, n.

the adjutant stork.

[Hind. *hargīla.*]

argali

är'gə-li, n.

the great wild sheep (*Ovis ammon*) of Asia.

[Mongol.]

argan

är'gan, n.

a Moroccan timber-tree of the family Sapotaceae: its oil-bearing seed.

[N. African pron. of Ar. *arjān.*]

argand

är'gand, n.

a burner admitting air within a cylindrical flame. — Also adj.

[Invented by Aimé *Argand* (1755–1803).]

argemone

är-jem-ō'nē, n.

the prickly poppy.

[Gr. *argemōnē*, a kind of poppy.]

arghan

är'gan, n.

pita fibre, or the plant yielding it.

[Origin unknown.]

arginine

ar'ji-nīn, n.

one of the essential amino-acids.

[Origin obscure.]

arkose

är-kōs', n.

a sandstone rich in feldspar grains, formed from granite, etc.

[Fr.]

armozeen, armozine

är-mō-zēn', n.

a kind of taffeta or plain silk, usu. black, used for clerical gowns.

[Fr. *armoisin.*]

armure

är'mūr, n.

a type of fabric with a pebbled surface.

[Fr.]

arolla

a-rol'ə, n.

the Swiss stone-pine or Siberian cedar (*Pinus cembra*).

[Fr. *arolle.*]

arpent

är'pənt, är-pã, n.

an old French measure for land still used in Quebec and Louisiana varying from about 50 to 35 ares (1¼ acres to 5/6 of an acre).

[Fr., — L. *arepennis,* said to be a Gallic word.]

arracacha

ar-a-käch'ə, n.

an umbelliferous plant
(*Arracacia*) of northern South
America, with edible tubers.
[Quechua *aracacha.*]

arrhenotoky

ar-ən-ot'ə-ki, n.

parthenogenetic production of
males alone.

[Gr. *arrēn,* male, *tokos,*
offspring.]

arriage

ar'ij, n.

a former feudal service in
Scotland, said to have been
rendered by the tenant with his
beasts of burden, later
indefinite.

arriero

ar-i-ā'rō, n.

a muleteer: — pl. **arrie'ros.**
[Sp.]

arris

ar'is, n.

a sharp edge on stone, metal,
etc. at the meeting of two
surfaces.
arris rail a wooden, etc. rail of
triangular section.

arrish, arish

är'ish, (*dial.*) n.

a stubble field.

[O.E. *ersc* (in compounds).]

arroba

a-rō'bə, ä-ro'bä, n.

a weight of 25 pounds (11·35kg)
or more, used in Spanish and
Portuguese regions.
[Sp. and Port., — Ar. *ar-rub',*
the quarter.]

arshin, arshine, arsheen

är-shēn', n.

an old measure of length, about
28 in. in Russia, about 30
inches (legally a metre) in
Turkey.
[Turkish.]

artel

är-tel', n.

a Russian workers' guild.
[Russ.]

aryballos

ar-i-bal'os, n.

a globular oil-flask with a neck.
adj. **aryball'oid.**
[Gr.]

asarum

as'ə-rəm, n.

the dried root of the wild ginger
(*Asarum canadense*).
n. **asarabacca** (*as-ə-rə-bak'ə;*

L. *bacca,* berry) a plant (*Asarum europaeum*), of the birthwort family, formerly used in medicine.

[L. *asarum* (— Gr. *asaron*), hazelwort.]

ascian

ash'i-ən, n.

an inhabitant of the torrid zone, shadowless when the sun is right overhead.

[Gr. *askios,* shadowless — *a-,* priv., *skiā,* a shadow.]

ascites

a-sī'tēz, n.

dropsy of the abdomen.
adjs. **ascit'ic** (-*sit'ik*), **ascit'ical.**

[Gr. *askītēs* — *askos,* belly.]

aspheterism

as-fet'ər-izm, (*Southey*) n.
denial of the right of private property.
v.i. **asphet'erise, -ize.**

[Gr. *a-,* priv., and *spheteros,* one's own.]

assart

as-ärt', (*hist.*) v.t.

to reclaim for agriculture by grubbing.
n. a forest clearing: assarted land: grubbing up of trees and bushes.

[A.Fr. *assarter* — L.L. *exsartāre*

— L. *ex,* out, *sar(r)īre,* to hoe, weed.]

assiento

as-ē-en'tō, (*hist.*) n.

a treaty (esp. that between Spain and Britain, 1713) for the supply of African slaves for Spanish American possessions: — pl. **assien'tos.**

[Sp. (now *asiento*), seat, seat in a court, treaty.]

assythment

ə-sīth'mənt, (*Scots law*; *obsolescent*) n.

indemnification by one who has caused a death, etc.

[M.E. *aseth,* amends — O.Fr. *aset,* adv. mistaken for objective of nom. *asez.*]

astatki

as-tat'kē, n.

the residue of petroleum-distillation, used as fuel.

[Russ. *ostatki,* pl. of *ostatok,* residue.]

asteism

as'tē-izm, n.

refined irony.

[Gr. *asty, -eōs,* a town; seen as a place of refinement.]

atabal

at'ə-bal, ä-tä-bäl', n.

a Moorish kettledrum.

[Sp., — Ar. *at-tabl*, the drum.]

atabeg, atabek

ät-ä-beg', -bek', ns.

a ruler or high official.

[Turk. *atabeg* — *ata*, father, *beg*, prince.]

atalaya

ä-tä-lä'yä, (Sp., — Ar.) n.

a watch-tower.

atap, attap

at'ap, n.

the nipa palm: its leaves used for thatching.

[Malay.]

athanor

ath'ə-nör, n.

an alchemist's self-feeding digesting furnace.

[Ar. *at-tannūr* — *al*, the, *tannūr*, furnace — *nūr*, fire.]

atimy

at'i-mi, n.

loss of honour: in ancient Athens, loss of civil rights, public disgrace.

[Gr. *atimiā* — *a-*, priv., and *timē*, honour.]

atman

ät'mən, n.

in Hinduism, the divine within the self.

[Sans. *ātman*, self, soul.]

atok, atoc

a-tok', n.

a species of skunk.

[Peruvian.]

atresia

ə-trēzh'(y)ə, n.

absence of, or closure of, a passage in the body.

[Formed from Gr. *trēsis*, perforation.]

attercop

at'ər-kop, (*obs.* or *dial*) n.

a spider: an ill-natured person.

[O.E. *attorcoppa* — *attor*, *ātor*, poison, and perh. *cop*, head, or *copp*, cup.]

austringer

ö'strin-jər, n.

a keeper of goshawks. — Also **a'stringer, ostreger** (*os'tri-jər; Shak.*).

[O.Fr. *ostruchier.*]

autoschediasm

ö-tō-sked'i-azm, or *-skēd'*, n.

anything extemporised.

v.t. **autosched'iaze** (-āz).
adj. **autoschedias'tic.**
[Gr. *autoschediasma*,
improvisation, *autoschediazein*,
to extemporize — *autoschedon*,
on the spot — *autos,* self,
schedios, off-hand.]

aventail, aventaile
av'ən-tāl, n.
the flap or movable part of a
helmet in front, for admitting air.
[O.Fr. *esventail,* air-hole — L.
ex, out, *ventus,* wind.]

averruncate
av'ər-ung-kāt, (*rare*) v.t.
to ward off: (wrongly) to uproot.
ns. **averruncā'tion;**
av'erruncātor an instrument
for cutting off branches of trees.
[L. *āverruncāre,* to avert, perh.
confused with *ēruncāre,* to
weed out.]

awhape
ə-(h)wāp', (*Spens.*) v.t.
to confound, amaze.
[Cf. Goth. *af-hwapjan,* to
choke.]

awmous
ö'məs, (*Scot.*) n.
alms.

[O.N. *almusa;* cf. O.E.
ælmysse, alms.]

ayu
ä'ū, ī'(y)ōō, **ai** *ī,* ns.
a small edible Japanese fish
(*Plecoglossus altevis*).
[Jap.]

azan
ä-zän', n.
the Muslim call to public prayer
made five times a day by a
muezzin.
[Ar. *'adhan,* invitation.]

azote
a-zōt', n.
an old name for nitrogen, so
called because it does not
sustain animal life.
adjs. **azot'ic** (*a-zot'ik*) nitric;
azō'tous nitrous.
v.t. **az'otise, -ize** to combine
with nitrogen.
[Gr. *a-,* priv., *zaein,* to live.]

azoth
äz'oth, n.
the alchemist's name for
mercury: Paracelsus's universal
remedy.
[From Ar. *az-zāūg — al,* the,
zāūg, from Pers. *zhīwah,*
quicksilver.]

azymous

az′i-məs, adj.

unfermented: unleavened.
ns. **az′ym** (*-im*), **az′yme** (*-īm*,
-im) unleavened bread;
az′ȳmite a member of any
church using unleavened bread
in the Eucharist.

[Gr. *azȳmos* — *a-*, priv., *zȳmē*,
leaven.]

B

babacoote

bab'ə-kōōt, n.

a large lemur, the indri or a closely related species.

[Malagasy *babakoto.*]

babassu

bab-ə-sōō', n.

a Brazilian palm (*Attalea*) or its oil-yielding nut.

[Prob. Tupí.]

babiroussa, -russa

bä-bi-rōō'sə, n.

a wild hog found in Celebes, etc., with great upturned tusks in the male, hence called the horned or deer hog.

[Malay *bābi,* hog, and *rūsa,* deer.]

babouche, babuche, baboosh

bə-bōōsh', n.

an Oriental heelless slipper.

[Fr., — Ar. *bābūsh* — Pers. *pā,* foot, *pūsh,* covering.]

baculine

bak'ū-līn, adj.

pertaining to the stick or cane — in flogging.

[L. *baculum.*]

badderlock

bad'ər-lok, (*Scot.*) n.

an edible seaweed (*Alaria*) resembling tangle. — Also **balderlocks** (*böl'dər-loks*).

[Poss. for **Balder's locks.**]

badious

bā'di-əs, (*bot.*) adj.

chestnut-coloured.

[L. *badius.*]

badmash, budmash

bud'mash, (*India*) n.

an evil-doer.

[Pers.]

baetyl

bē'til, n.

a magical or holy meteoric stone.

[Gr. *baitylos.*]

bagarre

ba-gär, (Fr.) n.

a scuffle, brawl, rumpus.

bagasse

bə-gas', n.

dry refuse in sugar-making.
n. **bagassō'sis** industrial disease caused by inhaling

bagasse.
[Fr.; Sp. *bagazo*, husks of
grapes or olives after pressing.]

baguio
bä-gē'ō, n.
a hurricane: — pl. **bagui'os.**
[Philippine Islands Sp.]

baht
bät, n.
the monetary unit of Thailand.
[Thai *bāt*.]

bajada, bahada
ba-hä'də, (*geol.*) n.
a slope formed by aggradation,
consisting of rock debris.
[Sp. *bajada*, a slope.]

baladin
ba-la-dɛ̃, (Fr.) n.
a public dancer: a mountebank:
— fem. **baladine** (*-dēn*).

balas
bal'as, n.
a rose-red spinel (usu. **balas
ruby**).
[O. Fr. *balais* (It. *balascio*) —
L.L. *balascus* — Pers.
Badakhshān, a place near
Samarkand where they are
found.]

balboa
bäl-bō'ə, n.
the monetary unit of Panama.
[Vasco Nuñez de *Balboa, c.*
1475–1517.]

balbutient
bal-bū'sh(y)ənt, adj.
stammering.
[L. *balbūtiēns, -entis* —
balbūtīre, to stutter.]

balibuntal
bal-i-bun'tl, n.
(a hat made of) fine,
closely-woven straw.
[From *Baliuag*, in the
Philippines, and *buntal*,
Tagálog for the straw of the
talipot palm.]

ballan
bal'ən, n.
a species of wrasse. — Also
ball'anwrasse'.
[Perh. Irish *ball*, spot.]

baloo, balu
bä'lōō, n.
in India, a bear.
[Hind. *bhālū*.]

balzarine
bal'zə-rēn, n.
a light dress material of mixed
cotton and worsted.
[Fr. *balzorine*.]

bam
bam, (*coll.*) n.
a hoax: a false tale.
v.t. to cheat or hoax.

banausic
ban-ö'sik, adj.
mechanic: befitting or savouring of an artisan: vulgar: materialistic. — Also **banau'sian**.
[Gr. *banausikos* — *banausos*, a handicraftsman.]

bandalore
ban'də-lōr, -lör, (*obs.*) n.
an 18th cent. toy resembling a yo-yo which, through the action of a coiled spring, returned to the hand when thrown down.
[Origin unknown.]

bandar
bun'där, n.
a rhesus monkey.
[Hind.]

bandelet
band'ə-let, (*archit.*) n.
a small flat moulding or fillet surrounding a column.
[Fr. *bandelette.*]

bandobast, bundobust
bun'dō-bust, (*Ind.*) n.
an arrangement, settlement.
[Hind and Pers. *band-o-bast*, tying and binding.]

bandoline
ban'dō-lēn, n.
a gummy substance used for stiffening the hair.

bandore
ban-dōr', -dör, n.
an Elizabethan wire-stringed instrument like a cittern, invented by John Rose. — Also **bando'ra**.
[Sp. *bandurria*, Fr. *mandore*; L. *pandura*, Gr. *pandourā*, a three-stringed lute.]

banteng, banting
ban'teng, -ting, ns.
an East Indian wild ox.
[Malay.]

banxring, bangsring
bangks'ring, n.
a tree-shrew.
[Jav. *bangsring.*]

baragouin
bä-rä-gwẽ, -gwin', n.
any jargon or unintelligible language.
[Fr.; from Bret. *bara*, bread, and *gwenn*, white, said to have originated in the Breton soldiers' astonishment at white bread.]

barbastel(le)

bär-bəs-tel', or *bär'*, n.
a hairy-lipped bat.
[Fr. *barbastelle.*]

barege, barège

bä-rezh', n.
a light, mixed dress-stuff.
n. **baregine** (*bar'i-jēn*) a
gelatinous mass of bacteria and
sulphur deposited in thermal
waters.
[*Barèges* in Hautes-Pyrénées.]

barghest, bargest, bargaist

bär'gest, -gäst, n.
a dog-like goblin portending
death.
[Perh. conn. with Ger.
Berggeist, mountain-spirit.]

barkhan, barkan, barchan(e)

bär-kän', n.
a crescent-shaped sand-dune,
of the type found in the
Turkestan deserts.
[Native word in Turkestan.]

barmbrack

bärm'brak, n.
a slightly sweet bread with dried
peel, currants, etc. in it.
[Ir. *bairigen* or *bairín, breac*,
speckled cake.]

barmkin

bärm'kin, (*arch.*) n.
a battlement, or a turret, on the
outer wall of a castle: the wall
itself.
[Orig. obscure.]

barp

bärp, (*Scot. dial.*) n.
a mound or cairn.
[Gael. *barpa*, a burial cairn.]

barrace

bar'as, (*obs.*) n.
the lists in a tournament.
[O.Fr. *barras — barre*, bar.]

barranca

bar-ang'kə, (*U.S.*) n.
a deep gorge. — Also
barran'co (pl. **barran'cos**).
[Sp. *barranco.*]

barrat

bar'ət, n. (*obs.*)
deceit, strife or trouble.
n. **barr'ator** one who
vexatiously stirs up lawsuits,
quarrels, etc.
adj. **barr'atrous.**
adv. **barr'atrously.**
n. **barr'atry** fraudulent
practices on the part of the
master or mariners of a ship to
the prejudice of the owners:
vexatious litigation: stirring up of
suits and quarrels, forbidden
under penalties to lawyers:

traffic in offices of church or state.

[O.Fr. *barat,* deceit; traced by some to Gr. *prattein,* to do, by others to a Celt. or a Scand. origin.]

barret

bar'it, n.

a flat cap: a biretta.
barr'et-cap.

[Fr. *barette.*]

barrico

bar-ē'kō, n.

a small cask: — pl. **barri'cos, -coes.**

[Sp. *barrica.*]

bartisan, bartizan

bär'ti-zan, -zan', n.

a parapet or battlement: a projecting gallery on a wall-face: (erroneously) a corbelled corner turret.
adj. **bar'tisaned** (or *-zand'*).

[Apparently first used by Scott, who found a reading *bertisene,* for **bratticing;** see **brattice.**]

basan

ba'zən, n.

a sheepskin roughly tanned and undressed.

[Ar. *bitanah,* lining.]

bascule

bas'kūl, n.

an apparatus of which one end rises as the other sinks.
bascule bridge a bridge that rises when a counterpoise sinks in a pit.

[Fr. *bascule,* see-saw.]

baselard

bas'ə-lärd, (*obs.*) n.

a dagger or hanger.

[A.Fr.]

basenji

bə-sen'jē, n.

a smallish erect-eared, curly-tailed African hunting dog that rarely barks.

[Bantu, pl. of *mosenji, musengi,* native.]

bashlyk

bash'lik, n.

a hood with long ends worn in Russia, esp. by soldiers.

[Russ. *bashlyk,* a Caucasian hood — Turk. — Turk. *baş,* a head.]

basoche

ba-sosh, (Fr.) n.

a mediaeval gild of clerks of the parliament of Paris, performers of mystery plays.

batata

bə-tä′tə, n.

the sweet-potato.

[Sp. from Haitian.]

bateleur

bat′lər, n.

a short-tailed African eagle.

[Fr., mountebank, app. from its characteristic movements.]

bathorse

bat′hörs, bät′ (formerly *bä′*), n.

a pack-horse carrying an officer's baggage.

[Fr. *bât,* pack-saddle.]

batta

bat′ə, n.

an allowance in addition to ordinary pay: subsistence money.

[Prob. Kanarese *bhatta,* rice.]

battology

bat-ol′ə-ji, n.

futile repetition in speech or writing.

adj. **battolog′ical.**

[Gr. *battologiā,* stuttering, said to be from *Battos,* who consulted the Delphic oracle about his defect of speech (Herodotus iv. 155), and *legein,* to speak.]

bausond

bös′ənd, adj.

of animals, having white spots, esp. on the forehead, or a white stripe down the face.

adj. **baus′on-faced.**

[O.Fr. *bausant,* black and white spotted.]

bavin

bav′in, n.

a fagot of brushwood.

bavin wits (*Shak.*) wits that blaze and die like bavins.

[Origin unknown.]

bawley

bö′li, (*Essex* and *Kent*) n.

a small fishing-smack.

[Origin obscure.]

bawn

bön, n.

a fortification round a house: an enclosure for cattle.

[Ir. *bábhun,* enclosure.]

bebeeru

bi-bē′rōō, n.

the greenheart tree of Guyana.

n. **bebee′rine** (*-rin, -rēn*) an alkaloid yielded by its bark, a substitute for quinine.

[Native name.]

bebung

bā'bōōng, (*mus.*) n.

a tremolo effect produced on the clavichord by fluctuating the pressure of the finger on the key.

[Ger.]

beccafico

bek-a-fē'kō, n.

a garden warbler or kindred bird, considered a delicacy *esp.* by the Italians: — pl. **beccafi'cos.**

[It., from *beccare*, to peck, and *fico*, a fig.]

bedeguar

bed'i-gär, n.

a soft spongy gall found on the branches of sweet-brier and other roses, called also the sweet-brier sponge.

[Fr. *bédeguar* — Pers. and Ar. *bādā-war*, lit. wind-brought.]

beenah

bē'nä, n.

a form of marriage (in Sri Lanka etc.) in which the man goes to live with his wife's relatives and the children belong to her group.

[Ar. *bīnah*, separate.]

befana, beffana

be-fä'nə, n.

an Epiphany gift.

[It. *La Befana*, a toy-bringing old woman, a personification of Epiphany, Gr. *epiphaneia*.]

beghard

beg'ärd, n.

in Flanders or elsewhere from the 13th century, a man living a monastic life without vows and with power to return to the world.

[Flem. *beggaert*, origin doubtful.]

beglerbeg

beg'lər-beg, n.

formerly, the governor of a Turkish province, in rank next to the grand vizier.

[Turk., lit. bey of beys.]

bekah

bē'kä, (*B.*) n.

a half-shekel.

[Heb.]

belah

bē'lä, n.

an Australian tree of the Casuarina genus.

[Aboriginal.]

belleter
bel'ə-tər, n.
a bell-founder.
[For *bellyetter* — **bell,** and O.E.
gēotan, to pour.]

bema
bē'mə, n.
the tribune or rostrum from
which Athenian orators made
their speeches: hence the apse
or chancel of a basilica.
[Gr. *bēma*, a step.]

benne
ben'ē, **benni, beni** *ben'i*, ns.
sesame.
ns. **benn'e-seed,
benn'i-seed, ben'iseed**
sesame seed.
[From Malay *bene*.]

benthos
ben'thos, n.
the flora and fauna of the
sea-bottom — opp. to *plankton*
and *nekton.*
adjs. **ben'thic; benthon'ic,
benthoal** *(ben-thō'əl)* living on
the sea-bottom.
ns. **benthopelagic**
(*-thō-pi-laj'ik*) (of marine fauna)
living just above the sea-bed;
ben'thoscope a submersible
sphere from which to study
deep-sea life.
[Gr. *benthos*, depth.]

berm
bûrm, n.
a ledge: the area of level
ground between the raised
mound of a barrow or other
earthwork and the ditch
surrounding it (*archaeol.*).
[Fr. *berme*; Ger. *Berme.*]

besognio
bi-zōn'yō, n.
a beggar: — pl. **besogn'ios.**
[It.; see **bezonian.**]

béton
bā'tō, n.
lime concrete: concrete.
[Fr.]

bezoar
bē'zōr, -zör, n.
a stony concretion found in the
stomachs of goats, antelopes,
llamas, etc., formerly esteemed
an antidote to all poisons.
adj. **bezoardic** (*bez-ō-ärd'ik*).
[Through Sp. *bezoar* and Ar.
bāzahr — Pers. *pādzahr*,
antidote — *zahr*, poison.]

bezonian
bi-zō'nyən, (*Shak.*) n.
a beggar.
[It. *bisogno*, need.]

bharal

bur'əl, n.

the blue sheep of the Himalaya, connecting the true wild sheep with the goats. — Also **burrel, burrell, burrhel, burhel.**

[Hind.]

bhisti, bheesty, bheestie, bhistee

bēs'tē, n.

an Indian water carrier.

[Urdu *bhīstī* — Pers. *behistī* — *bihisht*, paradise.]

bice

bīs, n.

a pale blue or green paint.

[Fr. *bis.*]

biffin

bif'in, n.

a variety of apple: such an apple slowly dried and flattened into a cake.

[For *beefing*, from its colour of raw beef.]

biga

bī'gə, bē'ga, (L.) n.

a two-horse chariot (in L. earlier in pl. form **bigae** *bī'jē, bē'gī* — *bi-, jugum*, yoke).

bigha

bē'gə, n.

a land measure in India, $\frac{1}{3}$ to $\frac{2}{3}$ of an acre.

[Hindi.]

bilander

bī'land-ər, n.

a two-masted hoy, having her mainsail bent to the whole length of her yard, hanging fore and aft, and inclined to the horizontal at an angle of about 45°. — Also **by'lander.**

[Du. *bijlander.*]

bilbo

bil'bō, n.

a rapier or sword: — pl. **bil'boes, -os.**

[From *Bilbao*, in Spain.]

bilboes

bil'bōz, n.pl.

a bar with sliding shackles.

[Perh. connected with the foregoing.]

bilian

bil'i-an, n.

a heavy ant-proof lauraceous timber tree of Borneo.

[Malay.]

bilimbi

bil-im'bi, n.

an East Indian tree of the wood-sorrel family: its acid fruit. — Also **bilim'bing, blim'bing.**

[Dravidian and Malay.]

bilirubin

bil-i-rōō'bin, n.

a reddish pigment in bile.
n. **biliver'din** a green pigment in bile.

[L. *bīlis*, bile, *ruber*, red, Fr. *verd*, green.]

billon

bil'ən, n.

base metal: esp. an alloy of silver with copper, tin, or the like.

[Fr.]

billyboy

bil'i-boi, n.

a bluff-bowed one-masted trading-vessel.

[Prob. conn. with **bilander**.]

bingle

bing'gl, n.

a hairstyle midway between bob and shingle. — Also v.t.

binturong

bin'tū-rong, n.

an East Indian prehensile-tailed carnivore, akin to the civet.

[Malay.]

birkie

birk'i, (*Scot.*) n.

a strutting or swaggering fellow: a fellow generally.

adj. active.

[Perh. conn. with O.N. *berkia*, O.E. *beorcan*, to bark.]

birlinn

bir'lin, n.

a chief's barge in the Western Isles.

[Gael. *birlinn* — O.N. *byrthingr* — *byrthr*, burden.]

bismar

bis', *biz'mər*, (*Orkney* and *Shetland*) n.

a kind of steelyard.

[O.N. *bismari*.]

bistort

bis'tört, n.

adderwort or snakeweed, a plant (*Polygonum bistorta*) of the dock family with twisted rootstock.

[L. *bistorta* — *bis*, twice, *tortus*, *-a*, *-um*, twisted.]

bistoury

bis'tər-i, n.

a narrow surgical knife for making incisions.

[Fr. *bistouri*.]

bito

bē'tō, n.

a tree (*Balanites aegyptiaca*; family Zygophyllaceae) of dry tropical Africa and Asia; its oil-yielding fruit: — pl. **bi'tos**.

bitterling

bit'ər-ling, n.

a small fish (*Rhodeus amarus*).

blay, bley

blā, n.

the bleak (fish).

[O.E. *blæge*.]

blende

blend, n.

a mineral, zinc sulphide.

[Ger. *Blende — blenden*, to deceive, from its resemblance to galena.]

blet

blet, n.

incipient internal decay in fruit without external sign: a part so affected.

v.i. to become soft or sleepy: — pr.p. **blett'ing;** pa.t. and pa.p. **blett'ed.**

[Fr.]

blewits

blū'its, n.

a kind of edible mushroom of the *Tricholoma* family, lilac-coloured when young.

bluette

blü-et, (Fr.) n.

a spark, flash: a short playful piece of music.

blunge

blunj, (*pottery*) v.t.

to mix (clay or the like) with water.

n. **blung'er** a machine for doing so: one who blunges.

[From *bl*end and pl*unge.*]

bobak, bobac

bō'bak, n.

a species of marmot.

[Pol. *bobak.*]

bobbery

bob'ər-i, n.

a noisy row.

[Perh. Hind. *bāp re,* O father.]

bobolink

bob'ō-lingk, n.

a North American singing bird.

[At first *Bob Lincoln,* from its note.]

bodach

bōd'əhh, bod', Gael. *bot',* (*Scot.*) n.

an old man, a churl: a goblin or spectre.

[Gael.]

bodgie

boj'i, (*Austr.*) n.

a delinquent youth, usu. a member of a teenage gang.

[From **bodge,** a clumsy worker.]

bodle,

also **boddle,** *bod'l, bōd'l,* n.

a 17th-century Scots copper coin, worth about one-sixth of an English penny, the smallest coin.

[Origin unknown.]

bodrag

bod'rag, (*Spens.*) n.

a hostile attack, a raid. — Also **bord'raging.**

[Perh. Ir. *buaidhreadh,* a disturbance.]

bogong

bō'gong, n.

a noctuid moth eaten by Australian Aborigines. — Also **bugong** (*bōō'-*).

[Aboriginal.]

bohea

bō-hē', n.

the lowest quality of black tea: black tea generally.

[From the *Wu-i* hills in China.]

bolide

bō'līd, n.

a large meteor, esp. one that bursts: a fireball.

[Fr., — L. *bolis, -idis* — Gr. *bolis,* missile.]

bonas(s)us

bon-as'əs, n.

a bison.

[L., — Gr. *bonasos, bonassos.*]

bonduc

bon'duk, n.

the nicker seed.

[Ar. *bonduq,* a kind of nut.]

bongrace

bon'grās, n.

a shade from the sun once worn by women on the front of the bonnet: a broad-brimmed hat or bonnet.

[Fr. *bonne* (*fem.*) good, *grâce,* grace.]

bonxie

bongks'i, (*Shetland*) n.

the great skua.

[O.N. *bunki,* heap.]

borachio

bor-ach'(i-)ō, n.

a Spanish wine-skin: a drunken fellow: — pl. **borach'ios.**

[Sp. *borracha, borracho.*]

borborygmus

bör-bə-rig'məs, n.

sound of flatulence in the intestines.

adj. **borboryg'mic.**

[Gr. *borborygmos.*]

bordar

börd'ər, n.

a villein who held his hut at his lord's pleasure.

[L.L. *bordārius*; of Gmc. origin.]

borecole

bōr'kōl, bōr', n.

kale.

[Du. *boerenkool*, lit. peasant's cabbage.]

boree

bö'rē, (*Austr.*) n.

any of several species of Acacia.

[Aboriginal.]

boreen

bō-rēn', n.

a lane: byroad.

[Ir. *bóithrín*.]

borrel, borrell, borel

bor'əl, (*arch.*) adj.

rustic, clownish.

[O.Fr. *burel*, coarse cloth worn by peasantry.]

bort, boart

bört, n.

diamond fragments or dust: a coarse diamond or semicrystallic form of carbon.

[Fr.]

boshta, boshter

bosh'tə, -tər, (*obs. Austr. coll.*) adjs.

very good.

bostangi

bos-tan'ji, n.

a Turkish palace guard.

[Turk. *bostanji*.]

botargo

bot-är'gō, n.

a relish made of mullet or tunny roe: — pl. **botar'gos, -goes.**

[It., — Ar. *butarkhah*.]

botryoid, -al

bot'ri-oid, -oid'əl, adjs.

like a bunch of grapes.
adj. **bot'ryose** botryoidal: racemose (*bot.*).
n. **Botrytis** (*bə-trī'tis*) a genus of fungi (fam. *Moniliaceae*), several of which cause plant diseases, and one of which (*Botrytis cinerea*) causes noble rot.

[Gr. *botrys*, a bunch of grapes.]

botte

bot, (Fr.) n.

a pass or thrust in fencing.

bouche

bōōsh, (Fr.) n.

the staff of cooks in a large house.

bouillotte

bōō-yot', n.

a gambling card game
resembling poker.

[Fr.]

bourasque

bōō-rask', n.

a tempest.

[Fr. *bourrasque*; It. *borasco*, a
storm.]

bourd

bōōrd, (*obs.*) n.

a jest, sport.

n. **bourd'er** (*obs.*) a jester.

[O.Fr. *bourde*, origin unknown.]

bourtree, boortree

bōōr'tri, (*Scot.*) n.

the elder-tree. — Also
bountree (*bōōn'tri*).
bour'tree-gun a pop-gun
made of an elder twig.

[Ety. unknown.]

boutade

bōō-täd', n.

a sudden outburst: a caprice.

[Fr., — *bouter*, to thrust.]

bovate

bō'vāt, (*hist.*) n.

an oxgang.

[L.L. *bovāta* — *bōs, bovis*, an
ox.]

bowat, bowet, buat

bōō'ət, (*Scot.*) n.

a lantern.

MacFarlane's buat (*Scott*) the
moon.

[L.L. *boeta*, box.]

boyau

bwo'yō, bwä'yō, boi'ō, (*fort.*) n.

a communication trench: — pl.
bo'yaux.

[Fr., bowel.]

boyg

boig, n.

an ogre: an obstacle, problem,
difficult to get to grips with.

[Norw. *bøig*.]

bozzetto

bot-set'tō, (*It.*) n.

a small model or sketch of a
projected sculpture: — pl.
bozzet'ti (*-tē*).

braccate

brak'āt, adj.

having feathered legs or feet.

[L. *brācātus*, wearing
breeches.]

braccio

brät'chō, n.

an obsolete Italian measure of
length, more than half a metre:
— pl. **braccia** (*brät'chä*).

[It., lit. arm.]

brack

brak, n.

a flaw in cloth.

brad

brad, n.

a small tapering nail with a side projection instead of a head.

[O.N. *broddr*, spike.]

braide

brād, (*Shak.*) adj.

dissembling, deceitful.

[O.E. *brǣgd*, falsehood — *bregdan*, to weave.]

braird

brārd, **breer** *brēr*, ns.

(orig. *Scot.*) the first shoots of corn or other crop.

vs.i. to appear above ground.

[O.E. *brerd*, edge.]

brancard

brangk'ərd, n.

a horse litter.

[Fr.]

branks

brangks, (*Scot.*) n.pl.,

rarely in sing., a bridle: a scold's bridle, having a hinged iron framework to enclose the head and a bit or gag.

[Ety. very obscure; O.Fr. *bernac* ; Ger. *Pranger,* pillory, Du. *prang,* fetter, have been compared.]

brasero

brä-sā'rō, n.

a brazier: a place for burning criminals or heretics: — pl. **braser'os.**

[Sp., — *brasa,* a live coal.]

brattice

brat'is, **brattish** *brat'ish,* **brettice** *bret'is,* ns.

in mediaeval siege operations, a fixed tower of wood: a covered gallery on a castle wall, commanding the wall-face below (in these senses also **bretesse** *bri-tes',* **bretasche** *bri-tash'):* a wooden partition: a wooden lining: a partition to control ventilation in a mine.

v.t. to furnish with a brattice.

ns. **bratt'icing, bratt'ishing** work in the form of brattices: cresting, or ornamental work along a ridge, cornice or coping (*archit.*).

bratt'ice-cloth strong tarred cloth used for mine brattices.

[O.Fr. *breteshe* — L.L. *bretachia*; cf. **bartisan.**]

braxy

brak'si, (*Scot.*) n.

a bacterial disease of sheep: applied loosely to various diseases of sheep: a sheep so infected: its flesh. — Also adj.

braxy mutton the flesh of a braxy sheep or generally of a sheep that has died of disease or accident.

[Prob. orig. pl. of *brack,* variant of **break.**]

breccia

brech'yə, n.

a rock composed of angular fragments.
adj. **brecciated** (*brech'i-ā-tid*) reduced to or composed of breccia.
[It.]

brecham

brehh'əm, (*Scot.*) n.

a horse-collar.
[O.E. *beorgan,* to protect, *hama,* covering.]

bregma

breg'mə, n.

the part of the skull where the frontal and the two parietal bones join — sometimes divided into the right and left bregmata: — pl. **breg'mata.**
adj. **bregmat'ic.**
[Gr.]

brehon

brē'hən, n.

an ancient Irish judge.
Brehon Law(s) the system of jurisprudence in use among the Irish until near the middle of the 17th century.

[Ir. *breitheamh,* pl. *breitheamhuin.*]

breloque

brə-lok', n.

an ornament attached to a watch-chain.
[Fr.]

brewis

brōō'is, (*arch.* and *dial.*) n.

broth, esp. beef broth: bread soaked in broth, fat, gravy, or the like.
[O.Fr. *broez,* influenced by O.E. *brīw,* bree.]

bridoon

brid-ōōn', n.

the light snaffle usual in a military bridle in addition to the ordinary bit, controlled by a separate rein.
[Fr. *bridon — bride,* a bridle.]

brigue

brēg, v.i.

to intrigue.
n. strife: intrigue.
n. **briguing** (*brēg'ing*) canvassing.
[Fr. *brigue.*]

brindisi

brin'di-zi, brēn-dē'zē, (It.) n.

a toast: a drinking-song.

brinjarry

brin-jär'i, n.

a travelling dealer in grain and salt, in Southern India.
[Hindi, *banjārā.*]

britzka, britzska, britska

brits'kə, **britschka** *brich'kə,* ns.

an open four-wheeled carriage with one seat.

[Polish *bryczka.*]

brocard

brōk'ärd, or *-ərd,* n.

an elementary law or principle: a canon: (*bro-kar*) a gibe (Fr.).

[Fr. *brocard,* L.L. *brocarda,* from *Brocard* or Burchard, Bishop of Worms, who published a book of ecclesiastical rules.]

brochan

brohh'ən, (*Scot.*) n.

gruel: sometimes porridge.

[Gael.]

brocket

brok'it, n.

a stag in its second year, with its first, dagger-shaped, horns.

[Fr. *brocard — broque,* a spike.]

brog

brog, (*Scot.*) n.

an awl.

v.t. to prick.

[Origin obscure.]

brolga

brol'gə, n.

a tall grey Australian crane. — Also **Australian crane, native companion.**

[Aboriginal.]

brommer

brom'ər, (*Afrik.*) n.

the bluebottle fly.

[Onomatopoeic.]

broose

(*Scott,* **brouze**), *brōōz, brüz,* (*Scot.*) n.

a race at a wedding.

[Derivation unknown.]

browst

browst, (*Scot.*) n.

a brewing.

[**brew.**]

brumby

brum'bi, (*Austr.*) n.

a wild horse.

[Origin unknown.]

bruxism

bruks'izm, n.

habitual grinding of the teeth.

[Gr. *brychein,* to gnash.]

buaze, bwazi

bū'āz, bwä'zi, ns.

an African fibre-yielding polygalaceous shrub

(*Securidaca*).
[Native name.]

bubinga
boo'bing-ə, n.
species of W. African tree, esp.
Didelotia africana, its hard wood
used in furniture-making.
[Bantu.]

buckra
buk'rə, n.
a word used by West Indian
and American Negroes for a
white man — said to mean
'demon' in a dialect of the
Calabar coast.

buddle
bud'l, n.
an inclined hutch for washing
ore.
v.t. to wash with a buddle.
[Origin obscure.]

budgeree
buj'ər-ē, (*Austr. obs. coll.*) adj.
good.
[Native word, *budgeri*.]

budgerow, budgero
(pl. **budgeros**) *buj'ər-ō*, (Hind.)
n.
a heavy keel-less barge.

bufflehead
buf'l-hed, n.
a N. American diving duck
resembling the golden-eye: a
stupid fellow.
[From **buffalo** and **head**.]

bufo
bū'fō, (*Ben Jonson*) n.
a black tincture in alchemy.
[L. *būfō*, toad.]

buirdly
bûrd'li, (*Scot.*) adj.
stalwart, large and well made.
[Poss. a variant of **burly**.]

buist
büst, (*Scot.*) n.
a box: a tar-box: an owner's
mark on sheep or cattle.
v.t. to mark thus.
[O.Fr. *boiste* (Fr. *boîte*), box.]

bullace
bool'is, n.
a shrub closely allied to the
sloe.
[Cf. O.Fr. *beloce*.]

bulse
buls, n.
a bag for or of diamonds, etc.
[Port. *bolsa* — L.L. *bursa*, a
purse.]

bumbo
bum'bō, n.
a mixture of rum or gin, water, sugar, and nutmeg, or similar drink: — pl. **bum'bos.**
[Perh. It. *bombo*, a child's word for drink.]

bummock
bum'ək, (*Orkney*) n.
a brewing of ale for a feast.
[Ety. unknown.]

bundook, bandook
bun'dōōk, (*mil. slang*) n.
a rifle.
[Hind. *bandūq.*]

bunnia, bunia
bun'i-ə, n.
a Hindu merchant.
[Hind.]

bunraku
bōōn-rä'kōō, n.
a Japanese form of puppet theatre in which the puppets, usu. about 3 ft (1 metre) high, are each manipulated by 3 men who remain visible throughout the performance.
[Jap.]

bunya
bun'yə, **bun'ya-bun'ya**, ns.
an Australian tree, *Araucaria bidwillii*, the cones of which contain large edible seeds.
[Aboriginal.]

bunyip
bun'yip, n.
a fabulous monster of Australian Aboriginal legend: an impostor.
[Aboriginal.]

buonamano
bwō'na-mä'nō, or **bonamano** *bo'na-*, (It.) n.
a tip: — pl. **b(u)o'nama'ni** (*-nē*).

buplever
bū-plev'ər, n.
hare's-ear (*Bupleurum*).
[Fr. *buplèvre* — L. *būpleurum* — Gr. *bous*, ox, *pleuron*, rib.]

buran
bōō-rän', n.
a violent blizzard blowing from the north-east in Siberia and Central Asia.
[Russ.]

burdash
bûr-dash', n.
a fringed sash worn by gentlemen in the time of Anne and George I.
[Origin unknown.]

burgoo

bûr-gōō', bûr'gōō, n.

a sailor's dish of boiled oatmeal with salt, butter, and sugar: a stew or thick soup for American picnics.

[Derivation unknown.]

burk(h)a

bōōr'kə, n.

a loose garment, with veiled eyeholes, covering the whole body.

[Urdu *burga'* — Ar.]

burl

bûrl, n.

a small knot in thread: a knot in wood. — v.t. to pick knots, etc., from, in finishing cloth.
n. **bur'ler**.
adj. **bur'ly**.
ns. **bur'ling-i'ron;
bur'ling-machine'**.

[O.Fr. *bourle*, tuft of wool.]

burrel

bur'əl, n.

a coarse russet cloth of mediaeval times.

bussu

bōōs'ōō, n.

a tropical American palm (*Manicaria*) with gigantic leaves and netted spathe that serves as cloth.

[Port. from Tupí *bussú*.]

bustee

bus'tē, n.

in India, a settlement or a collection of huts.

[Hind. *bastī*.]

bycoket

bī'kok-it, n.

a turned-up peaked cap worn by noble persons in the 15th century.

[O.Fr. *bicoquet*, prob. *bi-* (L. *bis*), double, *coque*, a shell.]

bywoner

bī'wōn-ər, bī'vōn-ər, n.

an authorised squatter on another's farm: a poor white parasite.

[Du. *bijwonen*, to be present.]

C

caatinga

kä-ting'gə, n.

in Brazil, open, comparatively
low forest, on white sandy soil
derived from granite.
[Tupí, white forest.]

cabas

kab'ä, n.

a woman's work-basket,
reticule, or handbag.
[Fr., flat basket.]

caboceer

kab-ō-sēr', n.

a West African headman.
[Port. *cabeceira* — *cabo* — L.
caput, head.]

cacafogo

kak-ə-fō'gō, **cacafuego** *-fū'gō*
(Sp. *kä-kä-fwä'gō*), (*obs.*) ns.

a spitfire, blusterer: — pls.
cacafog'os, -fueg'os.
[Sp. and Port. *cagar,* to void
excrement, Port. *fogo*, Sp.
fuego, fire.]

cacholong

kach'o-long, n.

a variety of quartz or of opal,
generally of a milky colour.
[Fr. from Kalmuck.]

cachucha

kə-chōō'chə, n.

a lively Spanish dance in 3–4
time, like the bolero.
[Sp.]

cacodyl

kak'ō-dil, n.

a colourless stinking liquid,
composed of arsenic, carbon,
and hydrogen.
adj. **cacodyl'ic.**
[Gr. *kakōdēs*, stinking, *hȳlē*,
matter.]

cacoepy

kak-ō'ə-pi, n.

bad or wrong pronunciation.
[Gr. *kakos*, bad, *epos*, word.]

cacoethes

kak-ō-ē'thēz, n.

a bad habit or itch.
[Gr. *kakoēthēs, -ĕs*, ill-disposed
— *kakos*, bad, *ēthos*, habit.]

cacolet

kak'ō-lā, n.

a military mule-litter.
[Fr., prob. from Basque.]

cadrans

kad'rənz, n.

an instrument by which a gem is adjusted while being cut.

[Fr. *cadran,* a quadrant, dial.]

caduac

kad'ū-ak, (*obs.*) n.

a casualty or windfall.

[Scot. — L. *cadūcum.*]

caespitose

sēs'pi-tōs, adj.

tufted: turf-like.

[L. *caespes, -itis,* turf.]

cafila, caffila, kafila

ka'fēl-a, kä', -fil-, -ä, n.

a caravan, caravan train.

[Ar. *qāfilah.*]

cagot

käg'ō, n.

one of an outcast class found scattered in the western Pyrenees, supposed to be the descendants of lepers.

[Fr.; origin unknown.]

cain, kain

kān, n.

in old Scots law, rent paid in kind, esp. in poultry, etc.: tribute.

cain'-hen a hen given up as cain.

pay the cain to pay the penalty.

[Ir. and Gael. *càin,* rent, tax.]

calamanco

kal-ə-mangk'ō, n.

a satin-twilled woollen stuff, chequered or brocaded in the warp: a garment made of this: — pl. **calamanc'os.**

[Du. *kalamink,* Ger. *Kalmank,* Fr. *calmande*; origin unknown.]

calamander

kal-ə-man'dər, n.

a hard and valuable cabinet-wood of the ebony genus, brownish with black stripes, brought from India and Sri Lanka.

[Prob. Sinh.]

calandria

kal-an'dri-ə, n.

a sealed vessel used in the core of certain types of nuclear reactor.

calash

kə-lash', n.

a light low-wheeled carriage with a folding top: a hood with hoops formerly worn by ladies over the cap.

[Fr. *calèche*; of Slav. origin.]

calavance

kal'ə-vans, n.

a name for certain varieties of pulse. — Also **car'avance**.

[Sp. *garbanzo*, chick-pea, said to be Basque *garbantzu*.]

caliche

kä-lē'chä, n.

Chile saltpetre.

[Sp.]

caligo

kal-ī'gō, n.

dimness of sight.

adj. **caliginous** (*kal-ij'i-nəs*) dim, obscure, dark.

n. **caliginos'ity**.

[L. *cālīgō, -inis*, fog.]

caliology

kal-i-ol'ə-ji, n.

the science of birds' nests.

[Gr. *kaliā, kalīā*, a nest, *logos*, discourse.]

calipash

kal'i-pash, n.

the part of a turtle close to the upper shell, a dull greenish fatty gelatinous substance.

n. **cal'ipee** the light-yellowish portion of flesh from the turtle's belly.

[Prob. from West Ind. words.]

calisaya

kal-i-sā'yə, n.

a variety of Peruvian bark.

callet

kal'it, (*Shak.*) n.

a scold, a woman of bad character, a trull.

[Origin obscure.]

callid

kal'id, adj.

shrewd.

n. **callid'ity** shrewdness.

[L. *callidus*, expert.]

calotte

kal-ot', n.

a plain skull-cap or coif worn by R.C. clergy.

[Fr.]

caloyer

kal'o-yər, n.

a Greek monk, esp. of the order of St Basil.

[Fr. — It. — Late Gr. *kalogēros.* — Gr. *kalos*, beautiful, *gēras*, old age.]

calp

kalp, n.

in Ireland, a dark shaly limestone occurring in the middle of the Carboniferous Limestone.

calumba

ka-lum'bə, n.

the root of an East African plant (*Jateorhiza columba,* fam. Menispermaceae) used as a stomachic and tonic.

[Perh. from *Colombo* in Sri Lanka.]

calver

kal'vər, v.t.

to prepare (salmon or other fish) when alive or freshly caught. adj. **cal'vered.**

calyptra

ka-lip'trə, n.

a Greek veil: a hood, covering, esp. that of a moss capsule, or of a root.

adj. **calyp'trate** capped.

n. **calyp'trogen** the group of cells giving rise to the root-cap.

[Gr. *kalyptrā,* a veil.]

camaieu

kam-a-yø', n.

a cameo: a painting in monochrome, or in simple colours not imitating nature: a style of printing pictures producing the effect of pencil-drawing: — pl. **camaieux** (*-yø'*).

[Fr.]

caman

kam'an, n.

a shinty stick.

n. **camanachd**

(*kam-an-ahh(k)'*) shinty.

[Gael.]

camass, camas, camash, quamash

kam'as, -ash, kwom'ash, kwam-ash', ns.

a small plant (*Camassia*) of the lily family growing in the north-western United States: its nutritious bulb.

cam'ass-rat a small gopher rodent that devours the bulbs.

[Chinook *kámass.*]

cambist

kam'bist, n.

one skilled in the science of financial exchange.

ns. **cam'bism, cam'bistry.**

[It. *cambista* — L. *cambīre,* to exchange.]

cambrel

kam'brəl, n.

a bent stick or rod for hanging a carcase: an animal's hock.

camouflet

kä-mōō-flā, n.

a mine to destroy an underground hostile gallery: an underground cavern filled with gas and smoke formed by a

bomb exploding beneath the
surface.

n. **cam'ouflage** (-fläzh) any
device or means (esp. visual)
for disguising, or for deceiving
an adversary: the use of such a
device or means.

v.t. and v.i. to deceive, to
counterfeit, to disguise.

[Fr. *camouflet,* a whiff of smoke
intentionally blown in the face,
an affront, a camouflet.]

camsho

kam'shō, **camshoch,
camsheugh**

kam'shuhh, (*Scot.*) adjs.
crooked.

camstairy, camsteerie,
camsteary

kam-stār'i, -stēr'i, (chiefly *Scot.*)
adjs.

perverse, unruly.
[Ety. dub.]

canaigre

kə-nā'gər, kə-nī'grē, n.
a Texan dock whose root is
used in tanning.
[Mexican Sp.]

canaster

kə-nas'tər, n.
a kind of tobacco, so called
from the rush basket in which it
was originally brought from
Spanish America.

[Sp. *canastra, canasta* — Gr.
kanastron.]

cancelier, canceleer

kan-si-lēr', (*Scott*) v.i.
of a hawk, to turn on the wing
before stopping. — Also n.

cangue, cang

kang, n.
a Chinese portable pillory borne
on the shoulders by petty
offenders.

[Fr. *cangue* — Port. *cango,* a
yoke.]

canities

ka-nish'i-ēz, n.
whiteness of the hair.
[L.]

capa

kä'pə, n.
a Spanish cloak: fine Cuban
tobacco for the outsides of
cigars.
[Sp.]

capelin

kap'ə-lin, n.
a small fish of the smelt family,
abundant off Newfoundland,
much used as bait. — Also
cap'lin.
[Fr. *capelan.*]

capeline

kap'ə-lin, n.
a small iron skullcap worn by
archers: a light woollen hood for
evening wear: a surgical

bandage for the head. — Also
cap'elline.
[Fr., — L.L. *capella* — *capa*, a
cap.]

capellet
kap'ə-lit, n.
a wen-like swelling on a horse's
elbow, or on the back part of his
hock.
[Fr., — L.L. *capella* — *capa*, a
cap.]

capias
kā'pi-as, ka', (*law*) n.
a writ which authorises the
arrest of the person named in it.
[L., you should seize, 2nd sing.
pres. subj. of *capĕre*, to take.]

caple, capul
kā'pl, n.
a horse.
[M.E. *capel*; cf. O.N. *kapall*; Ir.
capall; L.L. *caballus*, a horse.]

caponiere
kap-ō-nēr', n.
a covered passage across the
ditch of a fortified place. — Also
caponier'.
[Fr. *caponnière*, Sp. *caponera*,
capon-coop.]

capotasto
kap'ō-tas-tō, **capodastro**
kap'ō-das-trō, ns.
a movable bridge secured over

the fingerboard and strings of a
lute or guitar, to alter the pitch
of all the strings together: —
pls. **cap'otastos, -dastros.** —
Also **cap'ō:** — pl. **cap'os.**
[It. *capo tasto, dastro*, head
stop.]

capote
kə-pōt', n.
a long kind of cloak or mantle.
[Fr. dim. of *cape*, a cloak.]

capreolate
kap'ri-ō-lāt, adj.
tendrilled.
[L. *căprĕŏlus*, a tendril.]

caracara
kä-rä-kä-rä', or *kä-rä-kä'rä*, n.
a name for several South
American vulture-like hawks.
[Imit.]

carambola
ka-rəm-bō'lə, n.
a small East Indian tree
(*Averrhoa carambola*) of the
wood-sorrel family: its acrid
pulpy fruit used for tarts, etc.
[Port.]

carcajou
kär'kə-jōō, n.
the glutton or wolverene.
[Canadian Fr., prob. from an
Indian name.]

carcake

kär'kāk, (*Scot.*) n.

a kind of cake for Shrove
Tuesday.

[O.E. *caru,* grief, and **cake.**]

carcanet

kär'kə-net, n.

a collar of jewels: a jewelled
head-ornament (*obs.*).

[Fr. (and obs. Eng.) *carcan,* an
iron collar used for punishment
— L.L. *carcannum,* from Gmc.]

cardecu, cardecue

kär'di-kū, (*obs.*) n.

an old French silver coin.

[Fr. *quart d'écu,* quarter of a
crown.]

cardoon

kär-dōōn', n.

a Mediterranean plant close
akin to the true artichoke, its
leafstalks and ribs eaten like
celery.

[Obs. Fr. *cardon* — L. *carduus,*
a thistle.]

caribe

kä-rē'bā, n.

the piranha.

[Sp., Carib, savage, piranha.]

carlock

kär'lok, n.

a Russian isinglass.

[Russ. *karluk.*]

carnauba, carnahuba

kär-nä-ōō'bə, or *-now',* n.

a Brazilian palm (*Copernicia*):
its yellowish wax — also
Brazilian wax.

[Braz.]

carny, carney

kär'ni, (*dial.*) v.t. and v.i.

to coax, wheedle.
n. flattery: a flatterer.
adj. cunning, sly.

carr

kär, n.

(a copse in) boggy ground.

[O.N. *kjarr.*]

carrag(h)een

kar-ə-gēn', n.

a purplish-red North Atlantic
seaweed (*Chondrus crispus*)
and a related species (*Gigartina
mamillosa*), used for making
soup and a kind of blancmange,
as well as for size — also called
Irish moss.
n. **carragee'nan,
carrag(h)ee'nin** a colloid
prepared from red algae, used
in food processing,
pharmaceuticals, etc.

[Prob. Ir. *carraigín,* little rock —
carraig, rock.]

47

carritch

kar'ich, (*Scot.*) n.

a catechism.

[Fr. *catéchèse,* taken to be a plural.]

carriwitchet

kar-i-wich'it, n.

a quip: a quibble.

[Origin unknown.]

carthamine

kär'thə-min, n.

a dye got from safflower.

[L.L. *carthamus* — Ar. *qartum,* saffron.]

cartulary

kär'tū-lər-i, n.

a register-book of a monastery, etc.: one who kept the records: the place where the register is kept.

[L.L. *chartulārium* — L. *chartula,* a document — *charta,* paper.]

carucate

kar'ū-kāt, n.

as much land as a team of oxen could plough in a season.

n. **car'ucage** a tax on the carucate, first imposed by Richard I in 1198.

[L.L. *carrūcāta,* ploughland — *carrūca,* plough, from root of **car.**]

cascabel

kas'kə-bel, n.

the part behind the base-ring of a cannon.

[Sp.]

caschrom

kas'krōm, n.

a sort of spade with a bent handle, formerly used in the Scottish Highlands for tilling the ground — Also **cas crom.**

[Gael. *cas,* foot, handle, *chrom,* fem. of *crom,* bent, crooked.]

cassimere

kas'i-mēr, n.

a twilled cloth of the finest wools. — Also **ker'seymere.**

[Corr. of **cashmere.**]

cassonade

kas-o-nād', n.

unrefined sugar.

[Fr.]

cassone

kä-sō'nā, (It.) n.

a large chest, elaborately carved and painted.

cassumunar

kas-ōō-mū'nər, n.

an East Indian ginger.

[Origin unknown.]

catapan

kat'ə-pan, n.

the governor of Calabria and Apulia for the Byzantine emperor.

[Acc. to Littré, from Gr. *katepanō tōn axiōmatōn*, one placed over the dignities.]

catasta

kət-as'tə, n.

a block on which slaves were exposed for sale: a stage or place for torture.

[L.]

catawba

kə-tö'bə, n.

an American grape (*Vitis labrusca*): a red wine made from it.

[*Catawba* River in Carolina.]

catechu

kat'i-chōō, -shōō, n.

a dark extract of Indian plants (acacia, betel-nut, etc.) rich in tannin.

ns. **cat'echol** (*-kōl, -chōl*) a white crystalline phenol-alcohol derived from catechu; **catechō'lamine** (*-kō'lə-mēn, -chō'*) any of several sympathomimetic compounds (e.g. adrenaline and noradrenaline) that are derivatives of catechol.

[Cf. Malay *cachu*.]

cathexis

kə-thek'sis, (*psych*.) n.

a charge of mental energy attached to any particular idea or object: — pl. **cathex'es** (*-sēs*).

adj. **cathec'tic**.

[Gr. *kathexis*, holding.]

cattabu

kat'ə-bū, n.

a cross between common cattle and zebu.

[From *catt*le and ze*bu*.]

cattalo

kat'ə-lō, n.

a cross between the bison ('buffalo') and the domestic cow: — pl. **catt'alo(e)s**.

[From *catt*le and buff*alo*.]

catty

kat'i, n.

a unit of measurement used in S.E. Asia and China, equal to about 1·3 lb. avoirdupois in S.E. Asia and Hong Kong, and about 1·1 lb. avoirdupois (500 grammes) in China. — Also **kat'i, katt'i**.

[Malay *kati*.]

cavalla

kə-val'ə, **cavally** *kə-val'i*, ns.

an American fish of the scad family, or any of several related carangoid fish.

[Sp. *caballa* and Port. *cavalla,* mackerel.]

cavel

kāv'l, (*Scot.*) n.

a piece of wood, etc., used in casting lots: a lot.

[Du. *kavel.*]

cavendish

kav'ən-dish, n.

tobacco moistened and pressed into quadrangular cakes.

[Possibly from the name of the original manufacturer.]

cavesson

kav'əs-ən, n.

a nose-band for a horse.

[Fr. *caveçon* — It. *cavezzone* — L. *capitia, capitium,* a head-covering.]

cavie

kāv'i, (*Scot.*) n.

a hen-coop or cage.

[Cf. Du. *kevie*, Ger. *Käfig* — L. *cavus.*]

cedi

sed'i, n. **(new cedi)**

the unit of Ghana's decimal currency, equal to 100 (new) pesewas: — pl. **ced'is.**

cedula

sed'ū-lə, n.

a S. American promissory-note or mortgage-bond on lands.

[Sp.]

cembra

sem'brə, n. (also **cembra pine**)

the Swiss stone-pine.

[Modern L., from Ger. dial. *zember,* timber; cf. Ger. *Zimmer,* room.]

centner

sent'nər, n.

a hundredweight, usually of 50 kg.

[Ger., — L. *centēnārius.*]

cerasin

ser'ə-sin, n.

the insoluble portion of cherry-tree gum.

[L. *cerasus,* Gr. *kerasos,* the cherry-tree.]

cerastes

se-ras'tēz, n.

the North African horned viper, with a horny process over each eye: — pl. **ceras'tes.**

n. **Ceras'tium** the genus of mouse-ear chickweed, with horn-shaped capsules.

[Gr. *kerastēs* — *keras,* a horn.]

ceratoid
ser'ə-toid, adj.
horny.
[Gr. *keratoeidēs — keras*, horn,
eidos, form.]

ceresin, ceresine
ser'ə-sin, -sēn, ns.
a kind of hard, whitish wax
prepared from ozokerite.
[L. *cera*, wax.]

cerge
sûrj, n.
a large wax-candle burned
before the altar. — Also **cierge,
serge.**
[O.Fr., — L. *cēreus — cēra*,
wax.]

cerris
ser'is, n.
the Turkey oak (*Quercus
cerris*).
adj. **cerr'ial.**
[L. *cerreus.*]

cerumen
si-rōō'men, n.
ear wax.
adj. **ceru'minous.**
[L. *cēra*, wax.]

ceruse
sē'rōōs, or *si-rōōs'*, n.
white lead.
n. **cē'rus(s)ite** native lead

carbonate.
[Fr., — L. *cērussa*, conn. with
cēra, Gr. *kēros*, wax.]

chabouk
chä'bōōk, n.
a horsewhip.
[Pers. *chābuk.*]

chacma
chak'mə, n.
a large South African baboon.
[From Hottentot.]

chaft
chaft, chäft, (*Scot.*) n.
the jaw.
[O.N. *kjaptr*, cf. Sw. *kaft*, Dan.
kieft.]

chalaza
ka-lā'zə, n.
in a bird's egg, the string that
holds the yolk-sac in position
(*zool.*): the base of the ovule
(*bot.*).
adj. **chalazogamic**
(*kal-az-ō-gam'ik*).
n. **chalazogamy** (*-og'ə-mi*;
bot.) entrance of the pollen-tube
through the chalaza (opp. to
porogamy).
[Gr. *chalaza*, hail, lump.]

chalder
chöl'dər, n.
an old Scottish dry measure,
containing 16 bolls.
[Prob. a form of **chaldron.**]

chaldron

chöl'drən, n.

an old coal-measure, holding 36 heaped bushels (= 25½ cwt.).

[Fr. *chaudron*.]

challis, shalli

chal'is, shal'is, shal'i, ns.

a soft glossless silk and worsted fabric, later applied to other materials.

[Origin uncertain.]

chalumeau

shal-ū-mō', shal-ü-mō', n.

an early reed instrument that developed into the clarinet: the lowest register of the clarinet: — pl. **chalumeaux** (*-mōz'*).

[Fr., — O.Fr. *chalemel* — L.L. *calamellus*, dim. of *calamus*, a pipe, a reed.]

chamade

shə-mäd', n.

a drum or trumpet call for a parley or surrender.

[Fr.]

chamiso

shə-mē'sō, **chamise** *shə-mēz'*, ns.

a rosaceous shrub (*Adenostoma fasciculatum*) of California: — pls. **chami'sos, -mis'es.**

n. **chamisal'** a chamiso thicket.

[Sp. *chamiza*, cane.]

champak, champac

chum'puk, cham'pak, n.

an Indian tree (*Michelia champaca*) of the magnolia family, of great beauty, with oppressively scented flowers.

[Hind.]

champerty

cham'pər-ti, n.

an illegal bargain whereby the one party is to assist the other in a suit, and is to share in the proceeds.

n. **cham'part** the division of the produce of land, the right of the feudal lord.

[Norm. Fr. — L. *campī pars*, part of the field.]

chaparajos

shap-ə-rä'ōs, chä-pä-rä'hhos, **chaparejos** *-rä', -rē'*, ns.pl.

cowboy's leather riding leggings (short forms **chaps, shaps**).

[Mex. Sp.]

chaprassi

chu-präs'i, n.

an office messenger: a household attendant: an orderly.

[Hind. *chaprāsi*, badge-wearer, messenger — *chaprās*, a badge.]

charas, churrus

chär'əs, chur'əs, ns.

the resinous exudation of hemp, a narcotic and intoxicant.

[Hind.]

charneco

chär'ni-kō, (Shak.) n.

a kind of sweet wine.

[Prob. from a village near Lisbon.]

charpie

shär'pē, or *-pē',* n.

lint shredded down to form a soft material for dressing wounds.

[O.Fr. *charpir* — L. *carpĕre,* to pluck.]

charqui

chär'kē, n.

beef cut into long strips and dried in the sun — jerked beef.

[Quechua.]

chaton

shä-tō', n.

the head of a finger-ring.

[Fr.]

chatoyant

shat-wä-yä, shat-oi'ənt, adj.

with a changing lustre, like a cat's eye in the dark: iridescent.

n. **chatoyance** (*shat-wä-yäs, shat-oi'əns*).

[Fr.]

chatta

chät'ä, n.

an umbrella.

[Hind.]

chavender

chav'ən-dər, n.

the chub.

[Cf. **cheven.**]

chéchia

shä'shya, n.

a cylindrical skull-cap, worn by Arabs and adopted by French troops in Africa.

[Fr., — Berber *tashashit,* pl. *tishushai,* skull-cap.]

chelicera

kē-lis'ə-rə, n.

a biting appendage in Arachnida: — pl. **chēlic'erae** (*-rē*).

[Gr. *chēlē,* a crab's claw, *keras,* horn.]

chenar

chē-när', n.

the oriental plane (*Platanus orientalis*).

[Pers. *chinār.*]

chenet

shə-ne, (Fr.) n.

an andiron.

cherimoya, cherimoyer

cher-i-moi'ə, -ər, ns.

a Peruvian fruit (*Anona cherimolia*) resembling the custard-apple.

[Quechua.]

chernozem

chûr'nō-zem, n.

a very fertile soil of sub-humid steppe, consisting of a dark topsoil over a lighter calcareous layer.

[Russ., black earth.]

chevalet

shə-va'lā, she', n.

the bridge of a stringed instrument (*mus.*).

[Fr. dim. of *cheval,* a horse.]

cheven

chev'ən, n.

the chub. — Also **chev'in.**

[Fr. *chevin, chevanne.*]

cheverel, -il

chev'ər-əl, n.

a kid: soft, flexible kidskin leather.

adj. like kid leather, pliable.

ns. **chev(e)ron** (*shev'*; *obs.*) a kid glove; **chevrette** (*shəv-ret'*) a thin kind of goat-skin.

[Fr. *chevreau, chevrette,* a kid — *chèvre*; L. *capra,* a she-goat.]

chevesaile

chev'ə-sāl, n.

an ornamental collar of a coat.

[O.Fr. *chevesaile* — *chevece,* the neck.]

chewink

chə-wingk', n.

a large finch of eastern N. America, the red-eyed towhee.

[Imit.]

chiao

jow, n.

a coin of the People's Republic of China, one-tenth of 1 yuan: — pl. **chiao.**

[Chin.]

chica

chē'kə, n.

an orange-red dye-stuff, got by boiling the leaves of a South American Bignonia.

[From a native name.]

chicha

chēch'ə, n.

a South American liquor fermented from maize.

[Said to be Haitian.]

chickaree

chik-ə-rē', n.

an American red squirrel.

[From its cry.]

chillum

chil'um, n.

the part of a hookah containing the tobacco and charcoal balls: a hookah itself: the act of smoking it.

[Hind. *chilam.*]

chimer

chim'ər, **chimere** *chi-mēr'*, ns.

a long sleeveless tabard: the upper robe worn by a bishop.

[O.Fr. *chamarre*; cf. **cymar;** Sp. *zamarra*, *chamarra*, sheepskin.]

chinampa

chin-am'pə, n.

a 'floating garden', of earth piled on floating mats of twigs.

[Sp., — Nahuatl *chinamitl.*]

chinch

chinch, n.

the bed-bug in America.

[Sp. *chinche* — L. *cimex.*]

chincherinchee, chinkerinchee

ching'kə-rin-chē', chin-kə-rin'chē, n.

a white-flowered S. African plant of the star-of-Bethlehem genus. — Also (*coll.*) **chinks.**

[Said to be imitative of the flower-stalks rubbing together in the wind.]

chinkapin, chincapin, chinquapin

ching'kə-pin, n.

the dwarf chestnut of the U.S.

[Algonquian.]

chinovnik

chin-ov'nik, n.

a high official in the Russian civil service: a bureaucrat.

[Russ., — *chin*, rank.]

chiragra

kī-rag'rə, n.

gout in the hand.

adjs. **chirag'ric, -al.**

[Gr. *cheiragrā* — *cheir*, hand, *agrā*, a catching.]

chitarrone

kēt-ə-rō'nā, n.

a large lute-like instrument with a long neck.

[It.]

chittagong

chit'ə-gong, n.

an Indian variety of domestic fowl.

chitt'agong-wood' a cabinetmaker's wood, usu. that of *Chickrassia tabularis* (mahogany family).

[*Chittagong* in Bangladesh.]

chloasma

klō-az'mə, n.

a skin disease marked by
yellowish-brown patches.
[Gr. *chloasma*, greenness,
yellowness — *chloē*, verdure.]

chobdar

chōb'där, n.

in India, an usher.
[Pers.]

choenix, chenix

kē'niks, n.

in ancient Greece, a dry
measure equivalent to rather
more than a quart.
[Gr., in Rev. vi. 6.]

cholagogue

kol'ə-gog, n.

a purgative causing evacuations
of bile.
adj. **cholagog'ic** (*-gog'ik,
-goj'ik*).
[Gr. *cholē*, bile, *agōgos*,
leading.]

choli

chō'lē, n.

a short, short-sleeved blouse
often worn under a sari.
[Hindi *colī*; from Sans. but prob.
of Dravidian origin.]

choltry

chōl'tri, n.

a caravanserai: a shed used as
a place of assembly. — Also
choul'try.
[From Malayalam.]

choom

chōōm, (*Austr. coll.*) n.

an Englishman.

chout

chowt, n.

one-fourth part of the revenue,
extorted by the Mahrattas as
blackmail: blackmail, extortion.
[Hind. *chauth*, the fourth part.]

chowry, chowri

chow'ri, n.

an instrument used for driving
away flies.
[Hindi *caŭrī*.]

chrematist

krē'mə-tist, n.

a political economist.
adj. **chrematis'tic** pertaining
to finance, money-making, or
political economy.
n. sing. **chrematis'tics** the
science of wealth.
[Gr. *chrēmatistēs*, a
money-getter — *chrēma, -atos*,
a thing, possession, money.]

chufa

chōō'fə, n.

a sedge with edible tubers.

[Sp.]

chukor

chu-kör', **chukar** *-kär'*,

chik(h)or *chi-kör'*, ns. an Indian partridge.

[Hindi *cakor*.]

churinga

chōō-ring'gə, n.

a sacred amulet.

[Australian Aboriginal.]

chyle

kīl, n.

a white fluid, mainly lymph mixed with fats derived from food in the body.

n. **chylū'ria** (Gr. *ouron*, urine) the presence of chyle in the urine.

[Gr. *chȳlos*, juice — *cheein*, to pour.]

chyme

kīm, n.

the pulp to which food is reduced in the stomach.

n. **chymificā'tion** the act of being formed into chyme.

v.t. **chym'ify** to form into chyme.

adj. **chym'ous**.

[Gr. *chȳmos*, chyme, juice — *cheein*, to pour.]

cibation

si-bā'shən, (*obs.*) n.

the seventh of the twelve processes employed in the search for the philosopher's stone, 'feeding the matter': taking food, feeding.

[L. *cibātiō*, *-ōnis*, feeding.]

cidaris

sid'ə-ris, n.

a Persian tiara: (with *cap.*) a genus of sea-urchins, mostly fossil.

[Gr. *kidaris*.]

cilice

sil'is, n.

haircloth: a penitential garment made of haircloth.

adj. **cilicious** (*-ish'əs*).

[L., — Gr. *kilikion*, a cloth made of Cilician goat's hair.]

cimelia

sī-mē'li-ə, n.pl.

treasures.

[Gr. *keimēlia*.]

cimier

sē-myā', n.

the crest of a helmet.

[Fr.]

cippus
sip'əs, n.
the stocks: a monumental pillar:
— pl. **cippī.**
[L. *cippus,* a post.]

circumincession, -insession
sûr-kəm-in-sesh'ən, n.
the reciprocity of existence in
one another of the three
persons of the Trinity.
[L. *circum,* around, and
incessus, pa.p. of *incēdere,* to
go, proceed.]

ciselure
sēz'loōr, n.
the art or operation of chasing:
the chasing upon a piece of
metalwork.
n. **cis'eleur** (*-lər*), a chaser.
[Fr.]

citole
sit'ōl, sit-ōl', n.
a mediaeval stringed
instrument.

cladode
klad'ōd, (*bot.*) *n.*
a branch with the appearance
and functions of a leaf.
[Gr. *klados,* a shoot.]

clarabella
klar-ə-bel'ə, n.
an organ-stop of a sweet, fluty
tone.

[L. *clārus,* clear, *bellus,*
beautiful.]

clastic
klas'tik, (*geol.*) *adj.*
(of sedimentary rock) composed
of fragments of older rock,
fragmental.
[Gr. *klastos* — *klaein,* to break.]

cleithral, clithral
klī'thrəl, adj.
completely roofed over.
[Gr. *kleithron,* a bar.]

clem
klem, v.i. and *v.t.*
to starve.
[Dial. Eng. *clam*; Ger. *klemmen,*
to pinch.]

cleruch
kler'ōōk, -uk, (*Greek hist.*) *n.*
an allotment-holder in foreign
territory retaining his Athenian
citizenship.
n. **cler'uchy, cleruch'ia.**
[Gr. *klērouchos* — *klēros,*
allotment, *echein,* to have.]

clevis
klev'is, n.
a U-shaped piece of metal
through which tackle may pass,
fixed at the end of a beam.
[Ety. dub.]

clitellum

kli-, klī-tel'əm, n.

a glandular belt on a worm, secreting a cocoon: — pl. **clitell'a.**
adj. **clitell'ar.**
[L. *clītellae,* pack-saddle.]

cloam

klōm, n. and adj.

earthenware, clay, or made of such.
[O.E. *clām,* mud.]

cloqué

klo-kā', n.

an embossed material. — Also adj.
[Fr.]

clote

klōt, n.

the burdock: extended to other plants of burry character.
n. **clotbur** (*klot'bər*) the burdock: a species of Xanthium. — Also **clote'bur, cockle-bur.**
[O.E. *clāte.*]

clough

kluf, or *klow,* n.

a ravine: a valley.
[O.E. would be *clōh*; Scot. *cleuch.*]

clour

kloor, (*Scot.*) n.

a knock: a swelling caused by a knock, a bruise.
v.t. to knock: to raise a bump.
[Origin doubtful.]

clumber

klumb'ər, n.

a kind of spaniel, formerly bred at *Clumber,* in Nottinghamshire.

clunch

klunch, -sh, n.

a tough clay.
[Prob. related to **clump.**]

cly

klī, (*slang*) v.t.

to seize, steal.
cly'-fāk'er a pickpocket;
cly'-fāk'ing pocket-picking.
[Prob. related to **claw;** referred by some to Du. *kleed, a garment, to fake a cly,* to take a garment.]

clypeus

klip'i-əs, n.

the shield-like part of an insect's head.
adjs. **clyp'eal** of the clypeus;
clyp'eate, clyp'ēiform buckler-shaped.
[L. *clipeus* (*clypeus*), a round shield.]

coaita

kō-ī-tä′, n.

the red-faced spider monkey.

[Tupí.]

cobia

kō′bi-ə, n.

the sergeant-fish.

[Perh. of West Indian origin.]

coble, cobble

kōb′l, kob′l, ns.

a small flat-bottomed boat for use on rivers (*Scot.*): a single-masted sea-fishing boat with a flat bottom and square stern (*N.E. England*).

[Cf. W. *ceubal*, a hollow trunk, a boat.]

coccineous

kok-sin′i-əs, (*obs.*) adj.

bright red.

[L. *coccineus — coccum*, cochineal.]

cocco

kok′ō, **coco** *kō′kō*, ns.

the taro or other edible araceous tuber: — pls. **cocc′os, co′cos.**

cock-a-bondy

kok′ə-bon′di (coll. *kok-i-bun′di*), n.

a fly for angling.

[Welsh *coch a bon ddu*, red, with black stem.]

cockernony

kok-ər-non′i, (*obs. Scot.*) n.

the gathering of hair in a fillet: a coiffure: a pad of false hair: a starched cap.

[Origin obscure.]

cocket

kok′it, n.

the custom-house seal (*hist.*): a custom-house certificate.

[Origin doubtful.]

codilla

kō-dil′ə, n.

the coarsest part of hemp or flax.

[Dim. of It. *coda* — L. *cauda*, a tail.]

codille

kō-dil′, n.

a situation in ombre when the challenger loses.

[Fr.]

coehorn, cohorn

kō′hörn, n.

a small mortar for throwing grenades.

[Baron van *Coehoorn* (1641–1704).]

coffinite

kof′in-īt, n.

a uranium-yielding ore.

[From Reuben Clare *Coffin*, a worker of the ore in Colorado.]

coffle
kof'l, n.
a gang, esp. of slaves.
[Ar. *qāfilah,* a caravan.]

coggie, cogie
kog'i, kōg'i, (*Scot.*) n.
a small wooden bowl. — Also
cog.
[Dim. of **cogue.**]

cogue, cog
kōg, kog, (esp. *Scot.*) ns.
a round wooden vessel, usu. of
staves and hoops.
[Ety. dub.]

coho, cohoe
kō'hō, n.
a Pacific salmon, a species of
Oncorhynchus: — pl.
co'ho(e)s.
[Ety. unknown.]

cohune
kō-hōōn', n.
a Central and South American
palm (*Attalea cohune*) yielding
cohune nuts and **cohune oil.**
[From Amer. Sp.]

coistrel, coistril
kois'tril, n.
a groom (*obs.*): a knave
(*Shak.*).
[See **custrel.**]

colibri
kol'ib-rē, -lē', n.
a humming-bird.
[Sp. *colibrí,* Fr. *colibri,* said to
be the Carib name.]

colin
kol'in, n.
the Virginian quail.
[Ety. uncertain; perh. Sp.]

collieshangie
kol-i-shang'i, (*Scot.*) n.
a noisy wrangling: an uproar: a
disturbance.
[Origin unknown.]

colluvies
ko-lū', ko-lōō'vi-ēz, n.
accumulated filth: a rabble.
[L. *colluviēs,* washings —
colluĕre, to wash thoroughly.]

colocynth
kol'o-sinth, n.
a kind of cucumber (*Citrullus
colocynthis*): a cathartic drug
got from it.
[Gr. *kolokynthis.*]

colophony
kol-of'ə-ni, or *kol',* n.
rosin.
[Gr. *kolophōniā* (*rhētinē,* gum)
from *Kolophōn,* Colophon, in
Asia Minor.]

61

colugo

ko-lōō'gō, n.

the flying lemur: — pl.
colu'gos.

[Prob. from Malaysian word.]

colza

kol'zə, n.

cole-seed, yielding **col'za-oil.**

[Du. *koolzaad,* cabbage-seed.]

comedo

kom'i-dō, n.

a blackhead, a small,
black-tipped white mass
sometimes found in the
sebaceous glands: — pl.
com'edos.

[L. *comedō, -ōnis,* glutton —
comedĕre, to eat up, from its
wormlike appearance.]

commorant

kom'ər-ənt, n. and adj.

resident (esp. at a university).

[L. *commorāns, -antis,* pr.p. of
commorārī, to abide.]

commot,

commote *kum'ət,* (*hist.*) n.

a subdivision of a cantred.

[Mediaeval L. *commotum* — W.
cymwd.]

compesce

kəm-pes', (*arch. Scot.*) v.t.

to restrain.

[L. *compēscĕre.*]

conacre

kon'ā-kər, n.

the custom of letting land in
Ireland in small portions for a
single crop, for rent in money or
labour; a form of this is still
found in Eire. — Also
corn'acre.

v.t. to sublet in conacre.

n. **con'acreism.**

[**corn, acre.**]

confarreation

kən-far-i-ā'shən, n.

a Roman patrician mode of
marriage, in which a spelt cake
was offered up.

adj. **confarr'eāte.**

[L. *cōnfarreātiō* — *con-,* with,
fār, spelt.]

congiary

kon'ji-ər-i, n.

a gift to the Roman people or
soldiery, originally in corn, oil,
etc., later in money.

[L. *congiārium* — *congius,* the
Roman gallon.]

congou

kong'gōō, n.

a kind of black tea. — Also
con'go.

[Chinese *kung hu*, labour,
referring to that expended in
producing it.]

coniine

kō'ni-ēn, n.

a liquid, highly poisonous
alkaloid ($C_8H_{17}N$) found in
hemlock (*Conium*). — Also
cō'nia, cō'nine.

[Gr. *kōneion*, hemlock.]

conirostral

kōn-i-ros'trəl, adj.

having a strong conical beak.

[L. *cōnus* (Gr. *kōnos*), cone,
rōstrālis — *rōstrum*, a beak.]

conjee, congee

kon'jē, n.

water in which rice has been
boiled.

v.t. to starch with conjee.

[Tamil *kañji*.]

conspurcation

kon-spûr-kā'shən, (*obs.*) n.
defilement.

[L. *cōnspurcāre, -ātum*, to
defile.]

constuprate

kon'stū-prāt (*obs.*) v.t.
to ravish.

n. **constuprā'tion.**

[L. *cōnstuprāre* — *con-*, intens.,
stuprum, defilement, disgrace.]

contesseration

kon-tes-ər-ā'shən, n.

(the act of) forming friendship or
union — in Roman times by
dividing a square tablet as
token.

[From L. *contesserāre* — *con-*,
tessera, square stone, token
(*hospitalis*, given by guest to
host).]

contline

kont'līn, n.

the space between stowed
casks: a spiral interval between
the strands of a rope.

contrahent

kon'trə-hənt, adj.

entering into a contract.

n. a contracting party.

[L. *contrahēns, -entis* —
contrahĕre, to contract.]

contrayerva

kon-trə-yûr'və, n.

a tropical American plant of the
mulberry family, once esteemed
as an antidote: a Jamaican
birthwort of like reputation.

[Sp. (now *contrahierba*)—L.
contrā, against, *herba*, a herb.]

contubernal

(*Chaucer*, **contubernyal**)
kən-tūb'ər-nəl, adj.

living together (in the same
tent): pertaining to

63

companionship.

[L. *contubernālis* (*n.*) — *cum*, with, together, *taberna*, hut, tavern.]

coof

kōōf, køf, kif, (*Scot.*) n.

a lout.

[Origin obscure.]

coontie, coonty

kōōn'ti, n.

an American cycad yielding a sort of arrowroot.

[Seminole *kunti.*]

copacetic, copesettic

kō-pə-set'ik, (*U.S. slang*) adj.

sound: excellent.

interj. all clear.

[Origin obscure.]

copal

kō'pəl, n.

a hard resin got from many tropical trees, and also fossil.

[Sp., — Nahuatl *copalli,* resin.]

coparcener

kō-pär'sən-ər, n.

a joint heir to an undivided property.

n. and adj. **copar'cenery, -ary.**

copataine

kop'ə-tān, (*Shak.*) adj.

high-crowned like a sugar-loaf.

[Ety. obscure.]

copple

kop'l, (*obs.*) n.

a bird's crest.

n. **copp'le-crown.**

adj. **copp'le-crowned.**

coquito

kō-kē'tō, n.

a beautiful Chilean palm, *Jubaea spectabilis:* — pl. **coqui'tos.**

[Sp.; dim. of *coco,* coco-palm.]

corban

kör'bən, n.

anything devoted to God in fulfilment of a vow.

[Heb. *qorbān,* an offering, sacrifice.]

corcass

kör'kəs, n.

in Ireland, a salt-marsh, or readily flooded land by a river.

[Ir. *corcach.*]

corella

kə-rel'ə, n.

an Australian long-billed cockatoo.

[Aboriginal.]

corf

körf, n.

a coal-miner's basket, now usu. a tub or trolley: a cage for fish or lobsters: — pl. **corves** (*körvz*). — Also *dial.* **cauf** (*köf*): — pl. **cauves**.
corf'-house (*Scot.*) a salmon-curing house.
[Du., — L. *corbis*, basket.]

corium

kō'ri-əm, kö', n.

leather armour (*ant.*): the true skin, under the epidermis (*anat.*).
adjs. **coriā'ceous, co'rious** leathery.
[L. *corium* — Gr. *chorion*, skin, leather.]

corkir, korkir

kör'kər, (*Scot.*) n.

a lichen used for dyeing (red or purple).
[Gael. *corcur* — L. *purpura*, purple.]

cornage

körn'ij, (*hist.*) n.

a feudal service or rent fixed according to number of horned cattle — horngeld.
[O.Fr., — L. *cornū*, horn.]

corocore

kor'ō-kōr, -kör, -ō, n.

a Malay form of boat. — Also **cor'ocorō** (pl. **cor'ocoros**).
[Malay *kurakura*.]

corozo

kor-ō'sō, n.

a South American short-stemmed palm (*Phytelephas*) whose seed (**corozo nut**) gives vegetable ivory: also the cohune palm, or other: — pl. **corō'zos**.
[Sp. from an Indian language.]

corposant

kör'pə-zant, n.

St Elmo's fire, an electrical discharge forming a glow about a mast-head, etc.
[Port. *corpo santo* — L. *corpus sanctum*, holy body.]

corrade

kə-rād', kor-, (*geol.*) v.t.

to wear away through the action of loose solid material, e.g. pebbles in a stream or wind-borne sand.
n. **corrasion** (-*rā'zhən*).
[L. *corrādēre*, to scrape together — *con-*, together, *rādēre, rāsum*, to scratch.]

corrody, corody

kor'ō-di, n.

an allowance: a pension: originally the right of the lord to claim free lodging from the vassal.

[O.Fr. *conrei, conroi.*]

corsned

körs'ned, (*hist.*) n.

the ordeal of swallowing a piece of bread or cheese, taken to prove guilt if it stuck in the throat.

[O.E. *corsnæd — gecor* (cf. *coren,* pa.p. of *cēosan,* to choose) and *snæd,* a piece, from *snīdan,* to cut.]

coryza

ko-rī'zə, n.

a cold in the head: nasal catarrh.

[L., — Gr. *koryza.*]

coscinomancy

kos'i-nō-man-si, n.

an ancient mode of divination by a sieve and pair of shears.

[Gr. *koskinon,* a sieve, *manteiā,* divination.]

coshery

kosh'ər-i, n.

the ancient right of an Irish chief to quarter himself and his retainers on his tenantry — also **cosh'ering.**

v.i. **cosh'er** to live on dependants.

n. **cosh'erer.**

[Ir. *coisir,* a feast.]

costean

kos-tēn', v.i.

to dig down to bedrock in prospecting.

n. **costean'ing.**
costean'-pit.

[Said to be from Cornish *cothas,* dropped, *stean,* tin.]

costrel

kos'trəl, (*obs.* or *dial.*) n.

an eared bottle or small keg, to be hung at the waist.

[O.Fr. *costerel.*]

coteline

kōt-lēn', n.

a kind of muslin, corded or ribbed.

[Fr. *côte,* a rib — L. *costa.*]

coticular

kō-tik'ū-lər, (*obs.*) adj.

pertaining to whetstones.

[L. *cōticula,* dim. of *cos, cotis,* whetstone.]

cotta

kot'ə, n.

a surplice.

[L.L. *cotta.*]

cottabus

kot'ə-bəs, n.

an amusement in ancient Greece among young men, consisting in throwing wine into a vessel, success at which betokened fortune in love.

[L., — Gr. *kottabos*.]

cotyle

kot'i-lē, n.

an ancient Greek drinking-cup: a cup-like cavity (*zool.*): — pl. **cot'ylae** (*-lē*) or **cot'ylēs**. adjs. **cotyl'iform** (*bot.*) disc-shaped with raised rim; **cot'yloid** cup-shaped.

[Gr. *kotylē*.]

coucal

kōō'käl, n.

any member of a genus (*Centropus*) of common bush-birds in Africa, India and Australia, the lark-heeled cuckoos.

[Imit.]

coulisse

kōō-lēs', n.

a piece of grooved wood, as the slides in which the side-scenes of a theatre run — hence (in pl.) the wings.

[Fr. *couler*, to glide, to flow — L. *cōlāre*, to strain.]

courbaril

kōōr'bə-ril, n.

the West Indian locust-tree: its resin, gum anime.

[Fr. from Carib.]

coutil, coutille

kōō-til', n.

a strong cotton fabric used in mattresses, etc.

[Fr. *coutil*.]

cowan

kow'ən, (*Scot.*) n.

a dry-stone-diker: a mason who never served an apprenticeship: one who tries to enter a Freemason's lodge, or the like, surreptitiously.

[Origin doubtful.]

cozier, cosier

kō'zi-ər, (*Shak.*) n.

a cobbler.

[O.Fr. *cousere*, tailor — L. *cōnsuĕre*, to sew together.]

crame

krām, (*Scot.*) n.

a booth for selling goods.

[From Du. or Low Ger.]

cranreuch

krän'ruhh, (*Scot.*) n.

hoar-frost.

[Origin obscure; poss. from Gaelic.]

crants

krants, (*Shak.*) n.

the garland carried before the
bier of a maiden and hung over
her grave.

[Ger. *Kranz*, a wreath, a
garland.]

cratch

krach, n.

a crib to hold hay for cattle, a
manger. —n.pl. **cratch'es** a
swelling on a horse's pastern,
under the fetlock.

[Fr. *crèche*, manger; from a
Gmc. root, whence also **crib**.]

craton

krāt'on, (*geol.*) n.

any of the comparatively rigid
areas in the earth's crust.

[Gr. *kratos*, strength.]

creagh, creach

krehh, (*Scot.*) n.

a foray: booty.

[Gael. *creach.*]

creance

krē'əns, n.

the cord which secures the
hawk in training.

[Fr. *créance.*]

crémaillère

krā-mī-yer', n.

a zigzag line of fortification: a
rack railway.

[Fr., pot-hook.]

crepance

krē'pəns, n.

a wound on a horse's hind
ankle-joint, caused by the shoe
of the other hind-foot.

[L. *crepāre*, to break.]

crewels, cruel(l)s

krōō'əlz, (*Scot.*) n.pl.

the king's evil, scrofula.

[Fr. *écrouelles.*]

cringle

kring'gl, n.

a small piece of rope worked
into the bolt-rope of a sail, and
containing a metal ring or
thimble.

[Gmc.; cf. Ger. *Kringel.*]

crispin

kris'pin, n.

a shoemaker, from *Crispin* of
Soissons, the patron saint of
shoemakers, martyred 25
October 287.

crith

krith, n.

a unit of mass, that of 1 litre of
hydrogen at standard
temperature and pressure.

[Gr. *krīthē*, barleycorn, a small weight.]

crithomancy

krith'ō-man-si, n.

divination by the meal strewed over the victims of sacrifice.

[Gr. *krīthē*, barley, and *manteiā*, divination.]

crome, cromb

krōm, krōōm, (*dial.*) n.

a hook or crook.

v.t. to draw with a crome.

[Cf. Du. *kram*.]

cronet

krō'net, (*obs.*) n.

the hair growing over the top of a horse's hoof.

[coronet.]

croze

krōz, n.

the groove in the staves of a cask in which the edge of the head is set.

[Perh. O.Fr. *croz* (Fr. *creux*), groove.]

crubeen

krōō-bēn', krōō', n.

a pig's trotter, as food.

[Ir. *crúibín*, dim. of *crúb*, hoof.]

crucian, crusian

krōō'shən, n.

the German carp, without barbels.

[L.G. *karusse* (Ger. *Karausche*) — L. *coracīnus* — Gr. *korakīnos*, a black perch-like fish — *korax*, raven.]

crumen

krōō'mən, n.

a deer's tear-pit.

n. **cru'menal** (*Spens.*) a purse.

[L. *crumēna*, a purse.]

cruor

krōō'ör, n.

coagulated blood.

[L.]

cruset

krōō'sit, n.

a goldsmith's crucible.

[Cf. Fr. *creuset*, M.Du. *kruysel*, M.L.G. *krusel*.]

crusie, crusy, cruisie

krōōz'i, (*Scot.*) n.

an open iron lamp used with a rush wick.

[From **cruset**.]

crwth

krōōth, n.

the crowd, an old Welsh stringed instrument, four of its

six strings played with a bow, two plucked by the thumb.

[W. *crwth*, a hollow protuberance, a fiddle; Gael., Ir. *cruit*.]

cubica

kū'bi-kə, n.

a fine worsted for linings.

[Sp. *cubica*.]

cudbear

kud'bār, n.

a purple dyestuff, a powder prepared from various lichens.

[From Dr *Cuthbert* Gordon, who made it an article of commerce.]

cuffo

kuf'ō, (*old U.S. slang*) adv.

without any admission charge.

culch, cultch

kulch, (*S. England*) n.

rubbish: the flooring of an oyster-bed: oyster-spawn.

[Origin doubtful.]

cullet

kul'it, n.

waste glass, melted up again with new material.

[Fr. *collet* — L. *collum*, neck.]

culvertage

kul'vərt-tij, n.

degradation of a vassal to the position of a serf.

[O.Fr. *culvert*, a serf.]

cumshaw

kum'shö, n.

a gift, a tip.

[Pidgin-English.]

cunjevoi

kun'ji-voi, (*Austr.*) n.

a marine animal: a large-leaved araceous plant.

[Aboriginal.]

cupel

kū'pəl, n.

a small vessel used by goldsmiths in assaying precious metals: the movable hearth of a reverberatory furnace for refining.

v.t. to assay in a cupel: — pr.p. **cū'pelling**; pa.t. and pa.p. **cū'pelled**.

n. **cūpellā'tion** recovery of precious metal in assaying.

[L. *cūpella*, dim. of *cūpa*.]

curassow

kū'rə-sō, kū-räs'ō, n.

a large turkey-like S. American bird.

[From the island of *Curaçao*.]

curmurring

kər-mûr'ing, n.

a rumbling sound, esp. that made in the bowels by flatulence.

[Imit.]

curtana

kûr-tä'nə, -tā'nə, n.

a sword without a point, symbolic of mercy, carried at coronations.

[L. *curtus*, short.]

curtilage

kûr'til-ij, n.

a court or area of land attached to and including a dwelling-house, etc.

[O.Fr. *courtillage*.]

curule

kū'rōōl, adj.

like a camp-stool with curved legs, applied to the chair of a higher Roman magistrate.

[L. *curūlis* — *currus*, a chariot.]

custrel

kus'trəl, (*hist.*) n.

an attendant on a knight: a knave.

[O.Fr. *coustillier* — *coustille*, dagger; cf. **coistrel**.]

cutcha

kuch'ə, adj.

of dried mud: makeshift.

[Hindi *kaccā*, raw.]

cyathus

sī'ə-thəs, n.

the ancient Greek filling or measuring cup — about $\frac{1}{12}$ of a pint.

n. **Cyath'ea** a genus of tree-ferns, often with cup-shaped indusium, giving name to the family **Cyathea'ceae**.

adj. **cy'athiform** (or -*ath'*) cup-shaped.

ns. **cyath'ium** the characteristic inflorescence of the spurges (pl. **cyath'ia**); **Cyathophyll'um** (Gr. *phyllon*, leaf) a fossil genus of cup-corals.

[Gr. *kyathos*.]

cyesis

sī-ē'sis, n.

pregnancy: — pl. **cyē'ses** (-*sēz*).

[Gk. *kyēsis*.]

cylix

sil' or *sīl'iks*, n.

a shallow two-handled stemmed drinking cup: — pl. **cyl'ices** (-*sēz*). — Also **kyl'ix**.

[Gr. *kўlix, -ikos*.]

cyma

sī'mə, n.

an ogee moulding of the cornice (**cy'ma rec'ta** concave in front, convex behind; **cy'ma rever'sa** convex in front, concave behind).
ns. **cy'mograph** (improperly **cy'magraph**) an instrument for tracing the outline of mouldings; **cymā'tium** a cyma.

[Gr. *kyma,* a billow.]

cymar,

cimar *si-mär',* n.

a loose coat of various styles, formerly worn by women: an undergarment, a shift: a chimer.

[Fr. *simarre,* of comparable meanings, — Sp. *zamarra,* sheepskin.]

cymophane

sī'mō-fān, n.

cat's eye, a variety of chrysoberyl with wavy opalescence.
adj. **cymophanous** (*-mof'ə-nəs*) opalescent.

[Gr. *kȳma,* wave, *phainein,* to show.]

cynanche

si-nang'kē, n.

disease of the throat, esp. quinsy.

[Gr. *kyōn, kynos,* a dog, *anchein,* to throttle.]

cynegetic

sin-ē-jet'ik, adj.

relating to hunting.

[Gr. *kynēgetēs,* huntsman — *kyōn, kynos,* dog, *hēgetēs,* leader.]

D

dacker

dak'ər, **daker, daiker** *dā'kər,*
(*Scot.*) vs.i.
to lounge, saunter: to potter.
[Origin unknown.]

daddock

dad'ək, (*dial.*) n.
the heart of a rotten tree.

dagoba,

dagaba *dä'gə-bä,* n.
in Sri Lanka, a tope (for
Buddhist relics).
[Sinh. *dāgaba.*]

dahabiyah, -iyeh, -ieh, -eeah

dä-hä-bē'(y)ä, -ə, n.
a Nile sailing boat.
[Ar. *dhahabīyah,* golden.]

daimen

dem'ən, dām'ən, (*Scot.*) adj.
occasional.
[Origin obscure.]

dak

däk, **dawk** *dök,* ns.
in India, the mail-post: hence
mail, a letter, a parcel, etc.:
method of travelling like that of
the mail (orig. by relays of
bearers or horses).
dak bungalow a house for
travellers in India; **dak runner**
a runner or horseman who
carries mail.
[Hind. *dāk,* a relay of men.]

dalmahoy

däl'mə-hoi, -hoi', n.
a bushy bob-wig worn in the
18th cent.
[Said to be named from a
wearer.]

daman

dam'an, n.
the Syrian hyrax, the cony of
the Bible.
[Ar.]

dammar

dam'ər, n.
a copal used for making
varnish, obtained from various
conifers. — Also **damm'er.**
[Malay *damar.*]

dancette

dän-set', n.
a zigzag or indented line or
figure (*her.*): the chevron or
zigzag moulding common in
Romanesque architecture.

adj. **dancetté, -ee, -y**
(dän'set-i, or *-set')* deeply
indented.
[O.Fr. *dent, dant,* tooth, notch
— L. *dēns, dentis.*]

dandiprat, dandyprat
dan'di-prat, (*obs.*) n.
a silver three-halfpenny piece:
an insignificant person: a little
boy.
[Origin unknown.]

dannebrog
dan'e-brog, n.
the Danish national flag: the
second of the Danish orders
instituted by King Valdemar in
1219.
[Dan.]

dapsone
dap'sōn, n.
a drug widely used in the
treatment of leprosy, dermatitis,
etc.
[*di*aminodi*p*henylsulph*one.*]

darg
därg, (*Scot.*) n.
a day's work: a task.
[Contr. from *dawerk, day-wark,*
day-work.]

darga
dûr'gä, n.
(a structure over) a place where
a holy person was cremated or
buried.
[Hind. *dargāh.*]

daric
dar'ik, n.
an old gold or silver coin larger
than an English sovereign
named after *Darius* I of Persia.

dariole
da'rē-ōl, dar'yöl, n.
a shell of pastry, etc., or small
round mould: a dish comprising
such a shell and its filling.
[Fr.]

darshan
där'shən, n.
a blessing conferred by seeing
or touching a great or holy
person.
[Hindi.]

dartre
där'tər, n.
herpes.
adj. **dar'trous.**
[Fr.]

darzi
där'zē, dûr'zē, n.
a tailor.
[Hind. *darzī.*]

dassie

das'i, (*S. Afr.*) n.

the hyrax.

[Du. *dasje*, *dim.* of *das*, badger:
Afrik. *dassie.*]

dasyphyllous

das-i-fil'əs, adj.

having crowded, thick, or woolly
leaves.

[Gr. *dasys*, thick, bushy, hairy,
phyllon, leaf.]

datary

dā'tə-ri, n.

an officer of the papal court
charged with registering and
dating bulls, etc., and with
duties relating to the granting of
indults and graces: his office
(also **datā'ria**).

[L.L. *datārius* — L. *dăre*, to
give.]

daut, dawt

döt, (*Scot.*) v.t.

to pet.

n. **daut'ie, dawt'ie** a pet.

[Origin unknown.]

dealbate

dē-al'bāt, adj.

whitened.

n. **dealbā'tion.**

[L. *dealbāre*, *-ātum*, to
whitewash — pfx. *de-*, in sense
of over a surface, *albus*, white.]

deaner

dēn'ər, (*old slang*) n.

a shilling.

[Prob. L. *denārius.*]

deasil

dēz'l, des'l, desh'l, dēsh'l,
(*Scot.*) n.

sunwise motion — opp. to
withershins.

adv. sunwise. — Also
**dea'soil, dei's(h)eal,
dea'siul.**

[Gael. *deiseil.*]

debel

di-bel', (*Milt.*) v.t.

to conquer in war: — pr.p.
debell'ing; pa.t. and pa.p.
debelled'.

[L. *dēbellāre* — *dē*, down,
bellāre, to war — *bellum*, war.]

decussate

di-kus'āt, v.t.

to divide in the form of an X.
v.i. to cross in such a form: to
cross, intersect, as lines, etc.
adjs. **decuss'ate, -d** crossed:
arranged in pairs which cross
each other, like some leaves.
adv. **decuss'ately.**
n. **decussā'tion** (*dek-*).

[L. *decussāre, -ātum* —
decussis, a coin of ten asses
(*decem asses*) marked with X,
symbol of ten.]

deltiology

del-ti-ol'ə-ji, n.

the study and collection of picture postcards.
n. **deltiol'ogist.**

[Gr. *deltion*, small writing-tablet.]

delubrum

di-lū'brəm, -lōō', n.

a temple, shrine, sanctuary: a church having a font: a font.

[L. *dēlūbrum*.]

delundung

del'ən-dung, n.

the weasel-cat of Java and Malacca, a small carnivore akin to the civet.

[Javanese.]

dennet

den'it, n.

a light gig.

[Prob. a surname.]

desman

des'mən, n.

a Russian aquatic insectivore with long snout and musk-glands: a kindred Pyrenean species.

[Sw. *desman*, musk.]

devall

di-völ', v.i.

to sink, decline (*obs.*): to cease (*Scot.*).
n. (*Scot.*) a stop.

[Fr. *dévaler* — L. *dē-*, down, *vallis*, a valley.]

devanagari

dā-və-nä'gə-ri, n.

the character in which Sanskrit is usually written and printed: the official script for Hindi: used also for other Indian languages. — Also with *cap.*

[Sans. *devanāgari*, town-script of the gods; see **nagari.**]

devvel, devel

dev'l, (*Scot.*) n.

a hard blow.
v.t. to hit hard: to stun with a blow.

[Ety. dub.]

dewitt

di-wit', v.t.

to lynch — from the fate of Jan and Cornelius *De Witt* in Holland in 1672.

dharmsala

dûrm-sä'lä, n.

a building having a religious or charitable purpose, as a free or cheap lodging for travellers. — Also **dharmshala.**

[Hindi *dharmsālā* — Sans. **dharma**, *śālā*, hall.]

dharna

dûr'nä, n.

calling attention, esp. to injustice, by sitting or standing in a place where one will be noticed, esp. sitting and fasting at the door of an offender.
[Hindi.]

dhole

dōl, n.

the Indian wild dog.
[Supposed to be from an Indian language.]

diaconicon

dī-ə-kon'i-kən, n.

a sacristy for sacred vessels, in a Greek church, on the south side of the bema or sanctuary.
[Gr. *diākonikon*.]

diadochi

dī-ad'o-kī, n.pl.

the generals who became monarchs of the various kingdoms (Syria, Egypt, etc.) into which the empire of Alexander the Great split after his death (323 B.C.).
[Gr. *diadochos*, succeeding, a successor; *diadechesthai*, to succeed.]

diadrom

dī'ə-drom, n.

a course or passing: a vibration.
adj. (of leaf nerves) radiating fanwise.
[Gr. *dia*, across, *dromos*, a run.]

diapir

dī'ə-pēr, n.

an anticlinal fold in which the overlying rock has been pierced by material from beneath.
adj. **diapi'ric**.
n. **diapi'rism** the upward movement of material through denser rocks to form diapirs.
[Gr. *diapeirainein*, to pierce.]

diaskeuast

dī-ə-skū'ast, n.

a reviser: an interpolator.
[Gr. *diaskeuazein*, to make ready — *dia*, through, *skeuos*, a tool.]

dicacity

di-kas'i-ti, n.

raillery, pert speech.
adj. **dicacious** (*di-kā'shəs*).
[L. *dicāx*, sarcastic.]

dicast, dikast

dik'ast, n.

one of the 6000 Athenians annually chosen to act as judges.
n. **dicas'tery** their court.
adj. **dicas'tic**.
[Gr. *dikastēs* — *dikē*, justice.]

dickcissel

dik-sis'l, n.

the black-throated bunting, an American migratory bird.

[Imit. of call.]

didapper

dī'dap-ər, n.

the dabchick or little grebe: one who disappears and bobs up again.

[**dive** and **dapper,** a variant of **dipper;** cf. O.E. *dūfedoppa,* pelican.]

dido

dī'dō, (*slang*) n.

an antic, caper: a frivolous or mischievous act: — pl. **dī'does, dī'dos.**

act dido to play the fool; **cut up didoes** to behave in an extravagant way.

[Origin unknown.]

dieb

dēb, n.

a jackal of northern Africa.

[Ar. *dhīb.*]

dièdre

dē-edr', n.

a rock angle, or re-entrant corner, usu. with a crack in it.

[Fr.]

diffarreation

di-far-i-ā'shən, n.

a divorce from a Roman marriage by *confarreation.*

[L. *dif-* (*dis-*), asunder.]

digladiate

dī-glad'i-āt, v.i.

to fight with swords: to fence: to wrangle.

ns. **digladiā'tion; diglad'iātor.**

[L. *dīgladiārī,* to contend fiercely — *dis-*, this way and that, and *gladius,* sword.]

dilling

dil'ing, n.

a darling: the youngest child: the weakling of a litter.

[Origin doubtful.]

dimble

dim'bl, n.

a dell, dingle.

dinanderie

dē-nä-də-rē, n.

domestic decorative brassware, originally that made at *Dinant* in Belgium: extended to Indian and Levantine brassware.

[Fr.]

dinges

ding'əs, n.

an indefinite name for any person or thing whose name

one cannot or will not remember. — Also **ding'us.**
[Du., — Afrik. *ding*, thing; cf. Eng. **thingummy, thingumbob.**]

dinic
din'ik, adj.
relating to vertigo or dizziness.
n. a remedy for dizziness.
[Gr. *dīnos*, whirling.]

dinmont
din'mənt, n.
a Border name for a male sheep between the first and second shearing.
[Origin obscure.]

diota
dī-ō'tə, n.
a two-handled ancient vase.
[Gr. *dīōtos*, two-handled — *di-*, twice, *ous, ōtos*, ear.]

diploe
dip'lō-ē, (*anat.*) n.
the spongy tissue between the hard inner and outer tables of the skull.
[Gr. *diploē*, doubling, fold.]

dipsas
dip'sas, n.
a snake whose bite was believed to cause intense thirst: (pl. **dip'sades** (-*dēz*): (with *cap.*) a genus of non-venomous snakes.
[Gr. *dipsas* — *dipsa*, thirst.]

dirdum, dirdam
dir'dəm, (*Scot.*) n.
uproar: a scolding, punishment.
[Origin obscure.]

dirham
dûr-ham', də-ram', dē'ram, **dirhem** *dûr-hem'*, ns.
an oriental unit of weight, orig. two-thirds of an Attic drachma (usu. **dirhem**): (the following usu. **dirham**) the monetary unit of Morocco: a coin equal to this in value: a coin used in several N. African and Middle Eastern countries, with varying value. — Also **derham'.**
[Ar., Pers., and Turk. forms of the Greek *drachmē*, a drachma or dram.]

diriment
dir'i-mənt, adj.
nullifying.
[L. *dirimĕre.*]

disjaskit
dis-jas'kit, (*Scot.*) adj.
jaded: worn out.
[Prob. **dejected.**]

diss
dis, n.
an Algerian reedy grass (*Ampelodesma tenax*) used for

79

cordage, etc.

[Ar. *dīs.*]

dissepiment

di-sep'i-mənt, n.

a partition in an ovary (*bot.*): a partition partly cutting off the bottom of a coral cup (*zool.*). adj. **dissepimental** (*-ment'l*).

[L. *dissaepīmentum,* a partition — L. *dissaepīre* — *dis-,* apart, *saepīre,* to hedge in, to fence.]

distringas

dis-tring'gas, n.

an old writ directing a sheriff or other officer to distrain.

[Second pers. sing. pres. subj. of L. *dīstringĕre* .]

ditokous

dit'o-kəs, adj.

producing two at a birth or in a clutch.

[Gr. *di-,* twice, *tokos,* birth.]

dittany

dit'ə-ni, n.

an aromatic rutaceous plant (*Dictamnus albus*), secreting much volatile oil.

[O.Fr. *dictame* — L. *dictamnus* — Gr. *diktamnos*; prob. from Mt. *Diktē* in Crete.]

dittay

dit'ā, (*Scots law*) n.

an indictment, charge.

[O.Fr. *ditté* — L. *dictātum* .]

divellent

dī-vel'ənt, adj.

drawing asunder. v.t. **divell'icate** to pull in pieces: to pluck apart.

[L. *dī-,* apart, *vellĕre, vellicāre,* to pluck.]

dizzard

diz'ərd, n.

a blockhead.

[Perh. M.E. and O.Fr. *disour,* story-teller.]

doab

dō'äb, n.

a tongue of land between two rivers (esp. the Ganges and Jumna).

[Pers. *dōāb,* two waters.]

dobhash

dō'bash, n.

an interpreter.

[Hind. *dōbāshī, dūbhāshiya* — *dō, dū,* two,*bhāshā,* language.]

docimasy

dos'i-mə-si, n.

scrutiny: application of tests: assaying: examination of drugs. adj. **docimastic** (*-mas'tik*).

n. **docimol'ogy** the art of assaying.

[Gr. *dokimasiā*, examination — *dokimazein*, to test — *dechesthai*, to take, approve.]

dodman

dod'mən, (*dial.*) n.

a snail.

[Origin unknown.]

doilt

doilt, (*Scot.*) adj.

crazy, foolish. — Also **doiled.**

[Origin obscure.]

doit

doit, n.

a small Dutch coin worth about half a farthing: a thing of little or no value. — Also **doit'kin.**

[Du. *duit.*]

dolium

dō'li-əm, n.

a Roman earthenware jar for wine, oil, grain, etc.: — pl. **dō'lia.**

[L. *dōlium.*]

domett

dom'ət, -it, n.

a plain cloth with cotton warp and woollen weft.

[Perh. a proper name.]

donga

dong'gə, (orig. *S. Afr.*) n.

a gully made by soil erosion.

[Zulu, bank, side of a gully.]

donzel

don'zəl, (*obs.*) n.

a squire, aspirant to knighthood.

[It. *donzello* — L.L. *domnicellus*, dim. of L. *dominus*, lord.]

doolie

dōō'li, n.

a litter or palanquin.

[Hindi *dolī.*]

doorn

dōōrn, (*S. Afr.*) n.

thorn.

doorn-boom (*dōōrn'bōōm*) a S. African acacia.

[Du. *doorn*, thorn, *boom*, tree.]

dormy, dormie

dör'mi, adj.

in golf, as many holes up or ahead as there are yet to play.

[Conjecturally connected with L. *dormīre*, to sleep; the player who is *dormy* cannot lose though he go to sleep.]

dornick

dör'nik, n.

a kind of stout figured linen, originally made at *Doornik*, or Tournai, in Belgium.

dorse

dörs, n.

a small cod.

[Low Ger. *dorsch*.]

doseh

dō'se, n.

a religious ceremony at Cairo (abolished 1884), during the festival of the Prophet's birth, when the sheikh of the Sa'di dervishes rode on horseback over the prostrate bodies of his followers.

[Ar. *dawsah*, treading.]

dossil

dos'il, n.

a plug, spigot: a cloth roll for wiping ink from an engraved plate in printing: a pledget of lint for dressing a wound (*surg.*).

[O.Fr. *dosil* — L.L. *ducillus*, a spigot.]

doubletree

dub'l-trē, n.

the horizontal bar on a vehicle to which the whippletree (with harnessed animals) is attached.

douc

dōōk, n.

a variegated monkey of S.E. Asia.

[Fr., from Cochin name.]

doup

dowp, (*Scot.*) n.

the bottom section of an egg-shell: the buttocks: the bottom or end of anything. **can'dle-doup** a candle-end.

[Cf. O.N. *daup*, a hollow.]

dourine

dōō-rēn', *dōō'rēn*, n.

a contagious disease of horses due to a trypanosome.

[Fr. *dourin*.]

douzepers

dōō'zə-pār, n.pl.

the twelve peers of Charlemagne, or similar group: — sing. **dou'zeper, dou'cepere** (*Spens.*) a champion, great knight or noble.

[O.Fr. *douze pers*, twelve peers.]

dovekie

duv'ki, n.

the little auk or rotch: the black guillemot.

[Dim. of **dove**.]

dowf

dowf, (*Scot.*) adj.

dull, heavy, spiritless.
n. **dowf'ness**.

[Prob. O.N. *daufr*, deaf.]

dowie

dow'i, (*Scot.*) adj.

dull, low-spirited, sad: dismal.

[Prob. O.E. *dol*, dull.]

dowl, dowle

dowl, (*Shak.*) n.

a portion of down in a feather: a piece of fluff.

[Origin obscure.]

dowlas

dow'ləs, n.

a course linen cloth.

[From *Daoulas* or *Doulas*, near Brest, in Brittany.]

draff

dräf, n.

dregs: the refuse of malt after brewing.

adjs. **draff'ish, draff'y** worthless.

[Prob. related to Du. *draf*, Ger. *Treber*, *Träber*.]

drail

drāl, n.

the iron bow of a plough from which the traces draw: a piece of lead round the shank of the hook in fishing.

v.i. to draggle.

[Prob. a combination of **draggle** and **trail**.]

drammock

dram'ək, n.

meal and water mixed raw. — Also **dramm'ach.**

[Cf. Gael. *drama(i)g*, a foul mixture.]

dratchell

drach'l, (*dial.*) n.

a slut.

drazel

dräz'l, (*dial.*) n.

a slut.

[Origin unknown.]

dreikanter

dri'kān-tər, n.

a pebble faceted by wind-blown sand, properly having three faces: — pl. **drei'kanter(s).**

[Ger. *Dreikant*, solid angle — *drei*, three, *Kante*, edge.]

drevill

drev'il, (*Spens.*) n.

a foul person.

[Cf. M.Du. *drevel*, scullion.]

droger, drogher

drō'gər, n.

a W. Indian coasting vessel, with long masts and lateen sails.

[Du. *droogen*, to dry — orig. a vessel on which fish were dried.]

droich

drōhh, (*Scot.*) n.

a dwarf.

adj. **droich'y** dwarfish.

[Gael. *troich* or *droich*; orig.
from O.E.]

droil

droil, v.i.

to drudge.

[Perh. Du. *druilen*, to loiter.]

dromond

drom', *drum'ənd*, n.

a swift mediaeval ship of war.
— Also **drom'on.**

[O.Fr., — L.L. *dromō, -ōnis* —
Byzantine Gr. *dromōn* —
dromos, a running, *dramein*
(aor.) to run.]

drosometer

dros-om'i-tər, n.

an instrument for measuring
dew.

[Gr. *drosos*, dew, *metron*,
measure.]

druse

drōōz, n.

a rock cavity lined with crystals
(by geologists usu. called a
drusy cavity), a geode.

adj. **dru'sy** rough with,
composed of, minute crystals:
miarolitic.

[Ger. *Druse* — Czech. *druza*, a
piece of crystallised ore.]

druxy

druk'si, adj.

of timber, having decayed spots
concealed by healthy wood. —
Also **drick'sie.**

[Origin unknown.]

dudeen

dōō-dēn', -dhēn', n.

a short clay tobacco-pipe. —
Also **dudheen'.**

[Ir. *dúidín*, dim. of *dúd*, pipe.]

dukkeripen

dōōk-ə-rip'ən, n.

fortune-telling.

[Romany *drukeriben*.]

dumose

dū'mōs, adj.

bushy (also **dū'mous**).

n. **dumŏs'ity.**

[L. *dūmus*, a thorn-bush.]

dunderfunk

dun'dər-fungk, n.

ship-biscuit, soaked in water,
mixed with fat and molasses,
and baked in a pan. — Also
dan'dyfunk.

**duniewassal, dunniewassal,
duniwassal**

dōōn-i-wos'l, n.

a Highland gentleman of inferior
rank.

[Gael. *duine*, man, *uasal*, of
gentle birth.]

dunnage

dun'ij, n.

loose wood of any kind laid in the bottom of the hold to keep the cargo out of the bilge-water, or wedged between parts of the cargo to keep them steady: sailor's baggage.

[Ety. unknown.]

dupion

dū'pi-ən, -on, n.

a double cocoon, made by two silk-worms spinning together: a kind of coarse silk made from these cocoons.

[Fr. *doupion,* from It. *doppione,* double.]

dupondius

dū-pon'di-əs, (hist.) n.

an ancient Roman coin: — pl. **dupon'dii.**

[L.]

duppy

dup'i, n.

a ghost.

[West Indian Negro word.]

durgan

dûr'gən, n.

a dwarf, any undersized creature.

adj. **dur'gy.** (*-gi, -ji*).

[Related to **dwarf.**]

durn

dûrn, (dial.) n.

a doorpost. — Also **dern.**

[Prob. Norse.]

duro

dōō'rō, n.

a Spanish peso: — pl. **dur'os.**

[Sp. (*peso*) *duro,* hard (peso).]

durra

dōō'rə, n.

Indian millet, a grass (*Sorghum vulgare*) akin to sugar-cane, much cultivated for grain in Asia and Africa, or other species of the genus. — Also **dou'ra, dhu'rra, du'ra** and **dari** (*dur'i*).

[Ar. *dhurah.*]

dvandva

dvän'dvä, (gram.) n.

a compound word, each element being equal in status (e.g. *tragicomedy, bittersweet*).

[Sans. *dvaṁdva,* a pair.]

dvornik

dvor'nēk, dvör', n.

a Russian concierge or porter.

[Russ., caretaker — *dvor,* yard, court.]

dwale

dwāl, n.

deadly nightshade (*bot.*): a stupefying drink: a black colour (*her.*).

[O.N. *dvöl*, *dvali*, delay, sleep.]

dyschroa

dis'krō-ə, n.

discoloration of the skin from disease. — Also **dyschroia** (*-kroi'ə*).

[Pfx. **dys-**, and Gr. *chroā*, *chroiā*, complexion.]

dyscrasia

dis-krā'si-ə, -zhi-ə, -zhə, (*path.*) n.

a disordered condition of the body attributed originally to unsuitable mixing of the body fluids or humours.

[Pfx. **dys-**, and Gr. *krāsis*, a mixing.]

dyscrasite

dis'kras-īt, n.

a mineral composed of silver and antimony.

[Pfx. **dys-**, and Gr. *krāsis*, mixture.]

dysmelia

dis-mēl'i-ə, -mel', -yə, n.

the condition in which one or more limbs are misshapen or incomplete.

adj. **dysmel'ic.**

[Pfx. **dys-**, and Gr. *melos*, limb.]

dyvour

dī'vər, (*Scot.*) n.

a bankrupt.

n. **dyv'oury** bankruptcy.

[Perh. from Fr. *devoir*, to owe.]

dzeren

dzē'rən, n.

a Central Asian antelope.

[Mongolian.]

dziggetai

dzig'ə-tī, n.

a Central Asian wild ass (*Equus hemionus*), rather like a mule.

[Mongolian *tchikhitei*.]

E

eagre
ā′gər, ē′gər, n.
a bore or sudden rise of the tide in a river.
[Origin doubtful; hardly from O.E. *ēgor*, flood.]

ean
ēn, (*Shak.*) v.t. and v.i.
to bring forth.
n. **ean′ling** a young lamb.
[O.E. *ēanian*.]

easle, aizle
āz′l, (*Burns*) n.
hot ashes.
[O.E. *ysle*.]

eassel, eassil
ēs′l, (*Scot.*) adv.
eastward: easterly.
advs. **eass′elgate**, **eass′elward**.
[**east**.]

eatche
ēch, (*Scott*) n.
a Scots form of **adze**.

ébauche
ā-bōsh, (Fr.) n.
rough draft, sketch.

ébrillade
ā-brē-(l)yäd′, n.
the sudden jerking of a horse's rein when he refuses to turn.
[Fr.]

ecad
ek′ad, (*bot.*) n.
a plant form which is assumed to have adapted to its environment.
[*eco*logy, and suff. **-ad**.]

eccrisis
ek′ri-sis, n.
expulsion of waste or morbid matter.
n. **eccrit′ic** a medicine having the property of effecting this.
[Gr. *ekkrisis*, secretion — *ek*, out, and *krisis*, separation.]

ecdysis
ek′di-sis, n.
the act of casting off an integument, sloughing′.
n. **ecdysiast** (-*diz*′; *facet.*) a stripteaser.
[Gr. *ekdysis* — *ek*, out of, *dyein*, to put on.]

eclampsia

i-klamp'si-ə, n.

a condition resembling epilepsy: now confined to acute toxaemia with convulsive fits about the time of childbirth. — Also **eclamp'sy.**
adj. **eclamp'tic.**

[Gr. *eklampsis* — *eklampein*, to flash forth, to burst forth violently (as a fever) — *ek*, out of, *lampein*, to shine.]

ecostate

ē-kos'tāt, adj.

ribless.

[L. *ē*, from, *costa*, rib.]

ecru

e-, ā-krōō', -krü', n.

unbleached linen: its colour.
adj. like unbleached linen.

[Fr. *écru* — L. *ex*, intensive, *crūdus*, raw.]

ecthyma

ek-thī'mə, n.

a skin eruption in large pustules.

[Gr. *ekthȳma*, a pustule.]

écuelle

ā-kwel', or *ā-kü-el'*, n.

a two-handled soup bowl.

[Fr., — L. *scutella*, drinking-bowl.]

eddish

ed'ish, n.

pasturage, or the eatable growth of grass after mowing.

[Dubiously referred to O.E. *edisc*, a park.]

eident

ī'dənt, (*Scot.*) adj.

busy, diligent.

[M.E. *ithen* — O.N. *ithinn*, diligent.]

eigne

ān, adj.

first born.

[Fr. *aîné.*]

eirack

ē'rək, (*Scot.*) n.

a young hen.

[Gael. *eireag.*]

eisel(l)

ā'səl, ī'səl, (*obs.*) n.

vinegar.

[O.Fr. *aisil, aissil*, from L.L. dim. of L. *acētum*, vinegar.]

ekka

ek'ə, n.

a small one-horse carriage.

[Hindi — *ekkā*, one — Sans. *eka.*]

elaphine

el'ə-fīn, adj.
like or belonging to a red deer.
[Gr. *elaphos*, stag.]

elchi, eltchi, elchee

el'chē, -chi, ns.
an ambassador.
[Turk. *īlchī.*]

elemi

el'im-i, n.
a fragrant resinous substance
obtained from various tropical
trees, esp. a species of
Canarium.
[Perh. Ar.]

elsin

el'sin, **elshin** *el'shin*, (*Scot.*) ns.
an awl.
[From O.Du. *elssene* (mod.
els).]

elt

elt, (*dial.*) n.
a young sow.

elution

ē-, i-lōō'shən, -lū', (*chem.*) n.
purification or separation by
washing.
ns. **el'uant, eluent** a liquid
used for elution; **el'uate** liquid
obtained by eluting.
v.t. **elute'**.
n. **elu'tor** a vessel for elution.

[L. *ēlūtiō, -ōnis*, washing —
ēluĕre, ēlūtum — *ē*, from, *luĕre*,
to wash.]

elutriate

ē-, i-lōō'tri-āt, -lū', v.t.
to separate by washing into
coarser and finer portions.
ns. **elutriā'tion; elu'triātor**
an apparatus for elutriating.
[L. *ēlutriāre, -ātum*, to wash out,
ēluĕre — *ē*, from, *luĕre*, to
wash.]

emblements

em'bli-mənts, n.pl.
crops raised by the labour of
the cultivator, but not tree-fruits
or grass.
[O.Fr. *emblaer*, to sow with corn
— L.L. *imbladāre* — *in*, in,
bladum, wheat.]

emblic

em'blik, n.
an East Indian tree (*Phyllanthus
emblica*) of the spurge family:
its fruit, used for tanning. —
Also **emblic myrobalan.**
[Ar. *amlaj* — Pers. *amleh.*]

emicate

em'i-kāt, v.i.
to sparkle.
adj. **em'icant** sparkling:
flashing.
n. **emicā'tion.**
[L. *ēmicāre, -ātum.*]

emmet

em'it, (*arch.* and *dial.*) n.

the ant: in Cornwall, a tourist.

[O.E. *ǣmete.*]

emphractic

em-frak'tik, adj.

stopping the pores of the skin.
n. a substance with this
property.

[Gr. *emphraktikos,* obstructive
— *en,* in, *phrassein,* to stop.]

emphyteusis

em-fit-ū'sis, n.

in Roman law, a perpetual right
in a piece of land, for which a
yearly sum was paid to the
proprietor.

adj. **emphyteu'tic.**

[Gr., — *emphyteuein,* to
implant.]

emplecton

em-plek'ton, (*arch.*) n.

ashlar masonry filled up with
rubble. — Also (L.)
emplec'tum.

[Gr. *emplekton* — *en,* in,
plekein, to weave.]

emptysis

emp'ti-sis, n.

spitting, esp. of blood.

[Gr. *emptysis,* spitting — *en,* in,
ptyein, to spit.]

empyreuma

em-pir-ū'mə, n.

the burned smell and acrid taste
that come when vegetable or
animal substances are burned:
— pl. **empyreu'mata.**
adjs. **empyreumat'ic, -al.**
v.t. **empyreu'matise, -ize.**

[Gr. *empȳreuma, -atos,* embers
— *en,* in *pȳr,* fire.]

enantiodromia

en-an-ti-ō-drō'mi-ə, n.

the process by which something
becomes or is superseded by
its opposite, esp. the adopting
of values, beliefs, etc. opposite
to those previously held: the
interaction of such opposing
values, beliefs, etc.
adjs. **enantiōdrom'iacal,
-drōmī'acal;
enantiōdrō'mic.**

[Gr., — *enantios,* opposite,
dromos, running.]

enarthrosis

en-är-thrō'sis, (*anat.*) n.

a ball-and-socket joint.
adj. **enarthrō'dial.**

[Gr. *enarthrōsis* — *en,* in,
arthron, a joint.]

encaenia

en-sē'ni-ə, n.

the annual commemoration of
founders and benefactors at
Oxford, held in June.

[L., — Gr. *enkainia* (pl.), a feast

of dedication — *en,* in, *kainos,* new.]

encheason

en-chē'zn, (*Spens.*) n.

a reason, cause, or occasion.

[O.Fr. *encheson* — *encheoir,* to fall in; influenced by L. *occāsiō, -ōnis,* occasion.]

enchorial

en-kō'ri-əl, -kö', adj.

belonging to or used in a country (*rare*): used by the people, esp. (in ancient Egypt) demotic. — Also **enchoric** (*-kor'*).

[Gr. *enchōrios* — *en,* in, and *chōrā,* a place, country.]

encoignure

ā-kwa-nūr', -nūr', n.

a piece of, esp. ornamental, furniture, e.g. a cupboard or cabinet, made to fit into a corner.

[Fr., — *encoigner,* to fit into a corner — *en,* in, *coin,* a corner.

encolpion

en-kol'pi-on, n.

a reliquary, cross, etc., worn on the breast. — Also (Latinised) **encol'pium.**

[Gr., — *en,* in, on, *kolpos,* bosom.]

encolure

en(g)'kol-ūr', (*Browning*) n.

a horse's mane.

[Fr., horse's neck.]

encomienda

ān-kō-mē-ān'da, (Sp.) n.

a commandery.

n. **encomendero** (Sp.; *ān-kō-mān-dā'rō*) its commander: — pl. **encomender'os.**

energumen

en-ər-gū'mən, n.

one possessed: a demoniac.

[L.L. *energūmenus* — Gr. *energoumenos* — *energeein* — *en,* in, *ergon,* work.]

enew

e-nū', v.t.

in falconry, to drive or (*refl.*) plunge into water.

[O.Fr. *enewer* — *en,* in, O.Fr. *ewe* (Fr. *eau*), water.]

engouled

en-gōōld', (*her.*) adj.

of bends, crosses, etc., having ends that enter the mouths of animals.

[Fr. *engoulée* — *en,* in, O.Fr. *goule* (Fr. *gueule*), a beast's mouth.]

engrail

in-grāl', v.t.

to border with little semicircular indents (*her.*): to make rough (*arch.*).

v.i. to form an edging or border: to run in indented lines.

n. **engrail'ment** the ring of dots round the edge of a medal: indentation in curved lines (*her.*).

[O.Fr. *engresler* (Fr. *engrêler*) — *gresle*, slender — L. *gracilis.*]

engram

en'gram, less often **engramma** *en-gram'ə*, ns.

a permanent impression made by a stimulus or experience: a stimulus impression supposed to be inheritable: a memory trace.

adj. **engrammat'ic.**

[Ger. *Engramm* — Gr. *en*, in, *gramma*, that which is written.]

engrenage

ã-grə-näzh, (Fr.) n.

gearing (also *fig.*): a series of events, decisions, etc., each of which leads inevitably to further ones: the taking of such or decisions as moves towards some goal, thus avoiding the necessity of discussing the desirability of the goal itself.

enomoty

e-nom'o-ti, n.

a band of sworn soldiers, esp. the smallest Spartan subdivision.

[Gr. *enōmotiā* — *en*, in *omnynai*, to swear.]

ensiform

en'si-förm, adj.

sword-shaped.

[L. *ēnsis*, a sword, *förma*, form.]

entellus

en-tel'əs, n.

the hanuman monkey of India.

[App. from *Entellus* the old Sicilian in *Aeneid*, book V, from its old-mannish look.]

enzian

ent'si-ən, n.

a type of schnapps flavoured with gentian roots, drunk in the Tyrol.

[Ger. *Enzian*, gentian.]

éolienne

ā-ol-yen', n.

dress material of fine silk and wool.

[Fr.]

eothen

ē-ō'then, (*arch.*) adv.

from the east — the name given by Kinglake to his book of travel

in the East (1844).
[Gr. *ēōthen,* lit. from morn, at earliest dawn.]

epact

ē'pakt, n.

the moon's age at the beginning of the year: the excess of the calendar month or solar year over the lunar.
[Fr. *épacte* — Gr. *epaktos,* brought on — *epi,* on, *agein,* to bring.]

epaenetic

ep-ə-net'ik, **epainetic**
ep-ī-net'ik, (*arch.*) adjs.
eulogistic.
[Gr. *epainetikos* — *epainein,* to praise.]

epagoge

ep-ə-gō'gē, -jē, (*log.*) n.
induction.
adj. **epagŏg'ic.**
[Gr. *epagōgē* — *epi,* on, *agōgē,* leading.]

epagomenal

ep-ə-gom'ə-nəl, adj.
(esp. of days) intercalary.
[Gr. *epagomenos* — *epi,* upon, in, *agein,* to bring.]

epanodos

ep-an'o-dos, (*rhet.*) n.
recapitulation of the chief points in a discourse.
[Gr. *epanodos.*]

epedaphic

ep-ə-daf'ik, adj.
pertaining to atmospheric conditions.
[Gr. *epi,* above, *edaphos,* ground.]

epeolatry

ep-i-ol'ə-tri, n.
worship of words.
[Gr. *epos,* word, *latreiā,* worship.]

epha, ephah

ē'fə, n.
a Hebrew measure for dry goods.
[Heb.; prob. of Egyptian origin.]

ephialtes

ef-i-al'tēz, (*arch.*) n.
an incubus: a nightmare: — pl. -tes.
[Gr. *ephialtēs.*]

ephod

ef'od, n.
a kind of linen surplice worn by the Jewish priests: a surplice, generally.
[Heb. *ēphōd* — *āphad,* to put on.]

ephor

ef'ör, ef'ər, n.
a class of magistrates whose office apparently originated at

Sparta, being peculiar to the Doric states.

n. **eph'oralty.**

[Gr. *epi,* upon, and root of *horaein,* to see.]

epicede

ep'i-sēd, **epicedium** *ep-i-sē'di-əm* or *-dī',* ns.

a funeral ode: — pls. **ep'icedes, epicē'dia.** adjs. **epicē'dial, epicē'dian** elegiac.

[L. *epicēdīum* — Gr. *epikēdeion* — *epi,* upon, *kēdos,* care.]

epiclesis

ep-i-klē'sis, n.

in the Eastern church, an invocation of the Holy Spirit at the consecration of the elements (bread and wine): — pl. **epiclēsēs.**

[Gr. *epiklēsis,* invocation — *epikalein,* to summon.]

epidote

ep'i-dōt, n.

a greenish mineral, silicate of calcium, aluminium, and iron. n. **epidosite** (*ep-id'ə-sīt* a rock composed of epidote and quartz.
adj. **epidotic** (*-dot'*).
n. **epidotisā'tion, -z-.**
adj. **epid'otised, -ized** changed into epidote.

[Gr. *epididonai,* to give in

addition, superadd, from the great length of the base of the crystal.]

epilimnion

ep-i-lim'ni-ən, n.

the upper, warm layer of water in a lake.

[Gr. *epi,* upon, *limnion,* dim. of *limnē,* a lake.]

epilobium

ep-i-lōb'i-əm, n.

a willow-herb, a plant of the genus **Epilobium.**

[Gr. *epi,* upon, *lobos,* a pod, from the position of the petals.]

epinasty

ep'i-nas-ti, (*bot.*) n.

down-curving of an organ, caused by a more active growth on its upper side. — opp. to *hyponasty.*
adj. **epinas'tic.**
adv. **epinas'tically.**

[Gr. *epi,* upon, *nastos,* pressed close.]

epinosic

ep-i-nos'ik, adj.

unhealthy: unwholesome.

[Gr. *epi-,* and *nosos,* disease.]

epiphragm

ep'i-fram, n.

the disc with which certain molluscs close the aperture of

their shell.

[Gr. *epiphragma*, covering — *epiphrassein*, to obstruct.]

epispastic

ep-i-spas'tik, adj.

blistering.

n. a blistering agent.

[Gr. *epispastikos* — *epi*, upon, *spaein*, to draw.]

epistaxis

ep-i-stak'sis, n.

bleeding from the nose.

[Gr. *epistazein*, to shed in drops.]

epitonic

ep-i-ton'ik, adj.

overstrained.

[Gr. *epitonos* — *epi*, upon, *teinein*, to stretch.]

epitrachelion

ep'i-tra-kē'li-ən, n.

an Orthodox priest's or bishop's stole.

[Gr., on the neck — *epi*, upon, *trachēlos*, neck.]

epizeuxis

ep-i-zūk'sis, (*rhet.*) n.

the immediate repetition of a word for emphasis.

[Gr., joining on.]

eponychium

ep-o-nik'i-əm, n.

a narrow band of cuticle over the base of a nail.

[Gr. *epi*, on, *onyx*, *onychos*, nail.]

epopt

ep'opt, n.

one initiated into the Eleusinian mysteries.

[Gr. *epoptēs* — *epi*, upon, and root *op-*, to see.]

éprouvette

ā-prōō-vet', n.

an apparatus for testing the strength of gunpowder.

[Fr. *éprouver*, to try.]

epulation

ep-ū-lā'shən, n.

feasting.

adj. **ep'ulary.**

[L. *epulātiō*, *epulāris*, — *epulāri*, -*ātus*, to feast.]

epulis

e-pū'lis, n.

a tumour of the gums, either benign or malignant, and growing from the periosteum of the jaw.

[Gr. *epi*, upon, *oulon*, gum.]

epulotic
ep-ū-lot'ik, adj.
cicatrising.
n. a cicatrising medicament.
[Gr. *epoulōtikos* — *epi*, upon,
oulē, a scar.]

epyllion
e-pil'i-ən, n.
a poem with some resemblance
to an epic but shorter.
[Gr.; dim. of *epos*, word.]

eremacausis
er-i-mə-kö'sis, (*chem.*) n.
very slow oxidation.
[Gr. *ērema*, quietly, slowly,
kausis, burning — *kaiein*, to
burn.]

eremic
e-rē'mik, adj.
belonging to deserts.
[Gr. *erēmikos* — *erēmiā*,
desert, solitude.]

erf
ûrf, (*S. Afr.*) n.
a garden plot or small piece of
ground: — pl. **er'ven.**
[Du.; cf. O.E. *erfe*, inheritance.]

ergates
ûr'gə-tēz, **ergate** *ûr'gāt*, ns.
a worker ant, an undeveloped
female.
ns. **ergatan'dromorph** (Gr.

andromorphos, of male form) an
ant combining characters of
males and workers; **ergataner**
(*ûr-gə-tā'nər, -tä'nər*; Gr. *anēr*,
man) a worker-like wingless
male ant; **ergatoc'racy** (Gr.
kratos, power) rule by the
workers; **ergatogyne** (-*jī'nē*;
Gr. *gynē*, woman) a worker-like
wingless female ant.
adj. **er'gatoid** worker-like,
wingless but sexually perfect.
n. **er'gatomorph** an ergatoid
ant.
adj. **ergatomorph'ic.**
[Gr. *ergatēs*, workman —
ergon, work.]

ergodic
ər-god'ik, adj.
pertaining to the probability that
in a system any state will occur
again.
n. **ergodic'ity** (-*dis'*).
[Gr. *ergon*, work, *hodos*, way.]

eric
er'ik, n.
the blood-fine paid by a
murderer to his victim's family in
old Irish law. — Also **er'iach,
er'ick.**
[Ir. *eiric.*]

erinite
er'i-nīt, n.
a basic arsenate of copper
found in Cornwall and Ireland.
[*Erin*, Ireland.]

erotema

er-ō-tē′mə, **eroteme** *er′ō-tēm*,
erotesis *er-ō-tē′sis*, ns.
a rhetorical question.
adj. **erotetic** (*-tet′ik*)
interrogatory.
[Gr. *erōtēma, erōtēsis —
erōtaein*, to question.]

ers

ûrs, n.
the bitter vetch.
[Fr., — L. *ervum*.]

eruciform

e-rōō′si-förm, adj.
like a caterpillar.
[L. *ērūca*, caterpillar, *förma*,
form.]

eryngo

e-ring′gō, n.
the candied root of sea-holly:
the plant itself, a superficially
thistle-like umbellifer: — pl.
eryn′gos, -goes.
n. **Eryn′gium** (*-ji-əm*) a genus
of bristly plants including the
sea-holly (fam. Umbelliferae):
(without *cap*.) a plant of the
genus.
[Gr. *ēryngos*.]

escamotage

es-ka-mo-täzh, (Fr.) n.
juggling.

escarole

es-ka-rōl, -röl, n.
a broad-leaved, non-curly
endive.
[Fr.]

eschar

es′kär, n.
a slough or portion of dead or
disorganised tissue, esp. an
artificial slough produced by
caustics.
adj. **escharot′ic** tending to
form an eschar: caustic.
n. a caustic substance.
[L., — Gr. *escharā*, a hearth,
mark of a burn.]

esclandre

es-klä-dr′, n.
notoriety: any unpleasantness.
[Fr., — L. *scandalum*.]

escolar

es-kō-lär′, n.
an Atlantic and Southern fish of
spectacled appearance.
[Sp., scholar.]

escopette

es-kō-pet′, (*U.S.*) n.
a carbine.
[Sp. *escopeta*.]

escot

es-kot', (*Shak.*) v.t.

to pay for, to maintain.

[O.Fr. *escoter, escot,* a tax; of Gmc. origin.]

escribano

ā-skrē-bä'nō, (Sp.) n.

a notary: — pl. **escriba'nos.**

escroc

es-krō, (Fr.) n.

a swindler.

esemplastic

es-əm-plas'tik, adj.

unifying.

n. **esemplasy** (*es-em'plə-si*) the unifying power of imagination.

[Gr. *es,* into, *hen* (neut.), one, *plastikos,* moulding.]

esne

ez'ni, (*hist.*) n.

a domestic slave in O.E. times.

[O.E.]

esnecy

es'nə-si, (*obs.*) n.

the eldest daughter's right of first choice in dividing an inheritance.

[O.Fr. *ainsneece* (Fr. *aînesse*).]

espagnolette

es-pan-yō-let', n.

the fastening of a French window.

[Fr., dim. of *espagnol,* Spanish.]

espiègle

es-pē-eg'l', adj.

roguish, frolicsome: arch.

n. **espièg'lerie** roguishness: frolicsomeness.

[Fr., — Ger. *Eulenspiegel.*]

essoin, essoyne

es-oin', n.

an excuse for not appearing in court (*law*): an excuse (*Spens.*).

n. **essoin'er.**

[O.Fr. *essoine* (Fr. *exoine*), *es* — L. *ex,* out of, *soin,* care.]

essonite

es'ən-īt, **hessonite** *hes'ən-īt*, n.

cinnamon-stone.

[Gr. *hēssōn,* inferior (i.e. in hardness, to hyacinth which it resembles).]

estacade

es-tə-kād', n.

a dike of piles in a morass, river, etc., against an enemy.

[Fr., — Sp. *estacada.*]

estafette

es-tə-fet', n.

a military courier or express.

[Fr., — It. *staffetta* — *staffa*, stirrup; cf. O.H.G. *stapho*, a step.]

estoc

es-tok', n.

a short sword.

[Fr.]

estover

es-tō'vər, n.

a right to necessaries allowed by law, as wood to a tenant for necessary repairs, etc.

common of estovers the right of taking necessary wood from another's estate for household use and the making of implements of industry.

[O.Fr. *estover*, to be necessary, necessaries.]

estrade

es-träd', n.

a low platform.

[Fr., — Sp. *estrado*.]

estrapade

es-tra-pād', n.

a horse's attempt to throw its rider.

[Fr.]

estrepe

es'trēp, (*law*) v.t.

to commit waste (as a tenant) on lands, e.g. cutting down trees, etc.

n. **estrepe'ment.**

[M.Fr. *estreper* — L. *exstirpāre*, to root out.]

estro

es'trō, (It.) n.

enthusiasm, height of poetic inspiration.

etesian

e-tē'zh(y)ən, -zyən, adj.

periodical: blowing at stated seasons, as certain winds, esp. the north-west winds of summer in the Aegean.

[L. *etēsius* — Gr. *etēsios*, annual — *etos*, a year.]

ethmoid

eth'moid, adj.

like a sieve.

adj. **ethmoid'al.**

ethmoid bone one of the bones forming the anterior part of the brain-case.

[Gr. *ēthmos*, a sieve, and *eidos*, form.]

étrenne

(usu. in pl. **étrennes**) *ā-tren*, (Fr.) n.

New Year's gift.

étrier

ā-trē-yā′, n.

a small rope ladder of 1–4 rungs used as a climbing aid by mountaineers.

[Fr., stirrup.]

eulachon

ū′lə-kən, n.

the North Pacific candle-fish, so oily that it is dried for use as a candle. — Also **oolakan, oulakan, -chon, ulicon, -chon, -kon.**

[Chinook jargon, *ulâkân*.]

eupatrid

ū-pat′rid, n.

a member of the aristocracy in ancient Greek states.

[Gr. *eupatridēs — eu*, well, *patēr*, father.]

euphrasy

ū′frə-si, -zi, (*bot.*) n.

eyebright (*Euphrasia*) once thought good for disorders of the eyes.

[Gr. *euphrăsiā*, delight — *euphrainein*, to cheer — *eu*, well, *phrēn*, the mind.]

euphroe

ū′frō, (*naut.*) n.

the wooden block through which the lines of a crowfoot are rove. — Also **ū′phroe.**

[Du. *juffrouw — jong*, young, *vrouw*, woman.]

euripus

ū-rī′pəs, n.

an arm of the sea with strong currents, spec. that between Euboea and Boeotia: a ditch round the arena in a Roman amphitheatre.

[L., — Gr. *eurīpos.*]

eutexia

ū-tek′si-ə, n.

the property of being easily melted.

n. **eutec′tic** a mixture in such proportions that the melting-point (or freezing-point) is a minimum, the constituents melting (or freezing) simultaneously.

adj. of maximum fusibility: pertaining to a eutectic.

n. **eutec′toid** an alloy similar to a eutectic but involving formation of two or three constituents from another solid constituent. — Also adj.

eutectic point the temperature at which a eutectic melts or freezes.

[Gr. *eutēktos*, easily melted — *eu*, well, *tēkein*, to melt.]

eutrapelia

ū-trə-pē′li-ə, (*obs.*) **eutrapely** *ū-trap′ə-li,* ns.

wit, ease and urbanity of conversation.

[Gr. *eutrapelia — eutrapelos*, pleasant in conversation.]

ewest

ū′ist, (*Scot.*) adj. or adv.

near.

[App. from O.E. *on nēaweste*, in the neighbourhood, wrongly divided as *on ewest*.]

exarate

eks′ər-āt, adj.

containing grooves or furrows: said of pupae in which the wings and legs are free.

n. **exara′tion** (*rare*) the act of writing: composition.

[L. *exarātus* — *exarāre*, to plough up, to trace letters on a tablet.]

excambion

eks-kam′bi-on, (*Scots law*) n.

exchange of lands — also **excam′bium.**

v.t. **excamb′** to exchange.

[L.L. *excambiāre*.]

excipient

ek-sip′i-ənt, n.

a substance mixed with a medicine to give it consistence, or used as a vehicle for its administration.

[L. *excipiēns*, *-entis*, pr.p. of *excipĕre*, to take out, receive — *ex*, from, *capĕre*, to take.]

excubant

eks′kū-bənt, adj.

on guard.

[L. *excubāns*, *-antis*, pr.p. of *excubāre*, to sleep out, lie on guard — *ex*, *cubāre*, to lie.]

exeem, exeme

eks-ēm′, (*obs. Scot.*) v.t.

to release, exempt.

[L. *eximĕre* — *ex*, from, *emĕre*, to take.]

exenterate

eks-en′tər-āt, v.t.

to disembowel.
adj. (*-it*) disembowelled.
n. **exenterā′tion.**

[L. *exenterāre* — Gr. *exenterizein* — *ex*, from, and *enteron*, intestine.]

exequatur

eks-i-kwā′tər, n.

an official recognition of a consul or commercial agent given by the government of the country in which he is to be.

[L. *exequātur*, let him execute — the opening word.]

exergue

eks′ or *eks-ûrg′*, n.

a part on the reverse of a coin, below the main device, often filled up by the date, etc.
adj. **exer′gual.**

[Fr., — Gr. *ex*, out of, *ergon*, work.]

exies
ek'sāz, (*Scot.*) n.pl.
a fit, as of hysterics, ague.

exility
egz-, eks-il'i-ti, (*obs.*) n.
slenderness, smallness:
refinement.
[L. *exīlitās, -ātis — exīlis*,
slender.]

eximious
eg-zim'i-əs, (*arch.*) adj.
excellent, distinguished.
[L. *eximius — eximĕre — ex*,
from, *emĕre*, to take.]

exomis
eks-ō'mis, n.
a one-sleeved or (in Rome)
sleeveless garment —
(*Browning*) **exo'mion.**
[Gr. *exōmis — ex-*, out, *ōmos*,
shoulder.]

exon
eks'on, n.
an officer of the Yeomen of the
Guard.
[App. intended to express the
pronunciation of Fr. *exempt* .]

expiscate
eks-pis'kāt, (*Scot.*) v.t.
to find out by skilful means or
by strict examination.
n. **expiscā'tion.**
adj. **expis'cătory.**

[L. *expiscārī, expiscātus — ex*,
from, *piscārī*, to fish — *piscis*, a
fish.]

exsuccous
ik-suk'əs, adj.
sapless.
[L. *exsuccus — ex-, succus*,
juice.]

extine
eks'tin, -tēn, -tīn, (*bot.*) n.
the outer membrane of a
pollen-grain or spore. — Also
ex'ine.
[From the root of L. *exter*,
extimus, outer, outmost.]

exuviae
igz-, iks-ū'vi-ē, n.pl.
cast-off skins, shells, or other
coverings of animals: fossil
remains of animals (*geol.*).
adj. **exū'vial.**
v.i. **exū'viate** to shed, cast off,
for a new covering or condition.
n. **exuviā'tion** the act of
exuviating.
[L., *exuĕre*, to draw off.]

eyalet
ā-yä'let, n.
a division of Turkey — a *vilayet*.
[Turk., — Ar. *iyālah*.]

eyas

ī'əs, n.

an unfledged hawk.

adj. (*Spens.*) unfledged.

ey'as-mus'ket an unfledged male hawk: a child (*Shak.*).

[*An eyas* for *a nyas* — Fr. *niais* — L. *nīdus*, nest.]

eyra

ī'rə, n.

a South American wild cat.

[Guaraní.]

eyre

ār, (*hist.*) n.

a journey or circuit: a court of itinerant justices in the late 12th and 13th cents.

[O.Fr. *eire*, journey, from L. *iter*, a way, a journey — *īre*, *itum*, to go.]

F

facinorous

fa-, fǝ-sin'ǝ-rǝs, (*arch.*) adj.

atrociously wicked. — Also
facinē'rious (*Shak.*).
n. **facin'orousness**.

[L. *facinorōsus* — *facinus*, a
crime — *facĕre*, to do.]

facula

fak'ū-lǝ, n.

a spot brighter than the rest of
the surface, sometimes seen on
the sun's disc: — pl. **fac'ulae**
(*-lē*).
adj. **fac'ular**.

[L. *facula*, dim. of *fax*, torch.]

facundity

fǝ-kun'di-ti, n.

eloquence.

[L. *fācunditās, -ātis*.]

fahlband

fäl'bänt, n.

in crystalline rocks, a pale band
rich in metals; **fahl'erz** (*-erts*)
tetrahedrite: also tennantite;
fahl'ore (*-ōr, -ör*) tetrahedrite
or tennantite.

[Ger. *fahl*, dun-coloured, *Band*,
band, *Erz*, ore, and Eng. **ore**.]

faille

fāl, fīl, fä-y', n.

a soft, closely-woven silk or
rayon fabric with transverse
ribs.

[Fr.]

faitor

fā'tǝr, (*obs.*) n.

an impostor. — Often **fai'tour**.

[O.Fr. *faitor* — L. *factor, -ōris*,
doer.]

fakes, faikes

fāks, n.pl.

thin-bedded shaly or micaceous
sandstone or sandy shale.

falbala

fal'bǝ-lǝ, n.

a trimming or flounce: a
furbelow.

[Ety. dub.]

falcade

fal-kād', n.

the motion of a horse when he
throws himself on his haunches
in a very quick curvet.

[Fr., — L. *falcāta* (fem.) bent.]

falcate, -d

fal'kāt, -id, adjs.

bent like a sickle.

ns. **falcā'tion; fal'cūla** a falcate claw.

adjs. **falciform** (*fal'si-förm*) sickle-shaped; **fal'cūlate.**

[L. *falx, falcis*, a sickle.]

faldage

föld'ij, fald'ij, (*hist.*) n.

the right of the lord of a manor of folding his tenant's sheep in his own fields for the sake of the manure: a fee paid in commutation therefor.

[Law L. *faldāgium* — O.E. *fald*, fold.]

faldetta

fäl-det'ə, n.

a Maltese woman's combined hood and cape.

[It.]

famulus

fam'ū-ləs, n.

a private secretary or factotum: an attendant, esp. on a magician or scholar.

[L., a servant.]

fanal

fā'nəl, (*arch.*) n.

a lighthouse, a beacon.

[Fr., — Gr. *phanos*, a lantern, *phainein*, to show.]

fango

fang'gō, n.

a clay or mud from thermal springs in Italy, esp. at Battaglio, used in treatment of gout, rheumatism, etc.: — pl. **fang'os.**

[It., mud — Gmc.]

fanion

fan'yən, n.

a small flag, esp. for surveying. n. **fan'on** a cloth for handling holy vessels or offertory bread: a maniple: a short cape worn by the Pope when celebrating High Mass.

[O.Fr. *fanion, fanon* — L.L. *fanō, -ōnis*, banner, napkin — O.H.G. *fano*.]

fannel, fannell

fan'əl, n.

a maniple.

[L.L. *fanonellus, fanula*, dims. of *fanō*; see **fanion.**]

fantoccini

fan-to-chē'nē, n.pl.

marionettes: a marionette show.

[It., pl. of *fantoccino*, dim. of *fantoccio*, a puppet — *fante*, a boy — L. *īnfāns, -antis*.]

farandine, farrandine

far'ən-dēn, **ferrandine** *fer'*, (*obs.*) ns.

a cloth or a dress of silk with

wool or hair.
[Fr. *ferrandine*.]

fard

färd, n.

white paint for the face.
v.t. to paint with fard: to gloss
over: to trick out.
[Fr., of Gmc. origin.]

farruca

fa-rōō′ka, (Sp.) n.

a Spanish gypsy dance with
abrupt variations of tempo and
mood.

fascine

fas-ēn′, n.

a brushwood faggot, used to fill
ditches, protect a shore, etc.
[Fr., — L. *fascīna* — *fascis*, a
bundle.]

fastigiate

fas-tij′i-āt, adj.

pointed, sloping to a point or
edge: with branches more or
less erect and parallel (*bot.*):
conical.
adj. **fastig′iated.**
n. **fastig′ium** the apex of a
building: gable-end: pediment.
[L. *fastīgium*, a gable-end,
roof.]

fastuous

fas′tū-əs, (*arch.*) adj.

haughty: ostentatious.
[L. *fastuōsus* — *fastus*,
arrogance.]

fatiscent

fā-, fə-tis′ənt, adj.

gaping with cracks.
n. **fatis′cence.**
[L. *fatīscēns, -entis*, pr.p. of
fatīscĕre, to gape.]

fattrels

fat′rəlz, fät′, (*Scot.*) n.pl.

ends of ribbon.
[O.Fr. *fatraille*, trumpery.]

fautor

fö′tər, n.

a favourer: a patron: an abettor,
[L. *fautor* — *favēre*, to favour.]

fauvette

fō-vet′, n.

a warbler.
[Fr.]

faveolate

fə-vē′ō-lāt, adj.

honeycombed.
[L. *favus*, honeycomb.]

favus

fāv′əs, n.

a fungal skin disease, chiefly of
the scalp, giving a

honeycombed appearance.
adjs. **favose** (fə-vōs', fā'vōs)
honeycombed; **fā'vous** like a
honeycomb: relating to favus.
[L. *favus*, a honeycomb.]

faw
fö, n.
a gypsy.
[From the surname *Faa*.]

feague
fēg, (*obs.*) v.t.
to whip: to perplex.
[Cf. Du. *vegen*, Ger. *fegen*.]

fedelini
fed-e-lē'nē, n.
vermicelli.
[It.]

feis
fesh, n.
an ancient Irish assembly for
the proclamation of laws and
the holding of artistic,
intellectual and sports
competitions: an Irish festival on
the ancient model, including
sports events, folk music and
dancing: — pl. **feiseanna**
(fesh'ə-nə).
[Ir., festival, assembly.]

femerall
fem'ər-əl, n.
an outlet for smoke in a roof.
[O.Fr. *fumeraille* — L. *fūmus*,
smoke.]

fenks
fengks, **finks** fingks, ns.
the refuse of whale-blubber.
[Origin unknown.]

fennec
fen'ək, n.
a little African fox with large
ears.
[Ar. *fenek*.]

fent
fent, n.
a slit, crack: a remnant or odd,
short, or damaged piece of cloth
(*N. Eng.*).
fent'-merchant.
[O.Fr. *fente* — L. *findĕre*, to
cleave.]

feretory
fer'i-tər-i, n.
a shrine for relics carried in
processions.
[L. *feretrum* — Gr. *pheretron*,
bier, litter — *pherein*, to bear.]

fetwa
fet'wä, n.
a Muslim legal decision.
[Ar.]

fewter, feutre
fū'tər, n. (*obs.*)
a spear-rest.
v.t. (*Spens.*) to set in rest.
[O.Fr. *feutre*, felt, a felt-lined
socket.]

fianchetto

fyäng-ket′to, (*chess*) n.

the early movement of a
knight's pawn to develop a
bishop on a long diagonal: —
pl. **fianchet′ti** (*-tē*). — Also v.t.
[It., dim. of *fianco*, flank.]

fid

fid, n.

a conical pin of hard wood,
used by sailors to open the
strands of rope in splicing: a
square bar, with a shoulder,
used to support the weight of
the topmast or top-gallant mast.
[Origin unknown.]

fiddley

fid′li, n.

iron framework round a
hatchway opening.
[Origin obscure.]

fidibus

fid′i-bəs, n.

a paper spill for lighting a pipe,
etc.
[Ger.]

figuline

fig′ū-līn, -lin, adj.

of earthenware: fictile.
n. an earthen vessel.
[L. *figulīnus* — *figulus*, potter.]

filacer

fil′ə-sər, n.

formerly an officer who filed
writs. — Also **fil′azer.**
[O.Fr. *filacier* — *filace*, a file for
papers — apparently L. *fīlum*, a
thread.]

filander

fil-and′ər, n.

a threadlike intestinal worm in
hawks: (in pl.) the disease it
causes.
[O.Fr. *filandre* — L. *fīlum*,
thread.]

filasse

fil-as′, n.

vegetable fibre ready for
manufacture.
[Fr., — L. *fīlum*, thread.]

filature

fil′ə-chər, n.

the reeling of silk, or the place
where it is done.
n. **fil′atory** a machine for
forming or spinning threads.
[Fr., — L. *fīlum*, a thread.]

fimbria

fim′bri-ə, n.

a fringing filament.
adj. **fim′briate** fringed: having
a narrow border (*her*).
v.t. **fim′briate** to fringe: to
hem.
adj. **fim′briated.**

n. **fimbria'tion.**
[L. *fimbriae*, fibres, fringe.]

fimicolous
fim-ik'ə-ləs, adj.
growing on dung.
[L. *fimus*, dung, *colĕre*, to inhabit.]

fingan
fin-gän', n.
a small coffee-cup without a handle — used with a zarf. — Also **finjan** (*-jän'*).
[Egyptian *fingān*, Ar. *finjān*.]

finnesko, finnsko, finsko
fin'(e)-skō, ns.
a reindeer-skin boot with the hair on: — pl. **finn'eskō**, etc.
[Norw. *finnsko* — *Finn*, Lapp, *sko*, shoe.]

fiorin
fī'ə-rin, n.
a variety of creeping bent-grass (*Agrostis stolonifera*).
[Ir. *fiorthán*.]

firlot
fûr'lət, n.
an old Scottish dry measure, the fourth part of a boll.
[Earlier *ferthelot*; cf. O.N. *fiōrthe hlotr*, fourth lot.]

firn
firn, or *fûrn*, n.
snow on high glaciers while still granular.
[Ger. *firn*, of last year; cf. obs. Eng. *fern*, former.]

flacket
flak'it, n.
a flask, bottle.
[O.Fr. *flasquet*.]

flagitious
flə-jish'əs, adj.
grossly wicked: guilty oɪ enormous crimes.
adv. **flagi'tiously.**
n. **flagi'tiousness.**
[L. *flāgitiōsus* — *flāgitium*, a disgraceful act — *flagrāre*, to burn.]

flamfew
flam'fū, n.
a fantastic trifle.
[Fr. *fanfelue*.]

fletton
fle'tən, n.
a type of brick made near *Fletton* in Cambridgeshire, of a mottled yellow and pink colour, with sharp arrises.

flimp
flimp, (*slang*) v.t.
to rob while a confederate hustles.

[Cf. West Flem., *flimpe*, knock, rob.]

flittern

flit'ərn, (*dial.*) n.

an oak sapling.

flong

flong, n.

papier-mâché for stereotyping.

[Fr. *flan.*]

fogash

fog'osh, n.

the pike-perch.

[Hung. *fogas.*]

fogle

fōg'əl, (*slang*) n.

a silk handkerchief.

[Origin obscure.]

foin

foin, v.i.

to thrust with a sword or spear.
n. a thrust with a sword or spear.
adj. **foin'ingly.**

[O.Fr. *foine* — L. *fuscĭna*, a trident.]

fomes

fō'mēz, n.

a substance capable of carrying infection: — pl. **fomites** (*fō'mi-tēz*).

[L. *fōmes*, *-ĭtis*, touchwood.]

fontange

fō-tãzh', n.

a tall head-dress worn in the 17th and 18th centuries.

[Fr., from *Fontanges*, the territorial title of one of Louis XIV's mistresses.]

fonticulus

fon-tik'ū-ləs, n.

the depression just over the top of the breast-bone.

[L. *fonticulus*, dim. of *fōns*, fountain.]

forçat

för'sä, n.

in France, a convict condemned to hard labour.

[Fr.]

forfex

för'feks, n.

a pair of scissors, or pincers: the pincers of an earwig, etc.
adj. **for'ficate** deeply forked, esp. of certain birds' tails.
n. **Forfic'ūla** the common genus of earwigs.
adj. **forfic'ūlate** like scissors.

[L. *forfex*, *-icis*, shears, pincers.]

forinsec

fər-in'sek, adj.

(of feudal service) due to the lord's superior.
adj. **forin'secal** (*obs.*) foreign:

alien: extrinsic.

[L. *forīnsecus*, from without —
forīs, out of doors, *secus*,
following]

forlana

för-lä'nə, **furlana** *foor-*, ns.
a Venetian dance in 6-8 time.
[It. *Furlana*, Friulian.]

fossor

fos'or, n.
a grave-digger.
adj. **fossorial** (*-ō'ri-əl, -ö'*; *zool.*)
adapted for digging.
[L. *fossor* — *fodĕre*, to dig.]

fouat, fouet

foo'ət, (*Scot.*) n.
the house-leek.

foud

fowd, n.
a bailiff or magistrate in Orkney
and Shetland.
n. **foud'rie** his jurisdiction.
[O.N. *fōgeti*; Ger. *Vogt*; from L.
vocātus — *vocāre*, to call.]

fougade

foo-gäd', **fougasse** *foo-gäs'*,
(*mil.*) ns.
a piece of improvised artillery, a
small pit charged with powder
or shells and loaded with
stones.
[Fr.]

fourgon

foor-gō', n.
a baggage-wagon.
[Fr.]

frampold

fram'pōld, -pəld, (*obs.*) adj.
peevish, cross-grained: fiery. —
Also **fram'pal** (*Scott*).
n. **fram'pler** (*Scott*) a brawler.
[Ety. obscure.]

franion

fran'yən, n.
a paramour (*obs.*): a
boon-companion (*obs.*): a loose
woman (*Spens.*).
[Ety. dub.]

frankalmoign

frangk'al-moin, (*Eng. law*) n.
a form of land-tenure in which
no obligations were enforced
except religious ones, as
praying, etc.
[O.Fr. *franc*, free, *almoigne*,
alms.]

frass

fras, n.
excrement or other refuse of
boring larvae.
[Ger., — *fressen*, to eat.]

frazil
fraz'il, frā'zil, n.
ground-ice: ice in small spikes and plates in rapid streams.
[Canadian Fr. *frasil*; prob. Fr. *fraisil,* cinders.]

fredaine
frə-den, (Fr.) n.
an escapade, prank.

freemartin
frē'mär-tin, n.
a calf (twin with a bull) with internal male organs and external and rudimentary internal female: a similar animal of another species.
[Ety. unknown; perh. conn. with Ir. *mart,* a heifer.]

freit, freet
frēt, (Scot.) n.
an omen.
adj. **freit'y, freet'y**
superstitious.
[O.N. *frētt,* news.]

fremescent
frəm-es'ənt, (rare) adj.
growling, muttering.
n. **fremesc'ence.**
[L. *fremĕre,* to growl.]

fremitus
frem'i-təs, n.
a palpable vibration, as of the walls of the chest.
[L., a murmur.]

frescade
fres-kād', n.
a cool walk.
[Fr., — It. *frescata.*]

fris
frish, **friska** *frish'kö,* ns.
the quick movement of a csárdás.
[Hung.]

frisket
frisk'it, (print.) n.
the light frame between the tympan and the forme, to hold in place the sheet to be printed.
[Fr. *frisquette.*]

frist
frist, (obs.) n.
delay, respite.
v.t. to postpone: to grant time, as for payment.
[O.E. *first,* time, respite.]

froise
froiz, **fraise** *frāz,* ns.
a thick pancake, often with slices of bacon.
[Origin unknown.]

fronton
frun'tən, (archit.) n.
a pediment. — Also **frontoon** (*-toon'*).
[Fr., — It. *frontone.*]

fuero

fwā'rō, n.

a code or body of law or privileges, esp. in the Basque provinces, a constitution: — pl. **fue'ros.**

[Sp., — L. *forum*.]

fulham

fōōl'əm, n.

a die loaded at the corner. — Also **full'am, full'an.**

[Prob. the place name *Fulham*.]

fulvous

ful'vəs, adj.

dull yellow: tawny.

adj. **ful'vid.**

[L. *fulvus*, tawny.]

furacious

fū-rā'shəs, adj.

thievish.

ns. **fūrā'ciousness, fūracity** (*-ras'i-ti*).

[L. *fūrāx, -ācis* — *fūr*, thief.]

furfur

fûr'fûr, -fər (*Browning*, **furfair**), n.

dandruff, scurf.

n. **fūr'an** (*-an* or *-an'*) a colourless, liquid, heterocyclic compound, C_4H_4O, got from wood-tar or synthesised, and used in tanning and nylon production (also **fur'furan** *-fū-* or *-fə-*): any of a group of heterocyclic compounds derived from furan. — Also **fūr'ane** (*-ān*).

adj. **furfuraceous** (*fûr-fū-rā'shəs*) branny: scaly: scurfy.

ns. **furfural** (*fûr'fū-ral, -fə-ral*), in full **furfural'dehyde**, also called **fūr'al, fur'fūrol(e), fūr'ol(e)**, a liquid ($C_4H_3O \cdot CHO$) got by heating bran with dilute sulphuric acid; **furfuran** see **furan** above.

adj. **furfurous** (*fûr'fū-rəs, -fə-rəs*) furfuraceous.

[L. *furfur*, bran.]

furphy

fûr'fi, (*Austr.*) n.

a water cart: a rumour, false report.

[John *Furphy*, an Australian water cart manufacturer.]

furuncle

fū'rung-kl, n.

a boil.

adjs. **fūrun'cūlar, fūrun'cūlous.**

n. **fūruncūlō'sis** the condition of having many boils: a highly infectious disease of salmon and related fish.

[L. *fūrunculus*, lit. a little thief.]

fusarole, fusarol

fū'sə-rōl, or *-zə-*, (*archit.*) n.

an astragal moulding.

[Fr. *fusarolle* — It. *fusaruolo*,

spindle-whorl — L. *fūsus,*
spindle.]

fuscous

fus'kəs, adj.

brown: dingy. — Also (*Lamb*)
fusc.

[L. *fuscus.*]

fustanella

fus-tə-nel'ə, nⁱ

a white kilt worn by Greek and
Albanian men.

[Mod. Gr. *phoustanella,* dim. of
phoustani, Albanian *fustan* — It.
fustagno, fustian.]

fustigate

fus'ti-gāt, v.t.

to cudgel.
n. **fustigā'tion.**

[L. *fūstīgāre, -ātum* — *fūstis,* a
stick.]

futchel

fuch'əl, n.

a piece of timber lengthwise of
a carriage, supporting the
splinter-bar and the pole.

futhork, futhorc, futhark

foo'thörk, -thärk, ns.

the Runic alphabet.

[From the first six letters, *f, u, þ*
(*th*), *o* or *a, r, k.*]

fylfot, filfot

fil'fot, n.

a swastika, esp. one turned
counter-clockwise.

[Prob. from misunderstanding
of a manuscript, *fylfot* = fill-foot,
really meaning a device for
filling the foot of a painted
window.]

fyrd

fûrd, fērd, n.

the militia of Old English times.

[O.E. *fyrd,* army.]

G

gabbart
gab'ərt, (esp. *Scot.*) n.
a barge. — Also **gabb'ard.**
[Fr. *gabare* — Prov. and It.
gabarra.]

gabelle
gab-el', n.
a tax, esp. formerly in France,
on salt.
n. **gabell'er** a collector of
gabelle.
[Fr. *gabelle* — L.L. *gabella*,
gablum; of Gmc. origin.]

gaberlunzie
gab-ər-lün'i, -yi, later *-lun'zi*,
(*Scot.*) n.
a beggar's pouch: a strolling
beggar, orig. a bluegown.

gabion
gā'bi-ən, n.
a wickerwork or wire basket of
earth or stones used for
embankment work, etc. in
fortification and engineering: a
small curiosity (*Scott*).
ns. (*fort.*) **gā'bionade** a work
formed of gabions;
gā'bionage gabions
collectively.
adj. **gā'bioned** furnished with
gabions.

[Fr., — It. *gabbione*, a large
cage — *gabbia* — L. *cavea*, a
cage.]

gabnash
gab'nash, (*Scot.*) n.
prattle: chatter: a pert prattler.
[Cf. **nashgab.**]

gadi
gäd'ē, gud'ē, n.
an Indian throne.
[Marathi *gādī*, Bengali *gadī*.]

gadroon
gə-drōōn', n.
a boss-like ornament, used in
series in plate, etc., to form a
cable or bead.
adj. **gadrooned'.**
n. **gadroon'ing.**
[Fr. *godron*.]

galah
gə-lä', n.
an Australian cockatoo with pink
underparts: a fool.
[Aboriginal.]

galatea

gal-ə-tē'ə, n.

a cotton fabric usu. with coloured stripe.

[19th cent. H.M.S. *Galatea.*]

galdragon

gal'drə-gən, (*Scott*) n.

an obs. Shetland word for a sorceress, witch.

[O.N. *galdra-kona* — *galdr,* crowing, incantation, witchcraft, *kuna,* woman.]

galea

gal'i-ə, gāl'i-ə, (*biol.*) n.

a helmet-shaped structure.

adjs. **gal'eate, -d.**

[L. *galea,* a skin helmet.]

galimatias

gal-i-mā'shi-əs, -mat'i-äs, n.

nonsense: any confused mixture of unlike things.

[Fr.]

galiongee

gal-yən-jē', n.

a Turkish sailor.

[Turk. *qālyūnjī,* deriv. of *qālyūn* — It. *galeone,* galleon.]

galipot

gal'i-pot, n.

the turpentine that exudes from the cluster-pine.

[Fr.]

gallet

gal'ət, n.

a small pebble or stone chip.

v.t. to fill in mortar joints with gallets: — pr.p. **gall'eting;** pa.t. and pa.p. **gall'eted.**

[Fr. *galet,* a pebble — O.Fr. *gal.*]

galligaskins

gal-i-gas'kinz, n.pl.

wide hose or breeches worn in 16th and 17th centuries: leggings.

[O.Fr. *garguesque* — It. *grechesco,* Greekish — L. *graecus,* Greek.]

gallinazo

gal-i-nä'zō, n.

a turkey-buzzard or other vulture: — pl. **gallina'zos.**

[Sp., — *gallina* — L. *gallīna,* hen.]

gallinule

gal'i-nūl, n.

a water-hen.

[L. *gallīnula,* a chicken — *gallīna,* a hen.]

galliot, galiot

gal'i-ət, n.

a small galley: an old Dutch cargo-boat.

[Fr. *galiote* — L.L. *galea,* galley.]

gallipot

gal'i-pot, n.

a small glazed pot, esp. for medicine.

[Prob. a **pot** brought in **galleys.**]

gallise, -ize

gal'īz, v.t.

in wine-making, to bring to standard proportions by adding water and sugar to inferior must. — Also **gall'isise, -ize.**

[Ger. *gallisieren*, from the name of the inventor, Dr. L. *Gall.*]

gallivat

gal'i-vat, n.

a large two-masted Malay boat.

[Port. *galeota*; see **galliot.**]

galliwasp

gal'i-wosp, n.

a W. Indian lizard.

galopin

gal'ə-pin, n.

an errand boy (*Scott*): a kitchen boy (*obs.*).

[Fr.]

galut(h)

gä-lōōt', gō'ləs, n. (often *cap.*)

forced exile of Jews, esp. (diaspora) from Palestine.

[Heb. *gālūth*, exile.]

gamash

gəm-ash', n.

a kind of legging. — Also **gramash'** (*Scott*), **gramoche'** (*-osh'*; *Scott*).

[Fr. (now *dial.*) *gamache*, Prov. *garamacha*, apparently from *Ghadames*, famous for leather.]

gambeson

gam'bi-sən, n.

an ancient leather or quilted cloth coat worn under the habergeon.

[O.Fr., — O.H.G. *wamba*, belly.]

gambet

gam'bit, n.

the redshank.

[It. *gambetta*, ruff, *gambetta fosca*, spotted redshank.]

gambrel

gam'brəl, n.

the hock of a horse: a crooked stick for hanging a carcass, etc. **gambrel roof** a mansard roof.

[O.Fr. *gamberel*; cf. Fr. *gambier*, a hooked stick; connection with **cambrel** obscure.]

gambroon

gam-brōōn', n.

a twilled cloth of worsted and cotton, or linen.

[Prob. *Gambrun*, in Persia.]

gammock
gam'ək, (dial.) n.
a frolic, fun.
v.i. to frolic, to lark.

ganch, gaunch
gänsh, -ch, gönsh, -ch, v.t.
to impale: to lacerate.
n. impaling apparatus: a wound
from a boar's tusk.
[O.Fr. *gancher* — It. *gancio,* a
hook.]

gangue, gang
gang, n.
rock in which ores are
embedded.
[Fr., — Ger. *Gang* a vein.]

ganister, gannister
gan'is-tər, n.
a hard, close-grained siliceous
stone, found in the Lower Coal
Measures of N. England.
[Origin unknown.]

gapó
gä-pō', n.
riverside forest periodically
flooded: — pl. **gapós'**.
[Port. (*i*)*gapó* — Tupí *igapó,*
ygapó.]

garget
gär'git, n.
inflammation of the throat or
udder in cows, swine, etc.: (also
garget plant) pokeweed
(*U.S.*).

garron, garran
gar'ən, n.
a small horse.
[Ir. *gearran.*]

garuda
gur'ōō-dä, n.
(also with *cap.*) a Hindu
demigod, part man, part bird.
[Sans.]

gaur
gowr, n.
a species of ox inhabiting some
of the mountain jungles of India.
[Hindustani.]

gavelock
gav'ə-lək, n.
a javelin: a crow-bar.
[O.E. *gafeluc.*]

gayal, gyal
gī'al, n.
an Indian domesticated ox, akin
to the gaur, with curved horns.
[Hindi.]

gay-you
gī'ū, gā'ū, n.
a narrow flat-bottomed
Vietnamese boat with outrigger
and masts.
[Vietnamese *ghe hâu.*]

gean

gēn, n.

the European wild cherry.

[O.Fr. *guigne*.]

geason

gē'zn, (*obs.*) adj.

rare (*Spens.*): out of the way: wonderful.

[O.E. *gǣne*, *gēsne*, wanting, barren.]

geat

jēt, n.

the hole in a mould through which the metal is poured in casting.

[**jet**.]

gebur

gə-bōōr', *yə-bōōr'*, (*hist.*) n.

a tenant-farmer.

[O.E. *gebūr*.]

ged

ged, (*dial.*) n.

the pike or luce.

[O.N. *gedda*.]

gelada

jel'ə-də, *gel'*, *ji-läd'ə*, *gi-*, n.

an Ethiopian baboon, with a long mane.

[Poss. from Ar. *qilādah*, collar, mane.]

gelastic

jel-as'tik, adj.

pertaining to or provoking laughter.

[Gr. *gelastikos* — *gelaein*, to laugh.]

gena

jē'nə, n.

the cheek or side of the head. adj. **gē'nal**.

[L. *gĕna*.]

genappe

jə-nap', n.

a smooth worsted yarn used with silk in fringes, braid, etc.

[*Genappe* in Belgium.]

genipap

jen'i-pap, n.

a large West Indian tree (*Genipa americana*; Rubiaceae): its orange-sized, wine-flavoured fruit. — Also **gen'ip**.

[From Tupí.]

genizah

gə-nēz'ə, n.

a room adjoining a synagogue for the safe-keeping of old or damaged books, documents or valuables.

[Heb.]

geo, gio
gyō, (*Orkney, Shetland*) n.
a gully, creek: — pl. **geos, gios.**
[O.N. *gjā*.]

gerah
gē'rä, (*B.*) n.
the smallest Hebrew weight and
coin, 1/20 of a shekel.
[Heb. *gērāh*.]

geropiga
jer-ō-pē'gə, n.
a mixture of grape-juice,
brandy, etc., used to doctor
port-wine.
[Port.]

geta
gā'tə, n.
a Japanese wooden sandal with
a thong between the big toe
and the other toes: — pl. **ge'ta**
or **ge'tas.**
[Jap.]

ghazi
gä'zē, n.
a veteran Muslim warrior: a
slayer of infidels: a high Turkish
title.
[Ar. *ghāzi*, fighting.]

gibel
gib'əl, n.
the Prussian carp, without
barbules.

gibus
jī'bəs, n.
an opera-hat.
[Fr.]

gidgee, gidjee
gi'jē, (*Austr.*) n.
a small acacia tree, the foliage
of which at times emits an
unpleasant odour.
[Aboriginal.]

gilgie, jilgie
jil'gi, (*Austr.*) n.
a yabby.
[Aboriginal.]

gillaroo
gil-ə-rōō', n.
an Irish trout with thickened
muscular stomach.
[Ir. *giolla ruadh*, red lad.]

gingili, gingelly, jinjili
jin'ji-li, n.
a species of sesame: an oil got
from its seeds.
[Hind. *jinjalī*, prob. — Ar.
juljulān.]

ginglymus
jing'gli-məs (or *ging'-*), n.
a joint that permits movement in
one plane only: — pl.
ging'lymī.
adj. **ging'lymoid.**
[Latinised from Gr. *ginglymos*.]

girnel

gir'nl, (*Scot.*) n.

a granary (*obs.*): a meal chest.

[Variant of **garner.**]

gisarme

jē-zärm', *zhē-*, *gē-*, (*hist.*) n.

a type of long-staffed battle-axe carried by foot-soldiers.

[O.Fr. *guisarme*, prob. O.H.G. *getan*, to weed, *īsarn*, iron.]

gizz, jiz

jiz, (*Scot.*) n.

a wig.

[Origin unknown.]

gizzen

giz'n, (*Scot.*) v.i.

to shrink from dryness so as to leak: to wither.

adj. leaky: shrivelled.

[O.N. *gisna.*]

glabella

glə-bel'ə, n.

the part of the forehead between the eyebrows and just above their level: — pl. **glabell'ae** (-*bel'ē*).

adj. **glabell'ar.**

[L. *glaber*, bald, smooth.]

glareous

glā'ri-əs, adj.

gravelly: growing on gravel.

adj. **glā'real** growing on dry exposed ground.

[L. *glārea*, gravel.]

glede

glēd, **gled** *gled*, (*B.*) ns.

the common kite.

[O.E. *glida*, from *glīdan*, to glide.]

gleed

glēd, (*dial.*) n.

a hot coal or burning ember.

[O.E. *glēd*; cf. Du. *gloed*, Ger. *Glut*, Sw. *glöd.*]

gleet

glēt, n.

a viscous, transparent discharge from a mucous surface.

v.t. to discharge gleet.

adj. **gleet'y.**

[O.Fr. *glette*, *glecte*, a flux.]

glenoid, -al

glē'noid, -*əl*, adjs.

socket-shaped: slightly cupped. — Also n.

[Gr. *glēnoeidēs* — *glēnē*, a socket.]

gliff

glif, (*Scot.*) n.

a fright, a scare: a glimpse or other transient experience: a moment. — Also **glift.**

n. **gliff'ing** a moment.

[Ety. dub.]

glisk

glisk, (*Scot.*) n.

a glimpse.

[Perh. from the same root as
O.E. *glisian,* to shine.]

glogg

glog, n.

a Swedish hot spiced drink, of
wines, spirit, and fruit, often
served at Christmas.

[Sw. *glögg.*]

goanna

gō-an'ə, n.

in Australia, any large monitor
lizard.

[**iguana.**]

gobo

gō'bō, (chiefly *U.S.*) n.

a device used to protect a
camera lens from light: a device
for preventing unwanted sound
from reaching a microphone: —
pl. **gō'boes, gō'bos.**

[Origin obscure.]

godet

gō'dā, -det', n.

a triangular piece of cloth
inserted in a skirt, etc., e.g. to
make a flare.

[Fr.]

goel

gō'el, -āl, n.

the avenger of blood among the
Hebrews, the nearest relative,
whose duty it was to hunt down
the murderer.

[Heb.]

goety

gō'ə-ti, n.

black magic.

adj. **goetic** (*-et'*).

[Gr. *goēteiā,* witchcraft.]

goglet

gog'lit, n.

a water-cooler.

[Port. *gorgoleta.*]

gollan, golland

gol'ən(d), **gowland** *gow'lənd,*
ns.

a northern name for various
yellow flowers (marigold,
corn-marigold, globeflower,
etc.).

golomynka

go-lo-ming'kə, n.

a very oily fish found in Lake
Baikal, resembling the gobies.

[Russ.]

gombeen

gom'bēn', (*Ir.*) n.

usury.

gombeen'-man a grasping
usurer.

[Ir. *gaimbín.*]

gonfalon

gon'fə-lon, n.

an ensign or standard with streamers.

ns. **gonfalonier** (*-ēr'*) one who bears a gonfalon: the chief magistrate in some mediaeval Italian republics; **gon'fanon** a gonfalon: a pennon.

[It. *gonfalone* and O.Fr. *gonfanon* — O.H.G. *gundfano* — *gund*, battle, *fano* (Ger. *Fahne*), a flag; cf. O.E. *gūthfana*.]

gopura

gō'pōō-rə, **gopuram** *gō'pōō-rəm*, ns.

in Southern India, a pyramidal tower over the gateway of a temple.

[Sans. *gopura*.]

goral

gō'rəl, gö', n.

a Himalayan goat-antelope.

goramy, gourami, gurami

gō', gö', gōō'rə-mi, or *-rä'mi*, ns.

a large freshwater food-fish (*Osphromenus olfax*) of the Eastern Archipelago.

[Malay *gurāmī*.]

gorcock

gör'kok, n.

the red grouse cock.

[Origin obscure.]

gorcrow

gör'krō, n.

the carrion-crow.

[O.E. *gor*, filth, and **crow**.]

gorsedd

gor'sedh, n.

a meeting of bards and druids.

[W., throne.]

gossan, gozzan

gos', goz'ən, ns.

decomposed rock, largely quartz impregnated with iron compounds, at the outcrop of a vein esp. of metallic sulphides.

[Cornish miner's term; origin unknown.]

gourde

gōōrd, n.

the monetary unit of Haiti, consisting of 100 centimes.

[Fr. fem. of *gourd* — L. *gurdus*, dull, stupid.]

gourds

gōrdz, gördz, gōōrdz, n.pl.

a kind of false dice.

[Cf. O.Fr. *gourd*, swindle.]

gourdy

gōrd'i, görd', gōōrd', adj.

swollen in the legs (of a horse).

n. **gourd'iness**.

[O.Fr. *gourdi*, swollen.]

gowpen
gowp'ən, (*Scot.*) n.
the hollow of the two hands
held together: a double handful
(now usu. pl.).
n. **gow'penful.**
[O.N. *gaupn.*]

graddan
grad'ən, (*Scot.*) n.
parched grain.
v.t. to parch in the husk.
[Gael. *gradan.*]

graine
grān, n.
silkworm eggs.
[Fr.]

graip
grāp, (*Scot.*) n.
a three- or four-pronged fork
used for lifting dung or digging
potatoes.
[A form of **grope;** cf. Sw. *grep,*
Dan. *greb.*]

gralloch
gral'əhh, n.
a deer's entrails.
v.t. to disembowel (deer).
[Gael. *grealach.*]

grassum
grӓs'əm, (*Scots law*) n.
a lump sum paid by persons
who take a lease of landed
property — in England,
'premium' and 'fine'.
[O.E. *gærsum*, treasure, rich
gift, etc.]

graupel
grow'pəl, n.
frozen rain or snowflakes.
[Ger. *graupeln*, to sleet.]

greffier
gref'yā, n.
a registrar: a notary.
[Fr.]

gregale
grā-gä'lā, n.
a north-east wind in the
Mediterranean.
[It., — L. *graecus*, Greek.]

grego
grā'gō, grē'gō, n.
a Levantine hooded jacket or
cloak: an overcoat: — pl.
gre'gos.
[Port. *grego* or other deriv. of L.
graecus, Greek.]

grisgris, grigri, greegree
(also **gris-gris,** etc.) *grē'grē*, n.
African charm, amulet, or spell.
[Fr.; prob. of African origin.]

griskin

gris'kin, (*dial.*) n.

lean from a loin of pork.

grison

griz'ən, grīz'ən, -on, n.

a large grey S. American weasel: a grey S. American monkey.

[Fr., — *gris*, grey.]

grivet

griv'it, n.

a north-east African guenon monkey.

[Fr.; origin unknown.]

grockle

grok'l, (*dial.*) n.

a tourist.

[Origin unknown.]

groma

grōm'ə, n.

surveying instrument used by the Romans, in which plumblines suspended from the arms of a horizontal cruciform frame were used to construct right angles.

[L. *grōma*, a surveyor's pole, measuring rod.]

groser

grō'zər, **grosert, grossart** *-zərt*, **groset** *-zit*, (*Scot.*) ns.

a gooseberry.

[Fr. *groseille*.]

gru-gru, groo-groo

grōō'grōō, n.

a name for several tropical American palms akin to the coconut palm, yielding oil-nuts: an edible weevil grub (also **gru-gru worm**) found in their pith.

grume

grōōm, n.

a thick fluid: a clot.

adjs. **grum'ous, grum'ose** composed of grains.

[O.Fr. *grume*, a bunch — L. *grūmus*, a little heap.]

grunion

grun'yən, n.

a small Californian sea-fish which spawns on shore.

[Prob. Sp. *gruñon*, grunter.]

guan

gwän, n.

a large noisy American arboreal game-bird.

guanaco

gwä-nä'kō, n.

a wild llama. — Also **huana'co** (*wä-*): — pls. **guana'co(s), huana'co(s)**.

[Quechua *huanaco*.]

gub, gubbah

gub, gub'ə, ns.

a white man.

[Aboriginal term.]

gue, gu, gju

gōō, gū, ns.

a rude kind of violin used in Shetland.

[O.N. *gigja.*]

guereza

ger'ə-zə, n.

a large, long-haired, black-and-white African monkey, with a bushy tail: any species of the same genus (*Colobus*).

[App. of Somali origin.]

guimbard

gim'bärd, n.

a Jew's-harp.

[Perh. from Prov. *guimbardo,* a kind of dance — *guimba,* to leap, gambol.]

gumphion

gum'fi-ən, (obs. Scot.) n.

a funeral banner.

[**gonfanon.**]

gundy

gun'di, (Scot.) n.

a sweetmeat made of treacle and spices.

[Perh. variant of **candy.**]

gunyah

gun'yə, (Austr.) n.

an Australian Aborigine's hut: a roughly-made shelter in the bush.

[Aboriginal.]

gur, goor

gûr, gōōr, n.

an unrefined sweet cane sugar.

[Hindi, coarse sugar — Sans. *guda.*]

gurdwara

gûr'dwär-ə, n.

a Sikh place of worship.

[Punjabi *gurduārā* — Sans. *guru,* teacher, *dvāra,* door.]

gurge

gûrj, (Milt.) n.

a whirlpool.

[L. *gurges.*]

gurlet

gûr'lit, n.

a pickaxe with a head pointed at one end, bladed at the other.

gurrah

gur'ə, n.

a coarse Indian muslin.

[Hind. *gārhā,* thick.]

gurry

gur'i, n.

whale offal: fish offal.

[Origin unknown.]

gusla

gōōs'lǝ, **gusle** *-le*, **gusli** *-lē*, ns.

a one-stringed Balkan musical
instrument: a Russian
instrument with several strings.
n. **guslar'** a performer on it.

[Bulg. *gusla*, Serb. *gusle*, Russ.
gusli.]

guyot

gē'ō, n.

a flat-topped submarine
mountain.

[A. H. *Guyot*, Swiss-born Amer.
geologist.]

gytrash

gī'trash, (*dial.*) n.

a ghost.

H

haberdine

hab'ər-dēn, -dīn, -din, n.
dried salt cod.
[Old Du. *abberdaen,* also *labberdaen;* prob. from Le Labourd, or *Lapurdum,* Bayonne.]

haboob

hä-bōōb', n.
a sand-storm.
[Ar. *habūb.*]

hackamore

hak'ə-mōr, -mör, n.
a halter used esp. in breaking in foals, consisting of a single length of rope with a loop to serve instead of a bridle.
[Sp. *jáquima.*]

hackbolt

hak'bōlt, n.
the greater shearwater. — Also **hag'bolt, hag'den, hag'don, hag'down** (*hag'dən*).
[Origin obscure.]

hackbut

hak'but, **hagbut** *hag',* ns.
an arquebus.
n. **hackbuteer'.**

[O.Fr. *haquebute,* from O.Du. *hakebus.*]

hackee

hak'ē, n.
the chipmunk.
[Imit. of its cry.]

hackery

hak'ər-i, n.
an Indian bullock-cart.
[Perh. Bengali *hkārī,* shouting.]

hacklet

hak'lit, **haglet** *hag',* ns.
prob. the shearwater: the kittiwake.
[Origin unknown.]

hackmatack

hak'mə-tak, n.
an American larch.
[Indian word.]

hadith

had'ith, hä-dēth', n.
(often with *cap.*) the body of traditions about Mohammed, supplementary to the Koran.
[Ar. *hadīth.*]

haff

haf, n.

a lagoon separated from the sea by a long sandbar.

[Ger. *Haff,* bay.]

haiduk, heyduck

hī'dōōk, n.

a brigand: a guerrilla warrior: a liveried servant. ⟩

[Hung. *hajduk,* pl. of *hajdú.*]

hain

hān, (*Scot.*) v.t.

to save, preserve: to spare.

adj. **hained.**

n. **hain'ing** an enclosure.

[O.N. *hegna,* to enclose, protect; cf. Sw. *hägna*; Dan. *hegne.*]

haka

hä'kä, n.

a Maori ceremonial war-dance: a similar dance performed by New Zealanders, e.g. before a rugby game.

[Maori.]

hakam

häk'äm, n.

a sage: a rabbinical commentator, esp. one during the first two cents. A.D.

[Heb. *hākhām,* wise.]

halfa, alfa

(h)al'fə, ns.

N. African esparto.

[Ar. *halfā.*]

halfpace

häf'pās, n.

a landing or broad step: a raised part of a floor.

[O.Fr. *halt* (Fr. *haut*), high, *pas,* step.]

halicore

hal-īk'o-rē, n.

the dugong.

[Gr. *hals,* sea, *korē,* girl.]

halieutic

hal-i-ū'tik, adj.

pertaining to fishing.

n. sing. **halieu'tics** the art of fishing: a treatise thereon.

[Gr. *halieutikos — halieus,* fisher — *hals,* sea.]

hallali

hal'ə-lē, n.

a bugle-call.

hallan

häl'ən, (*Scot.*) n.

a partition or screen between the door and fireplace in a cottage.

n. **hallan-shäk'er** (or -*shäk'ər*) a sturdy beggar.

hälleflinta

hel'ə-flin-tə, n.

a very compact rock composed of minute particles of quartz and feldspar.

[Sw., hornstone.]

halteres

hal-tēr'ēz, n.pl.

the rudimentary hind-wings of flies.

[Gr. *haltērĕs*, dumb-bells held by jumpers — *hallesthai*, to jump.]

hamate

hā'māt, adj.

hooked.

[L. *hāmātus* — *hāmus*, hook.]

hamble

ham'bl, v.t.

to mutilate, make useless for hunting (by cutting the balls of a dog's feet).

v.i. to limp, to stumble (*dial.*).

[O.E. *hamelian*.]

hamesucken

hām'suk-n, (*Scots law*) n.

the assaulting of a man in his own house.

[O.E. *hāmsōcn* — *hām*, home, *sōcn*, seeking, attack; cf. Ger. *Heimsuchung*, affliction.]

hamfatter

ham'fat-ər, n.

a third-rate minstrel, variety artist, actor.

v.t. and v.i. to act badly or ineffectively.

[Perh. from an old Negro minstrel song, The *Hamfat* Man.]

hammal, hamal

hum-äl', n.

an Eastern porter.

[Ar. *hammāl*.]

hamza, hamzah

häm'zä, ham'zə, n.

in Arabic, the sign used to represent the glottal stop.

[Ar. *hamzah*, a compression.]

handjar, hanjar

han'jär, n.

a Persian dagger. — Also **khanjar**.

[Pers. and Ar. *khanjar*.]

hanepoot

hän'ə-pōōt, (*S.Afr.*) n.

a kind of grape. — Also **haanepoot, honeypot**.

[Du. *haane-poot* — *haan*, cock, *poot*, foot.]

haoma

how'ma, n.

a drink prepared from the haoma vine, used in Zoroastrian ritual: (*cap.*) a deity, personification of haoma.

[Avestan.]

haptic

hap'tik, adj.

pertaining to the sense of touch. n. sing. **hap'tics** science of studying data obtained by means of touch.

[Gr. *haptein,* to fasten.]

hards

härdz, **hurds** *hûrdz,* ns.pl.

coarse or refuse flax or hemp: tarred rags used as torches (*Scott*).

ns. **hard'en, herd'en, hurd'en** a coarse fabric made from hards.

[O.E. *heordan.*]

hareld

har'ld, n.

the long-tailed duck, *Clangula hyemalis.*

[Mod. Icel. *havella* — *hav,* sea.]

harman

här'mən, (*old thieves' slang*) n.

a constable: (in pl.) the stocks. n. **har'man-beck** a constable.

[Origin obscure.]

harmost

här'most, n.

a Spartan governor of a subject city or province.

n. **har'mosty** the office of harmost.

[Gr. *harmostēs.*]

harn

härn, n.

a coarse linen fabric.

hartal

här'tal, hûr'täl, (*India*) n.

a stoppage of work in protest or boycott.

[Hindi *hartāl.*]

hassar

has'ər, n.

a South American nest-building land-walking catfish (in the American sense).

[Amer. Indian origin.]

hatti-sherif

ha'ti-she-rēf', (*hist.*) n.

a decree signed by the Sultan of Turkey.

[Pers. *khatt-i-sharīf,* noble writing, from Ar.]

haurient, hauriant

hö'ri-ənt, (*her.*) adj.

rising as if to breathe.

[L. *hauriēns, -entis,* pr.p. of *haurīre,* to draw up, drink.]

haustellum

hös-tel'əm, n.

a sucking proboscis or its sucking end, as in flies: — pl. **haustell'a**.

adj. **haus'tellate** having a haustellum.

n. **haustō'rium** the part by which a parasitic plant fixes itself and derives nourishment from its host: — pl. **haustō'ria**.

[L. *haurīre, haustum*, draw up, drink.]

havelock

hav'lək, n.

a white cover for a military cap, with a flap over the neck.

[From Gen. Henry *Havelock*, 1795–1857.]

helcoid

hel'koid, adj.

ulcerous.

[Gr. *helkos*, an ulcer.]

helminth

hel'minth, n.

a worm.

n. **helminthī'asis** infestation with worms.

adjs. **helmin'thic**;
helmin'thoid worm-shaped;
helmintholog'ic, -al.

ns. **helminthol'ogist**;
helminthol'ogy the study of worms, esp. parasitic.

adj. **helminth'ous** infested with worms.

[Gr. *helmins, -inthos*, a worm.]

heortology

hē-ört-ol'ə-ji, n.

the study of religious feasts.

adj. **heortological** (*-ə-loj'i-kl*).

n. **heortol'ogist**.

[Gr. *heortē*, a feast, *logos*, discourse.]

herdic

hûr'dik, n.

a low-hung two- or four-wheeled carriage with back entrance and side seats.

[From the inventor, P. *Herdic* (1824–88), of Pennsylvania.]

herling, hirling

hûr'ling, (*dial.*) n.

a young sea-trout, a finnock.

hership

hûr'ship, (*Scot.*) n.

plundering: plunder.

[O.E. *here*, army, or *hergan*, to harry; cf. O.N. *herskapr*, warfare.]

hiccatee, hicatee

hik-ə-tē', n.

a West Indian freshwater tortoise.

[From a native name.]

hickwall

hik'wöl, (*dial.*) n.

the green woodpecker.

[Origin obscure.]

hielaman

hē'lə-man, n.

an Australian Aboriginal narrow shield of bark or wood.

[Native word *hīlaman*.]

himation

hi-mat'i-on, n.

the ancient Greek outer garment, oblong, thrown over the left shoulder, and fastened either over or under the right.

[Gr.]

hirrient

hir'i-ənt, adj.

roughly trilled.

n. a trilled sound.

[L. *hirriēns, -entis,* pr.p. of *hirrīre,* to snarl.]

hirsel

hûr', hir'sl, (Scot.) n.

a stock of sheep: a multitude: the ground occupied by a hirsel of sheep.

v.t. to put in different groups.

[O.N. *hirzla,* safe-keeping — *hirtha,* to herd.]

hirstie

hirs', hûrs'ti, (obs. Scot.) adj.

dry: barren.

hirudin

hir-ōōd'in, n.

a substance present in the salivary secretion of the leech which prevents blood-clotting.

n.pl. **Hirudinea** (*-in'i-ə*) a class of worms, the leeches.

n. and adj. **hirudin'ean.**

adjs. **hirud'inoid; hirud'inous.**

[L. *hirūdō, -inis,* a leech.]

hoastman

hōst'man, n.

a member of an old merchant guild in Newcastle, with charge of coal-shipping, etc.

[O.Fr. *hoste* — L. *hospes,* stranger, guest.]

hobday

hob'dā, v.t.

to cure a breathing impediment in (a horse) by surgical operation.

adj. **hob'dayed.**

[After Sir Frederick *Hobday* (1869–1939).]

hodmandod

hod'mən-dod, n.

a shelled snail.

n. **hodd'y-dodd'y** (*obs.*) a dumpy person: a duped husband: a noodle.

hogger

hog'ər, (Scot.) n.

a footless stocking worn as a gaiter: a short connecting-pipe.

[Origin obscure.]

hoggin, hogging

hog'in, n.

sifted gravel: a mixture
containing gravel.

[Origin uncertain.]

hoolachan

hōō'lə-hhən, **hoolican**
hōō'li-kən (*Scot.*) ns.

a Highland reel, esp. the reel of
Tulloch.

[Gael. (*ruidhle*) *Thulachain,* the
reel of Tulloch, in Strathspey.]

hoolock

hōō'lək, n.

a small Assamese gibbon.

[Said to be native name,
hulluk.]

horme

hör'mē (*psych.*), n.

goal-directed or purposive
behaviour.

hormic theory theory stressing
the importance of instinctive
impulses and purposive striving.

[Gr. *hormē,* animal impulse.]

horst

hörst, (*geol.*) n.

a block of the earth's crust that
has remained in position while
the ground around it has either
subsided or been folded into
mountains by pressure against
its solid sides.

[Ger.]

hospodar

hos'po-där, (*hist.*) n.

a prince or governor, esp. of
Moldavia or Wallachia. — Also
gos'podar.

[Rum. *hospodár,* of Slav.
origin.]

howdie, howdy

how'di, (*Scot.*) n.

a midwife.

[Poss. O.E. *hold,* gracious.]

huckaback

huk'ə-bak, n.

a coarse linen or cotton with
raised surface, used for towels,
etc.

[Origin unknown.]

huia

hōō'yə, hōō'ē-ə, n.

a New Zealand bird
(*Heteralocha acutirostris*) akin
to the crows and starlings, now
prob. extinct.

[Maori; imit.]

huma

hōō'mə, n.

a fabulous restless bird.

[Pers. *humā,* phoenix.]

humhum

hum'hum, n.

a kind of plain, coarse cotton
cloth used in the East Indies.

huso

hū'sō, n.

the great sturgeon: — pl.
hu'sos.

[O.H.G. *hûso.*]

hutia

hōō-tē'ə, n.

the hog-rat.

[Sp. *hutia,* from Taino.]

huzoor

huz-ōōr', n.

an Indian potentate, or (loosely)
any person of rank or
importance.

[Ar. *hudūr,* the presence.]

hydyne

hī'dīn, n.

an American rocket-launching
fuel.

hyleg

hī'leg, n.

the ruling planet at the hour of
birth.

[Origin obscure; cf. Pers. *hailāj,*
nativity.]

hypaethral

hip-ē'thrəl, or *hīp-,* adj.

roofless, open to the sky.
n. **hypae'thron** an open court.

[Gr. *hypo,* beneath, *aithēr,*
upper air, sky.]

hypural

hī-pū'rəl, adj.

situated beneath the tail.

[Gr. *hypo,* under, *ourā,* tail.]

hyson

hī'son, n.

a very fine sort of green tea.
hy'son-skin the refuse of
hyson tea removed by
winnowing.

[From Chin.]

I

ichnite

ik'nīt, **ichnolite** *ik'nə-līt*, ns.
a fossil footprint.
n. **ichnography** (*ik-nog'rə-fi*) a
ground plan: the art of drawing
ground plans.
adjs. **ichnographic**
(*-nō-graf'ik*), **-al.**
adv. **ichnograph'ically.**
n. **ichnol'ogy** footprint lore:
the science of fossil footprints.
[Gr. *ichnos*, a track, footprint.]

igarapé

ē-gä-rä-pā', n.
a canoe waterway in Brazil.
[Tupí.]

ihram

ē-räm, ēhh'räm, n.
the scanty garb worn by Muslim
pilgrims on drawing near
Mecca: the holy state it
betokens.
[Ar. *ihrām*.]

illipe

il'i-pi, **illupi** *il-ōō'pi*, n.
the mahwa tree (Sapotaceae)
yielding **illipe nuts** and **oil.**
[Tamil *illuppai*.]

imbroccata

im-bro-kä'tə, n.
in fencing, a thrust.
[It.]

impavid

im-pav'id, (*rare*) adj.
fearless.
adv. **impav'idly.**
[L. *impavidus* — *im-* (*in-*), not,
pavidus, fearing.]

inchpin

inch', insh'pin, (*obs.*) n.
a deer's sweetbread.

incony, inconie

in-kun'i, (*Shak.*) adj.
fine, delicate, pretty.
[Origin unknown.]

incus

ing'kəs, n.
one of the bones in the middle
ear, so called from its fancied
resemblance to an anvil: — pl.
incudes (*ing-kū'dēz*, or *ing'*).
adj. anvil-shaped.
[L. *incūs, incūdis*, an anvil; see
incuse.]

incuse

in-kūz', v.t.

to impress by stamping, as a coin.

adj. hammered.

n. an impression, a stamp.

[L. *incūsus*, pa.p. of *incūdĕre* — *in*, on, *cūdĕre*, to strike: to work on the anvil.]

indagate

in'də-gāt, (*arch.*) v.t.

to search out.

n. **indagā'tion**.

adj. **in'dagātive**.

n. **in'dagātor**.

adj. **in'dagātory**.

[L. *indāgāre, -ātum*, to trace.]

induciae

in-dū'si-ē, (*Scots law*) n. sing.

the time limit within which (after a citation) the defendant must appear in court or reply.

[L. *indūciae, -tiae*, truce, delay.]

induline

in'dū-lin, -lēn, -līn, n.

any one of a class of coal-tar dyestuffs, giving blues, etc.

infangthief

in'fang-thēf, n.

in old English law, the right of taking and fining a thief within the boundary of one's own jurisdiction.

[O.E. *infangenethēof* — *in*, in,
the root of *fōn*, to seize, *thēof*, thief.]

infarct

in-färkt', n.

a portion of tissue that is dying because blood supply to it has been cut off.

n. **infarc'tion**.

[Mediaeval L. *īnfarctus* — *in*, in, *far(c)tus* — *farcīre*, to cram, stuff.]

infaust

in-föst', adj.

unlucky: ill-omened.

[L. *īnfaustus* — *in-*, not, *faustus*, propitious.]

inficete

in-fi-sēt', (*rare*) adj.

not facetious: rudely jesting.

[L. *īnficētus* — *in-*, not, *facētus*, courteous, witty.]

infula

in'fū-lə, n.

a white-and-red fillet or band of woollen stuff, worn by the ancient Romans upon the forehead in religious rites: a lappet in a mitre: — pl. **in'fulae** (*-ē*).

[L. *īnfula*.]

infundibular

in-fun-dib'ū-lər, adj.

funnel-shaped. — Also
**infundib'ulate,
infundib'uliform.**

[L. *īnfundibulum,* a funnel — *in,*
in, *fundĕre,* to pour.]

ingluvies

in-glōō'vi-ēz, n.

the crop or craw of birds.
adj. **inglu'vial.**

[L. *inglŭviēs.*]

inguinal

ing'gwin-əl, adj.

relating to the groin.

[L. *inguinālis — inguen,
inguinis,* the groin.]

inqilab

in'ki-läb, n.

in India, Pakistan, etc.,
revolution.

[Urdu.]

inquiline

in'kwi-līn, adj.

living in the abode of another.
n. animal so living.
ns. **in'quilinism, inquilin'ity.**
adj. **inquilī'nous.**

[L. *inquilīnus,* tenant, lodger —
incola, inhabitant — *in,* in,
colĕre, to inhabit.]

inquinate

in'kwin-āt, v.t.

to defile.
n. **inquinā'tion.**

[L. *inquināre, -ātum.*]

inro

in'rō, n.

a small Japanese container for
pills and medicines, once part of
traditional Japanese dress: —
pl. **in'rō.**

[Jap., seal-box.]

inselberg

in'zəl-bûrg, in'səl-berg, (*geol.*)
n.

a steep-sided eminence arising
from a plain tract, often found in
the semi-arid regions of tropical
countries: — pl. **inselberge**
(-*gə*).

[Ger., island-hill.]

insulse

in-suls', adj.

insipid: stupid.
n. **insul'sity** (*Milt.*) stupidity.

[L. *īnsulsus — in-,* not, *salĕre,*
to salt.]

intertie

in'tər-tī, n.

in roofing, etc., a short timber
binding together upright posts.

[Origin obscure.]

intertrigo

in-tər-trī'gō, n.

an inflammation of the skin from chafing or rubbing: — pl. **intertri'gos.**

[L. *intertrīgō* — *inter*, between, *terĕre, trītum*, to rub.]

inust

in-ust', (*obs.*) adj.

burned in.

n. **inustion** (*inus'chən*; *obs.*) burning in: cauterisation.

[L. *inūrĕre, inūstum*.]

inwick

in'wik, n.

in curling, a stroke in which the stone glances off the edge of another stone, and then slides close to the tee.

v.i. **inwick'** to make an inwick.

inyala

in-yä'lə, **nyala** *n-yä'lə*, ns.

a S. African antelope.

[Bantu.]

irade

i-rä'de, n.

a written decree of the Sultan of Turkey.

[Turk., — Ar. *irādah*, will.]

isabel

iz'ə-bel, n. and adj.

dingy yellowish-grey or drab. — Also **isabell'a, isabell'ine**

(*-in, -īn*).

[Origin unknown: too early in use to be from *Isabella*, daughter of Philip II, who did not change her linen for three years until Ostend was taken; an etymological connection with Isabella of Castile, to whom a similar legend is ascribed, is chronologically possible but by no means certain.]

ish

ish, (*Scots law*) n.

issue, liberty of going out: expiry.

[O.Fr. *issir*, to go out — L. *exīre* — *ex*, out of, *īre*, to go.]

isobront

ī'sō-bront, n.

a contour line marking simultaneous development of a thunderstorm.

[Pfx. **iso-,** and Gr. *brontē*, thunder.]

isochor, isochore

ī'sō-kōr, -kör, n.

a curve representing variation of some quantity under conditions of constant volume.

adj. **isochoric** (*-kor'ik*).

[Pfx. **iso-,** and Gr. *chōrā*, space.]

isolecithal

ī-sō-les'i-thəl, adj.

(of the ova of mammals and some other vertebrates) having the yolk distributed evenly through the protoplasm.
[Pfx. **iso-**, Gr. *lekithos*, egg-yolk.]

issei

ēs'sā', n.

a Japanese immigrant in the U.S.A.
[Jap., first generation.]

istle

ist'li, **ixtle** *ikst'li*, ns.

a valuable fibre obtained from Agave, Bromelia, and other plants.
[Mexican Sp. *ixtle* — Nahuatl *ichtli*.]

Iyyar

ē'yär, n.

the eighth month of the Jewish year (second of the ecclesiastical year).
[Heb.]

J

jabiru

jab'i-rōō̄, -rōō̄', n.

a large Brazilian stork: extended to other kinds.

[Tupí *jabirú*.]

jaçana

zhä-sə-nä', **jacana** *jak'ə-nə*, ns.

a long-toed swamp bird of the tropics.

[Port., from Tupí.]

jacchus

jak'əs, n.

a South American marmoset (*Callithrix*).

[L. *Iacchus* — Gr. *Iakchos*, Bacchus.]

jaconet

jak'ə-net, n.

a cotton fabric, rather stouter than muslin — different from the fabric orig. so named which was imported from *Jagannāth* (Puri) in India: a thin material with waterproof backing used for medical dressings.

jaggery

jag'ə-ri, n.

a coarse, dark sugar made from palm-sap or otherwise.

[Hindi *jāgrī*, Sans. *śarkarā* .]

jaghir, jaghire, jagir

jä-gēr', n.

the government revenues of a tract of land assigned with power to administer.

n. **jaghir'dar** the holder of a jaghir.

[Hind. and Pers. *jāgīr*.]

jambee

jam-bē', n.

an 18th-century light cane.

[*Jambi* in Sumatra.]

jambiya(h)

jam-bē'yä, n.

a type of Middle Eastern curved, double-edged dagger.

[Ar.]

jambone

jam'bōn, n.

a lone hand in euchre, played only by agreement, in which the player lays his cards on the table and must lead one chosen by his opponent, scoring 8

points if he takes all the tricks.
[Origin unknown.]

jamdani

jäm'dä-nē, n.
a variety of Dacca muslin
woven in design of flowers.
[Pers. *jāmdānī.*]

jampan

jam'pan, n.
an Indian sedan-chair.
n. **jampanee'**, **jampani** *(-ē')*
its bearer.
[Beng. *jhāmpān.*]

janker

jang'kər, (*Scot.*) n.
a long pole on wheels for
transporting large logs
suspended from it.
[Origin unknown.]

jann

jän, n.pl.
the least powerful order of jinn:
(sing.) a jinni.
[Ar. *jānn.*]

jargoon

jär'gōōn', **jargon** *jär'gən,* ns.
a brilliant colourless or pale
zircon.
n. **jargonelle'** an early pear
(orig. a gritty kind).
[Fr. *jargon.*]

jark

järk, (*cant*) n.
a seal on a document (usu.
counterfeit document): a pass,
safe-conduct.
jark'man a swindling beggar,
a begging-letter writer.

jarrah

jar'ə, n.
a Western Australian timber
tree, *Eucalyptus marginata.*
[Aboriginal.]

jarta, yarta

yär'tə, (*Shetland*) n.
lit. heart, used as an
endearment. — Also adj. —
Also (*Scott*) **yar'to.**
[O.N. *hjarta,* heart.]

jarul, jarool

jə-rōōl', n.
the Indian bloodwood
(*Lagerstroemia*), a lythraceous
tree.
[Beng. *jarūl.*]

jarvey, jarvie

jär'vi, (*slang*) n.
a hackney-coach driver: a
jaunting-car driver.
[Earlier *Jarvis*, poss. from St
Gervase, whose emblem is a
whip.]

jasey, jasy, jazy

jā'zi, n.

a wig, orig. of worsted.

jataka

jä'tə-kə, n.

a nativity, the birth-story of Buddha.

[Sans. *jātaka — jāta,* born.]

javel

jav'əl, (Spens.) n.

a worthless fellow.

[Origin unknown.]

jeistiecor

jēs'ti-kōr, -kör, (obs.; Scot.) n.

a close-fitting garment.

[Fr. *juste au corps,* close-fitting to the body.]

jemima

ji-mī'mə, (coll.) n.

an elastic-sided boot.

[An appropriate woman's name.]

jenneting

jen'it-ing, n.

a kind of early apple.

[Prob. St John's apple — Fr. *Jeannet,* dim. of *Jean,* John; not from *June-eating.*]

jeofail

jef'āl, (obs.) n.

an error in pleadings, or the acknowledgment of a mistake.

[A.Fr. *jeo fail,* I mistake.]

jequirity

jə-kwr'i -ti, n.

Indian liquorice: (also **jequirity bean**) its seed, otherwise crab's-eye, prayer-bead.

[Origin obscure.]

jerid, jereed

jer-ēd', n.

a blunt Oriental javelin: a tournament in which it is used.

[Ar. *jarīd.*]

jerque, jerk

jûrk, v.t.

to search (as a vessel) for concealed or smuggled goods: to examine (as a ship's papers). *ns.* **jerqu'er, jerk'er; jerqu'ing, jerk'ing.**

[Poss. It. *cercare,* to search.]

jesserant

jes'ə-rənt, **jazerant** *jaz', (hist.) ns.*

splint armour.

[O.Fr. *jaseran(t), jazeran* — Sp. *jacerina.*]

jettatura

jet-ə-tōō′rə, n.

the spell of the evil eye.

[It. *iettatura*, a Neapolitan word — L. *ējectāre* — *jactāre*, freq. of *jacĕre*, to throw.]

jingal, gingall, gingal

jin(g)′göl, -göl′, n.

a large Chinese or Indian swivel-musket.

[Hind. *janjāl*.]

jirble

jir′, jûr′bl, (*Scot.*) v.t. and v.i.

to pour splashingly or unsteadily.

jocko

jok′ō, n.

a chimpanzee: — pl. **jock′os.**

[Fr., from a W. African word *ncheko*.]

jockteleg

jok′tə-leg, (*Scot.*) n.

a large clasp-knife.

[The suggested *Jacques de Liège* lacks confirmation.]

joskin

jos′kin, n.

a clown, yokel.

[Thieves' cant.]

jota

hhō′tä, n.

a Spanish dance in triple time.

[Sp.]

jotun

yō′tən, **jötunn** *yœ′tən*, ns.

a giant.

[O.N. *jötunn*.]

jougs

jōōgz, jugz, n.pl.

an iron neck-ring — the old Scottish pillory.

[Prob. O.Fr. *joug*, a yoke — L. *jugum*.]

jubate

jōō′bāt, (*zool.*, etc.) adj.

maned.

[L. *jubātus* — *juba*, mane.]

jud

jud, n.

a mass of coal holed or undercut so as to be thrown down by wedges.

[Origin unknown.]

jumar

jōō′mär, n.

a clip used in mountaineering, which grips the rope when weight is applied, and runs freely along the rope when the weight is taken off: a climb using these.

v.i. to climb using jumars.
[Swiss name.]

jumart
joo'märt, -mərt, n.
the fabled offspring of a bull and
a mare, or stallion and cow.
[Fr.]

jumbal, jumble
jum'bl, n.
a thin, crisp, sweet cake,
formerly made in the shape of a
ring.

jupati
joo'pə-tē or *-tē',* n.
a species of raphia palm.
[Tupí.]

K

kaama
kä′mə, n.
the hartebeest.
[Of Hottentot or Bantu origin.]

kabaya
kä-bä′yə, n.
a loose tunic.
[Malay, from Pers. or Ar.]

kabeljou, kabeljouw
kob′, kub′l-yō, n.
a large South African fish,
Johnius hololepidotus.
[Afrik.]

kachahri, kacheri
kuch′ə-ri, kuch-er′i, n.
an Indian magistrate's office or
courthouse. — Also **cutcherry**.
[Hindi *kacahrī*.]

kago
käg′ō, n.
a Japanese basketwork
palanquin: — pl. **kag′os**.
[Jap. *kago*.]

kai
kä′ē, kī, (*N. Zealand*, etc.) n.
food.
n. **kai′kai** food: feast.

v.t. to eat.
[Maori; also in other Polynesian
languages.]

kaimakam
kī-mä-käm′, n.
a Turkish lieutenant-colonel or
lieutenant-governor.
[Turk. *kaymakam* — Ar.
qā′imaqām.]

kajawah
kä-jä′wä, n.
a camel litter or pannier.
[Pers.]

kaka
kä′kə, n.
a New Zealand parrot (*Nestor
meridionalis*).
ns. **ka′ka-beak, -bill** the New
Zealand glory-pea (*Clianthus*);
ka′kapō the New Zealand
owl-parrot, large-winged but
almost flightless: — pl.
ka′kapōs.
[Maori *kaka*, parrot, *po*, night.]

kaki
kä′kē, n.
the Japanese persimmon, or
Chinese date-plum.
[Jap.]

kala-azar

kä'lä-ä-zär', n.

a tropical fever, characterised by bloodlessness, and ascribed to a protozoan parasite.

[Assamese *kālā*, black, *āzār*, disease.]

kalamdan

kal'am-dan, n.

a Persian writing-case.

[Pers. *qalamdān — qalam*, a pen, *dān*, holding.]

kalamkari

kal-am-kä'rē, n.

a method of colouring and decorating by several dyeings or printings: a chintz so treated.

[Pers. *qalamkārī*, writing, painting, etc. — *qalam*, pen.]

Kaliyuga

käl-i-yōō'gə, n.

in Hindu mythology, the present (fourth) age of the world, of universal degeneracy.

[Sans.]

Kallima

kal'i-mə, n.

an Oriental genus of butterflies, mimicking dead leaves.

[Gr. *kallimos*, beautiful.]

kalong

kä'long, n.

a large fruit-bat.

[Malay *kālong*.]

kalpa

kal'pə, n.

a day of Brahma, a period of 4320 million years. — Also **cal'pa.**

[Sans., formation.]

kalpak

käl'päk, or *-päk'*, n.

a triangular Turkish or Tatar felt cap. — Also **calpac, calpack.**

[Turk. *qālpāq.*]

kalpis

kal'pis, n.

a water-vase.

[Gr.]

kalumpit

kä-lōōm-pēt', n.

a Philippine tree of the myrobalan genus: its edible fruit.

[Tagálog.]

kalyptra

ka-lip'trə, n.

a veil worn by Greek women.

[Gr.]

kamala

kä'mä-lä, n.

an orange dyestuff got from the fruit-hairs of an East Indian tree of the spurge family (*Mallotus philippinensis*): the tree itself. — Also **kamela, kamila** (*kä-mä'lä, -mē'lä*).

[Sans. *kamala*; Hind. *kamēlā, kamīlā.*]

kami

kä'mi, n.

a Japanese lord, national god, demigod, or deified hero (or any of their supposed descendants, as the mikados and, formerly, the imperial family), or any natural force or power.

[Jap., superior.]

kamichi

kä'mē-shē, n.

the horned screamer, a South American bird.

[Fr., from Carib.]

kana

kä'nä, n.

Japanese syllabic writing, as distinguished from Japanese written in Chinese characters.

[Jap.]

kaneh, caneh

kä'ne, n.

a Hebrew measure of 6 cubits' length.

[Heb. *qāneh*, reed, cane.]

kang

kang, n.

a large Chinese water-jar: a platform (e.g. of brick) for sleeping on that can be warmed by a fire underneath.

[Chin.]

kanga, khanga

kang'gə, n.

in East Africa, a piece of cotton cloth, usually brightly decorated, wound around the body as a woman's dress.

[Swahili.]

kans

käns, n.

an Indian grass which is allied to sugar-cane.

[Hindi *kās*.]

kantar, cantar

kan-tär', n.

a varying weight in Turkey, Egypt, etc., approximately a hundredweight.

[Ar. *qintār*.]

kanten

kan'tən, n.

agar-agar jelly.

[Jap.]

kantikoy, canticoy

kan'ti-koi, **cantico** (*-kō*; pl. **can'ticos**) ns.

an American Indian religious dance: a dancing-match.

v.i. to dance as an act of worship.

[From Algonquian.]

kanzu

kan'zōō, n.

a long white garment worn by men in central East Africa.

[From Swahili.]

kaoliang

kä-ō-li-ang', n.

sorghum grain of several varieties: a spirituous liquor made from it.

[Chin., tall grain.]

karaka

kə-ra'kə, n.

a New Zealand tree with edible orange fruit whose seeds are poisonous until treated.

[Maori.]

kaross

kä-ros', n.

a S. African skin blanket.

[Perh. a Hottentot modification of Du. *kuras*, cuirass.]

karri

kar'ē, n.

a Western Australian gum-tree (*Eucalyptus diversicolor*): its red timber.

[Aboriginal.]

katakana

kat-ä-kä'nä, n.

a Japanese syllabary.

[Jap.]

kavass

kä-väs', n.

an armed attendant in Turkey.

— Also **cavass**.

[Ar. *qawwās*.]

kea

kē'ə, n.

a New Zealand parrot that sometimes kills sheep.

[Maori.]

keb

keb, (*Scot.*) v.i.

to cast a lamb prematurely.

n. a ewe that has cast its lamb.

[Cf. Ger. *Kibbe*, *Kippe*, ewe.]

kebbie

keb'i, (*Scot.*) n.

a shepherd's crook: a crook-handled walking-stick.

kebbock, kebbuck

keb'ək, (*Scot.*) n.

a cheese.

[Origin unknown; Gael. *cabag*, a cheese, may be derived from this word.]

kebele

kə-bā'lā, n.

a self-governing association found in towns in Ethiopia. — Also **kabe'le** (*kä-*).

[From Amharic.]

keech

kēch, (*Shak.*) n.

a lump of fat.

keeling

kē'ling, (*Scot.*) n.

a codfish.

[Origin unknown.]

keelivine, keelyvine

kē'li-vīn, (*Scot.*) n.

a lead pencil.

keeshond

kās'hond, *-nt*, n.

a medium-sized dog of the spitz group once common on Dutch barges.

[Du., — *kees*, terrier, *hond*, dog.]

keeve, kieve

kēv, n.

a large tub.

[O.E. *cȳf*, vat.]

kef

kāf, n.

a state of dreamy repose: something, as Indian hemp, smoked to produce this. — Also **kaif** (*kīf*), **kif** (*kif, kēf*).

[Ar. *kaif*, pleasure.]

keffel

kef'l, (*dial.*) n.

a horse, nag.

[W. *ceffyl*; cf. **caple**.]

kefir, kephir

ke'fər, n.

an effervescent drink of low alcoholic content, made from fermented cow's milk.

[Native name in the Caucasus.]

keitloa

kāt'lō-ə, n.

a two-horned rhinoceros.

[Tswana *kgetlwa*.]

keltie, kelty

kel'ti, (*Scot.*) n.

a bumper, esp. one imposed as a penalty on one who does not drain his glass completely.

kemple

kem'pl, (*Scot.*) n.

forty bottles of hay or straw.

[Origin obscure.]

kennet

ken'it, (*obs.*) n.

a small hunting dog.

[O.N.Fr. *kennet*, dim. — L. *canis*, dog.]

kentledge

kent'lij, n.

pig-iron in a ship's hold for ballast. — Also **kint'ledge**.

[Origin unknown.]

kermis

kûr'mis, n.

a fair in the Low Countries: in America, an indoor fair. — Also **ker'mess, kir'mess.**

[Du. *kermis* — *kerk*, church, *mis*, mass.]

kerygma

kə-rig'mə, n.

(preaching of) the Christian gospel, esp. in the way of the early Church.

adj. **kerygmat'ic.**

[Gr. *kērygma*, proclamation, preaching.]

keta

kē'tə, n.

a Pacific salmon, the dog-salmon.

[Russ. *keta.*]

kgotla

hhö'tlə, kgot'lə, n.

an assembly of tribal elders in Botswana: the place of such assembly.

[Bantu.]

khaddar

kud'ər, n.

in India, hand-spun, hand-woven cloth. — Also **khadi.**

[Hind. *khādar, khādī.*]

kharif

kə-rēf', (*India*) n.

crop sown before the monsoon to ripen in autumn.

[Hind. *kharīf* — Ar., gathered.]

kheda, keddah

ked'ə, n.

an enclosure for catching wild elephants: the operation of catching wild elephants.

[Hindi *khedā.*]

khoja, khodja

kō'ja, also **hodja**, *hō'*, ns.

an Eastern title of respect: a professor or teacher.

[Turk. and Pers., *khōjah, khwājah.*]

khor

kōr, kör, n.

a dry watercourse: a ravine.

[Ar. *khurr, khorr.*]

khud

kud, n.

a pit, hollow: a ravine.

[Hindi *khad.*]

khutbah

kōōt'bä, n.

a Muslim prayer and sermon delivered in the mosques on Fridays. — Also **khot'bah, khot'beh.**

[Ar.]

kiang, kyang

kyang, ki-ang', n.

a Tibetan wild ass.

[Tibetan *rkyang.*]

kiaugh

kyöhh, kyähh, (Scot.) n.

care, trouble. — Also **kaugh** (*köhh, kähh*).

kibitka

ki-bit'kə, n.

a Russian covered wagon or sledge: a Central Asian felt tent.

[Russ.]

kiblah

kib'lä, n.

the point toward which Muslims turn in prayer. — Also **keb'lah.**

[Ar. *qiblah.*]

kiddle

kid'l, n.

a stake-fence set in a stream for catching fish. — Also **kid'el, kett'le.**

[O.Fr. *quidel*; cf. Bret. *kidel.*]

kie-kie

kē'kē, n.

a New Zealand climbing plant (*Freycinetia banksii*) of the screw-pine family.

[Maori.]

kier, keir

kēr, n.

a bleaching vat.

[Cf. O.N. *ker,* tub.]

kierie

kē'rē, (S.Afr.) n.

a stick.

[Prob. Hottentot.]

kikumon

kik'ōō-mon, n.

the chrysanthemum badge of the Japanese imperial family.

[Jap. *kiku,* chrysanthemum, *mon,* badge.]

kilfud-yoking

kil-fud'-yōk'ing, (*Scot.*) n.

a fireside disputation.

[Scot. *kilfuddie*, the aperture for feeding a kiln, and **yoking**.]

killadar

kil'ə-där, n.

the commandant of a fort or garrison.

[Hind. (Pers.) *qil'adār*.]

killas

kil'əs, n.

clay slate.

[Cornish miners' term.]

killcrop

kil'krop, n.

an insatiate child: a changeling.

[L.G. *kîlkrop*; Ger. *Kielkropf*.]

killdeer

kil'dēr, n.

the largest North American ring-plover. — Also **kill'dee**.

[Imit.]

killick, killock

kil'ik, -ək, ns.

a small anchor: its fluke: in the Royal Navy, a leading seaman (from his badge, bearing the symbol of an anchor).

[Origin obscure.]

killogie

ki-lō'gi, (*Scot.*) n.

the space before the fireplace of a kiln.

killut

kil'ut, n.

in India, a robe of honour or other ceremonial present. — Also **kell'aut, khal'at, khil'at**.

[Hind. and Pers. *khil'at*.]

kinchin

kin'chin, n.

a child in thieves' slang. **kin'chin-cove** (*obs.*) a boy; **kin'chin-lay** the robbing of children; **kin'chin-mort** (*obs.*) a girl.

[Appar. Ger. *Kindchen*, little child.]

kincob

king'kəb, n.

a rich silk fabric embroidered with gold or silver thread, made in India.

[Hind. and Pers. *kimkhāb*.]

kino

kē'nō, n.

an astringent exudation from various tropical trees: — pl. **kin'os**.

[App. of W. African origin.]

kirbeh

kir'be, n.

a skin for holding water.

[Ar. *qirba.*]

kirimon

kē'ri-mon, n.

one of the two imperial crests of Japan, bearing three leaves and three flowers of Paulownia.

[Jap.]

kisan

kē'sän, (India) n.

a peasant.

[Hindi *kisān.*]

kistvaen, cistvaen

kist'vīn, n.

a chest-shaped burial-chamber made of flat stones.

[W. *cist,* chest, and *maen,* stone, *m* being aspirated.]

klendusic

klen-dū'sik, adj.

of plants, able to withstand disease by means of some protective mechanism.

n. **klendū'sity.**

[Gr. *kleidoein,* to lock up — *kleis,* a key.]

klinostat

klī'nō-stat, n.

a revolving stand for experimenting with growing plants.

[Gr. *klīnein,* to incline, *statos,* standing.]

klipdas

klip'dus, n.

the Cape hyrax.

[Du., lit. rock-badger.]

kloof

klōōf, (S.Afr.) n.

a mountain ravine.

[Du., cleft.]

knag

nag, n.

a knot in wood: a peg.

n. **knagg'iness.**

adj. **knagg'y** knotty: rugged.

[Cf. Dan. *knag,* Ger. *Knagge.*]

knawel

nö'əl, n.

a cornfield weed (*Scleranthus*) of the chickweed family.

[Ger. *Knauel* or *Knäuel.*]

knitch

nich, (dial.) n.

a faggot.

[O.E. *gecnycc,* bond.]

knosp

nosp, n.

the unopened bud of a flower: an architectural ornament resembling that.

[Ger. *Knospe.*]

koa

kō'ə, n.

a Hawaiian acacia.

[Hawaiian.]

kob

kob, n.

an African water-antelope.

[Wolof.]

koban

kō'ban, **kobang** *kō'bang*, ns.

an obsolete Japanese oblong gold coin, rounded at the corners.

[Jap. *ko-ban*.]

koff

kof, n.

a small Dutch sailing-vessel.

[Du. *kof*.]

koftgar

koft'gär, n.

one who inlays steel with gold. n. **koftgari** (*koft-gur-ē'*) such work — sometimes **koft'work**.

[Hind. from Pers. *koftgar*.]

kokra

kok'rə, n.

the wood of an Indian tree (*Aporosa*) of the spurge family, used for making flutes, clarinets, etc.

kok-saghyz

kok'-sä'gēz, n.

a species of dandelion (*Taraxacum kok-saghyz*) from the Tien Shan, grown in Russia, etc., for rubber-making.

kokum

kō'kəm, n.

an East Indian tree (*Garcinia indica*).

kokum butter an edible fat got from its nuts.

[Marathi *kokamb*, mangosteen.]

kolinsky

ko-lin'ski, n.

(the fur of) a species of mink, (*Mustela sibirica*), found in eastern Asia.

[Russ. *kolinski*, of the Kola Peninsula.]

kolo

kō'lō, n.

a Serbian dance or dance-tune: — pl. **kō'los.**

[Serb., wheel.]

konimeter

kon-im'i-tər, n.

an instrument for measuring dust in air.

ns. **koniol'ogy** the study of dust in the air and its effects; **kon'iscope** an instrument for estimating the dustiness of air.

[Gr. *konis*, dust, *metron*, measure, *skopeein*, to look at.]

kora

kō'rə, kö', n.

the water-cock (*Gallicrex*).

[Origin uncertain.]

korora

kō'rō-rə, n.

the fairy penguin or little (blue) penguin (*Eudyptula minor*), smallest of all the penguins.

[Maori.]

koruna

ko-rōō'nə, n.

the standard monetary unit of Czechoslovakia, 100 halers.

kotwal, cotwal

kōt'wäl, n.

a chief constable or magistrate of an Indian town.

[Hind. *kotwāl*.]

kreng

kreng, n.

the carcass of a whale after the blubber has been removed. — Also **krang**.

[Du.]

krimmer

krim'ər, n.

tightly curled grey or black fur from a Crimean type of lamb. — Also **crimm'er**.

[Ger. *Krim*, Crimea.]

kuku

kōō'kōō, n.

a large fruit-eating pigeon of New Zealand (*Hemiphaga novaeseelandiae*), the wood-pigeon.

[Maori.]

kulan, koulan

kōō'län, n.

the onager, or a nearly related wild ass of the Kirghiz Steppe.

[Kirghiz.]

kumara

kōō'mə-rə, n.

sweet potato.

[Maori.]

kumari

kōō-mar'i (*Ind.*) n.

Miss (title of respect).

kurbash, kourbash

kōōr'bash, n.

a hide whip used in the East.

v.t. to whip with a kurbash.

[Ar. *qurbāsh*.]

kurgan

kōōr-gän', n.

a sepulchral barrow.

[Russ. from Tatar.]

kurrajong

kur'ə-jong, n.

a name for various Australian trees with fibrous bark. — Also **curr'ajong.**

[Aboriginal.]

kurta, khurta

kōōr'tä, n.

a loose-fitting collarless shirt or tunic worn in India.

[Hindi.]

kurvey

kûr-vā', (*rare S.Afr.*) v.i.

to transport goods.

n. **kurvey'or** transport rider.

[Du. *karwei,* work — Fr. *corvée.*]

kwacha

kwach'ə, n.

the basic unit of currency in Zambia and Malawi.

[Native name, meaning 'dawn'.]

kyat

kyät, kē-ät', n.

the monetary unit of Burma.

kylie, kiley, kyley

kī'li, n.

a boomerang.

[Aboriginal.]

kylin

kē'lin, n.

a fabulous animal figured in the decoration of Chinese pottery.

[From Chinese *ch'ī lin.*]

kyllosis

kil-ō'sis, n.

club-foot.

[Gr. *kyllōsis.*]

kyloe

kī'lō, n.

one of the cattle of the Hebrides.

[Origin unknown.]

kyphosis

kī-fō'sis, n.

a hunchbacked condition.

adj. **kyphotic** (*-fot'ik*).

[Gr. *kȳphōsis* — *kȳphos,* a hump.]

L

lablab

lab'lab, n.

a tropical bean (*Dolichos lablab*) with edible pods.

[Ar. *lablāb*.]

labrys

lab'ris, lāb'ris, n.

the double-headed axe, a religious symbol of ancient Crete, etc.

[Gr., from Lydian; perh. conn. with **labyrinth**.]

ladanum

lad'ə-nəm, n.

a resin exuded from Cistus leaves in Mediterranean countries. — Also **lab'danum**.

[L. *lādanum, lēdanum* — Gr. *lādanon, lēdanon* — *lēdon*, the Cistus plant, prob. — Pers. *lādan*.]

lagan

lag'ən, n.

wreckage or goods at the bottom of the sea: later taken to mean such goods attached to a buoy with a view to recovery. — Also **ligan** (*lī'gən*).

[O.Fr. *lagan*; falsely associated with L. *ligāmen*, a tying.]

lagena

lə-jē'nə, (*ant.*) n.

a narrow-necked bottle.

adj. **lage'niform** flask-shaped.

[L. *lagēna* — Gr. *lagȳna*.]

laggen, laggin

lag', läg'ən, (*Burns*) n.

the angle between the side and bottom of a wooden dish.

n. **lagg'en-gird** a hoop at the bottom of a wooden vessel.

lagniappe

lan'yap, n.

something given beyond what is strictly required: a gratuity.

[Louisiana Fr., from Amer. Sp. (Quechua *yápa*, addition).]

laika

lī'kə, n.

any of several similar breeds of working dog, originating in Finland, small and reddish-brown.

laisse

les, n.

a tirade or string of verses on one rhyme.

[Fr.]

lalang

lä'läng, n.

a coarse grass, *Imperata arundinacea*, of the Malay archipelago.

[Malay.]

lamantin

lä-man'tin, n.

the manatee.

[Fr.]

lamboys

lam'boiz, (*ant.*) n.pl.

kilted flexible steel-plates worn skirt-like from the waist.

[Perh. Fr. *lambeaux*, flaps; or a blunder for *jambeaux*.]

lamiger, lammiger

lam'i-jər, (*dial.*) n.

a cripple.

lamington

lam'ing-tən, (*Austr.*) n.

a piece of sponge-cake, coated in chocolate and coconut.

[From Lord *Lamington*, Governor of Queensland (1895–1901).]

lammer

läm', lam'ər, (*Scot.*) n.

amber.

[Fr. *l'ambre*, the amber.]

lammergeier, lammergeyer

lam'ər-gī-ər, n.

the great bearded vulture of southern Europe, etc.

[Ger. *Lämmergeier* — *Lämmer*, lambs, *Geier*, vulture.]

lammy, lammie

lam'i, n.

a thick quilted jumper worn in cold weather by sailors.

[Perh. **lamb**.]

lancegay

läns'gā, (*obs.*) n.

a kind of spear.

[O.Fr., — *lance*, a lance, *zagaye*, a pike.]

landamman(n)

land'am-an (Ger. *länt'äm-än*), n.

the chief magistrate in some Swiss cantons.

[Ger. *Landammann* — *Land*, land, and *Amtmann*, bailiff — *Amt*, office, and *Mann*, man.]

langspel, langspiel

läng'späl, -spēl, ns.

an old Shetland cithern.

[Norw. *langspill* — *lang*, long, *spill*, play, instrument.]

laniary

lā'ni-ər-i, adj.

fitted for tearing.

[L. *laniārius*, of a butcher — *lanius*, a butcher.]

lanner

lan'ər, n.

a kind of falcon, esp. the female.

n. **lann'eret** the male lanner.

[Fr. *lanier,* possibly — L. *laniārius,* tearing, or from *lānārius,* a weaver (a mediaeval term of reproach).]

lanterloo

lant'ər-lōō, (*obs.*) n.

a card game, ancestral form of loo.

[Fr. *lanturlu* (a meaningless refrain).]

lanugo

lan-ū'gō, n.

down: an embryonic woolly coat of hair: — pl. **lanū'gos.**

adjs. **lanū'ginose** (-*jin*-), **lanūginous** downy: covered with fine soft hair.

[L. *lānūgō, -inis,* down — *lāna,* wool.]

larrigan

lar'i-gən, n.

a long boot made of oiled leather worn by lumbermen, etc.

[Origin unknown.]

larrikin

lar'i-kin, (*Austr.*) n.

a rough or hooligan. — Also adj.

n. **larr'ikinism.**

[Origin doubtful; a connection with '*larking* about' has been suggested but remains unsubstantiated.]

lashkar

lash'kär, n.

a camp of Indian soldiers (*obs.*): a body of armed Indian tribesmen, a force.

[Hind., army, camp.]

lassu

losh'ōō, n.

the slow movement of a csárdás.

[Hung.]

lat

lät, n.

in India, an isolated pillar.

[Hindi *lat.*]

laund

lönd, (*Shak.*) n.

a glade: a grassy place.

[O.Fr. *launde, lande;* prob. Celt.]

lauwine

lö'win, (*Byron*) n.

an avalanche.

[Ger. *La(u)wine,* perh. — *lau,* tepid.]

laveer

lä-vēr', (*arch.*) v.i.
to beat to windward.
[Du. *laveeren.*]

leasow, leasowe

lē'sō, -zō, (*dial.*) n.
pasture.
v.t. and v.i. to pasture.
[O.E. *lǣs*, a meadow, in
oblique cases *lǣswe.*]

lebbek

leb'ek, n.
an Old World tropical
mimosaceous timber tree
(*Albizzia lebbek*).
[Origin unknown.]

ledden

led'n, (*Spens.*) n.
language, dialect, speech.
[O.E. *lēden, lēoden*, language
— *lēode*, people, confused with
lǣden, Latin — L. *Latīnum*,
Latin.]

leger

lej'ər, (*obs. cant*) n.
one who sells short weight in
charcoal: one who swindles by
scamping work, using bad
materials, or the like.
n. **leg'ering.**
[Poss. Fr. *léger,* light.]

leglin, leglan, leglen

leg'lən, (*Scot.*) n.
a milking-pail.
cast a leglin girth to have an
illegitimate child.
[Cf. **laggen.**]

leister

lēs'tər, (*Scot.*) n.
a salmon-spear.
v.t. to spear with a leister.
[O.N. *ljōstr;* Dan. *lyster.*]

lek

lek, n.
a unit of Albanian currency =
100 qintars: a coin or note of
this value.

lekythos

lē'ki-thos, (*ant.*) n.
a narrow-necked Greek flask.
[Gr. *lēkythos.*]

leno

lē'nō, n.
a thin muslin-like fabric: — pl.
lē'nos.
[Perh. Fr. *linon.*]

lenocinium

lē-nō-sin'i-əm, (*Scots law*) n.
connivance at one's wife's
adultery.
[L. *lēnōcinium*, enticement —
lēnō, a pander.]

lentic

len'tik, (*ecology*) adj.

associated with standing water: inhabiting ponds, swamps, etc.

[L. *lentus,* slow.]

lentigo

len-tī'gō, n.

a freckle: (usu.) freckles: — pl. **lentigines** (*len-tij'i-nēz*). adjs. **lentig'inose, lentig'inous** (*bot.*) minutely dotted.

[L. *lentīgō, -inis,* a freckle — *lēns,* a lentil.]

lentisk

len'tisk, n.

the mastic tree.

[L. *lentiscus.*]

lentor

len'tör, (*arch.*) n.

sluggishness: viscidity. adj. **len'tous.**

[L. *lentus,* slow.]

lepton

lep'ton, n.

the smallest ancient Greek coin, translated mite in the N.T. (pl. **lep'ta**): a modern Greek coin, 1/100th of a drachma (pl. **lep'ta**): any of a group of subatomic particles with weak interactions, electrons, negative muons, tau particles and neutrinos (opp. to **baryon**) (pl.

lep'tons).

adjs. **lepton'ic** of or pertaining to leptons; **leptocephal'ic** (Gr. *kephalē,* head) narrow-skulled.

n. **leptoceph'alus** the larva of an eel.

adj. **leptocerc'al** (Gr. *kerkos,* tail) slender-tailed.

n. **leptodac'tyl** (Gr. *daktylos,* finger, toe) a bird or other animal with long slender toes.

adj. **leptodac'tylous** slender-toed.

n. **lep'tome** phloem or bast.

adjs. **leptophyll'ous** (*bot.*) with long slender leaves; **lep'torrhine** (Gr. *rhīs, rhīnos,* nose) narrow-nosed.

n. **lep'tosome** (Gr. *sōma,* body) a person with a slight, slender physical build: an asthenic.

adjs. **leptosō'mic, leptosomatic** (*-sə-mat'ik*).

n. **leptospīrō'sis** (Gr. *speira,* a coil) a disease of animals or man caused by bacteria of the genus **Leptospī'ra.**

adj. **leptosporan'giate** having each sporangium derived from a single cell (opposed to *eusporangiate*).

n. **lep'totene** (*-tēn*) the first stage of meiotic prophase in which long, slender, single-stranded chromosomes develop.

[Gr. *leptos,* neut. *lepton,* slender.]

leu

le'oo, n.

the monetary unit of Rumania.
— Also (*rare*) **ley** (*lā*): — pl. **lei**
(*lā*).

[Rum., lion.]

lev, lew

lef, n.

the monetary unit or franc of
Bulgaria: — pl. **leva** (*lev'ä*).

[Bulg., lion.]

levin

lev'in, (*arch.*) n.

lightning.

[M.E. *leuen(e)*, prob. — O.N.]

lewis

loo'is, n.

a dovetail iron tenon for lifting
blocks of stone (also
lew'isson): a freemason's son.

[Ety. dub.]

liang

lyang, n.

a Chinese ounce or tael.

[Chin.]

libeccio

li-bet'chō, n.

the south-west wind. — Also
(*Milt.*) **libecchio** (It. *li-bek'i-ō*):
— pl. **libecc(h)'ios**.

[It., — L. *Libs*; Gr. *Lips, Libos*.]

lichanos

lik'a-nos, (*anc. Gr. mus.*) n.

the string or the note struck by
the forefinger.

[Gr. *lichanos*, forefinger,
lichanos — *leichein*, to lick.]

lierne

li-ûrn', n.

a cross-rib or branch-rib in
vaulting.

[Fr.]

likin

lē-kēn', n.

formerly, a Chinese transit duty.

[Chin.]

limation

lī-mā'shən, n.

filing.

[L. *līma*, a file.]

limicolous

lī-mik'ə-ləs, adj.

living in mud.
adj. **lī'mous** (*arch.*) muddy:
slimy.

[L. *līmus*, mud, *colĕre*, to dwell.]

limmer

lim'ər, (*dial.*, esp. *Scot.*) n.

a rogue or thief: a hussy, a
jade.

[Origin obscure.]

limosis

lī-mō'sis, n.
a morbidly ravenous appetite.
[Gr. *līmos,* hunger.]

lindworm

lind'wûrm, (myth.) n.
a wingless dragon.
[Adapted from Sw. and Dan.
lindorm.]

lingel, lingle

ling'gl (chiefly *Scot., ling'l*), *n.*
a shoemaker's waxed thread.
[O.Fr. *lignoel* — a dim. from L.
līnea.]

linhay, linny

lin'i, (dial.) n.
a shed, open in front.
[Origin obscure.]

linin

lī'nin, n.
a substance which forms the
network of a cell nucleus.
[L. *līnum,* thread, net.]

linsang

lin'sang, n.
a civet-like animal of Borneo
and Java: applied also to
kindred animals of the
Himalayas, Burma, and West
Africa.
[Javanese *linsan.*]

lippitude

lip'i-tūd, (arch.) n.
soreness of the eyes.
[L. *lippitūdō — lippus,*
blear-eyed.]

lippy, lippie

lip'i, n.
an old Scottish dry measure,
the fourth part of a peck.
[Dim. from O.E. *lēap,* a basket.]

liripoop

lir'i-pōōp, (obs.) n.
the long tail of a graduate's
hood: a part or lesson
committed to memory: a silly
person. — Also **lir'ipipe** (*-pīp*).
[L.L. *liripipium*; origin unknown.]

lirk

lirk, (Scot.) n.
a fold: a wrinkle.
v.i. to wrinkle.
[Origin unknown.]

lissotrichous

lis-ot'ri-kəs, adj.
smooth-haired.
[Gr. *lissos,* smooth, *thrix,
trichos,* hair.]

lixiviation

liks-iv-i-ā'shən, n.
leaching.
adjs. **lixiv'ial, lixiv'ious.**
v.t. **lixiv'iate.**

n. **lixiv′ium** lye.
[L. *lixīvium*, lye.]

lockram
lok′rəm, n.
a coarse linen said to have
been made at *Locronan*
(Ronan's cell) in Brittany.

locuplete
lok′ū-plēt, adj.
well-stored.
[L. *locuplēs, -ētis.*]

logie
lō′gi, (*Scot.*) n.
the space before a kiln fire.
[Origin unknown; cf. **killogie**.]

logothete
log′ō-thēt, n.
a chancellor, esp. in the
Byzantine Empire and in
Norman Sicily.
[Gr. *logothetēs,* an auditor.]

loma
lō′mə (*zool.*) n.
a membranous fringe or flap.
[Gr. *lōma, -atos.*]

lomentum
lō-ment′əm, n.
a pod that breaks in pieces at
constrictions between the
seeds: — pl. **loment′a.** —
Also **lō′ment** (-*mənt*).

adj. **lomentā′ceous.**
[L. *lōmentum*, bean-meal (used
as a cosmetic) — *lavāre, lōtum,*
to wash.]

longan
long′gan, n.
a tree (*Nephelium longana*) akin
to the lychee: its fruit.
[Chin. *lung-yen,* dragon's eye.]

lorcha
lör′chə, n.
a light vessel of European build,
but rigged like a Chinese junk.
[Port.]

lordosis
lör-dō′sis, n.
abnormal curvature of the spinal
column, the convexity towards
the front.
adj. **lordot′ic** affected with,
relating to lordosis.
[Gr. *lordōsis* — *lordos,* bent
back.]

lorette
lör-et′, n.
a courtesan.
[Fr., from the church of their
district in Paris, Notre Dame de
Lorette.]

loriot
lō′ri-ət, lö′, n.
the golden oriole.
[Fr. *loriot* — *l′,* the, O.Fr. *oriol*

— L. *aureolus*, dim. of *aureus*, golden — *aurum*, gold.]

lota, lotah
lō'tä, n.

in India, a small brass or copper pot.

[Hindi *lotā*.]

loure
lōōr, n.

an old slow dance, or its tune, usu. in 6–4 time, sometimes included in suites.

[Fr., bagpipe.]

loy
loi, n.

a long, narrow spade with footrest on one side of the handle.

lubra
lōō'bra, (*Austr.*) n.

an Aboriginal woman.

[Aboriginal.]

lucarne
lōō-, lū-kärn', n.

a dormer-window, esp. in a church spire.

[Fr. (of unknown origin).]

luce
lōōs, lūs, n.

a freshwater fish, the pike.

[O.Fr. *lus* — L.L. *lūcius*.]

lucigen
lōō', lū'si-jən, n.

a lamp burning oil mixed with air in a spray.

[L. *lūx, lūcis*, light, and root of L. *gignĕre, genitum*, to beget.]

lucumo
lōō', lū'kū-mō, n.

an Etruscan prince and priest: — pl. **lu'cumos**, (L.) **lucumōn'es** (*-ēz*).

[L. *lŭcŭmō*, from Etruscan.]

lues
lōō', lū'ēz, n.

a pestilence: now confined to syphilis.

adj. **luetic** (*-et'ik*; an etymologically unjustifiable formation).

[L. *lŭēs*.]

luge
lōōzh, lüzh, n.

a light toboggan.

v.i. to glide on such a sledge. — pr.p. and n. **lug'ing, luge'ing**.

[Swiss Fr.]

lumbang
lōōm-bäng', n.

the candle-nut tree or other species of Aleurites, whose nuts yield **lumbang'-oil'**.

[Tagálog.]

lungi

lōōn'gē, n.

a long cloth used as loin-cloth, sash, turban, etc.

[Hind. and Pers. *lungī.*]

lunt

lunt, (Scot.) n.

a slow-match or means of setting on fire: a sudden flame, blaze: smoke.

v.t. to kindle: to smoke.

v.i. to blaze up: to emit smoke: to smoke tobacco.

[Du. *lont,* a match; cf. Ger. *Lunte.*]

lupulin

lōō'pū-lin, n.

a yellow powder composed of glands from hop flowers and bracts, used as a sedative.

adjs. **lu'puline, lupulinic** (*-lin'ik*).

[L. *lupus,* hop-plant.]

Lurgi

lōōr'gi, adj.

pertaining to a German plant that enables coal-gas to be made from low-grade coal.

lustring

lus'tring, n.

a glossy silk cloth. — Also **lus'trine, lutestring** (*lōōt', lūt'string*).

[Fr. *lustrine* — It. *lustrino.*]

lutz

lōōts, n.

in figure-skating, a jump (with rotation) from the back outer edge of one skate to the back outer edge of the other.

[Poss. Gustave *Lussi* of Switzerland, born 1898, the first exponent.]

luz

luz, n.

a bone supposed by Rabbinical writers to be indestructible, probably the sacrum.

lyam

lī'əm, **lime, lyme** *līm, ns.*

a leash: a lyam-hound.

n. **ly'am-hound, lime'-hound, lyme'-hound** a bloodhound.

[O.Fr. *liem* (Fr. *lien*) — L. *ligāmen* — *ligāre,* to tie.]

lymphad

lim'fad, n.

a Highland galley.

[Gael. *longfhada.*]

lytta

lit'ə, n.

a cartilaginous or fibrous band on the under surface of the tongue in carnivores — the worm of a dog's tongue.

[Gr.]

M

maar

mär, n. (*geol.*)

a crater that has been formed by a single explosion and so does not lie in a cone of lava.

[Ger.]

machair

ma'hhər, n.

a low-lying sandy beach or boggy links affording some pasturage.

[Gael.]

machan

ma-chän', n.

a shooting-platform up a tree.

[Hindi *macān*.]

maconochie

mə-kon'ə-hhi, (*mil.*) n.

tinned meat and vegetable stew: tinned food.

[Packer's name.]

mactation

mak-tā'shən, n.

slaying, esp. of a sacrificial victim.

[L. *mactātiō, -ōnis*.]

madarosis

mad-ə-rō'sis, n.

loss of hair, esp. of the eyebrows or eyelashes.

[Gr. *madarōsis — madaros*, bald, *madaein*, to fall off.]

madefy

mad'i-fī, v.t.

to moisten.

n. **madefac'tion.**

[L. *madefacĕre, -factum — madēre*, to be wet.]

madid

mad'id, adj.

wet, dank.

[L. *madidus — madēre*, to be wet; akin to Gr. *madaein*.]

madoqua

mad'ō-kwə, n.

a very small Abyssinian antelope.

[Amharic *midaqua*.]

madroño

ma-drō'nyō, n.

a handsome evergreen Arbutus tree of North California: — pl. **madrō'ños.** — Also **madrō'ña** (-*nyə*).

[Sp. *madroño*.]

magilp, megilp

mə-gilp', n.

a vehicle used by oil-painters, consisting of linseed-oil and mastic varnish.

[Origin unknown.]

magnes

mag'nēz (arch.) n.

lodestone.

mag'nesstone *(Spens.).*

[L. and Gr. *magnēs*.]

magot

mag'ət, mä-gō', n.

the Barbary ape, a macaque, the only European monkey: a small grotesque figure, in Chinese or Japanese workmanship.

[Fr.]

mahmal

mä'mäl, n.

the empty litter sent to Mecca in the hadj.

mahoe

mä'hō-i, n.

the whitewood tree of New Zealand.

[Maori.]

mahseer, mahsir

mä'sēr, n.

a large fish found in the rivers of Northern India.

[Hind. *mahāsir*.]

mahua, mahwa

mä'(h)wä, n.

a kind of butter-tree (*Bassia,* or *Illipe, latifolia*) with edible flowers.

mahua butter a fat got from its seeds. — Also **mowa, mowra.**

[Hindi *mahūā*.]

mahzor, machzor

mahh-zör', mähh', n.

the Jewish prayer-book used for festivals and other special occasions: — pl. **ma(c)hzorim** *(-ēm')*.

[Heb. *mahzor*, a cycle.]

makimono

mäk-i-mō'nō, n.

a roll, as of silk, esp. a long picture or writing rolled up and not hung: — pl. **makimō'nos.**

[Jap., — *maki*, roll, scroll, *mono*, thing.]

malacia

mal-ā'shi-ə, n.

pathological softening: perverted appetite.

[Gr. *malakiā*, softness.]

malacology

mal-ə-kol'ə-ji, n.

the study of molluscs.

adj. **malacological** *(-kə-loj')*.

n. **malacol'ogist.**

[Gr. *malakos*, soft, *logos*, discourse.]

malacophilous

mal-ə-kof'i-ləs, (*bot.*) adj.

pollinated by snails.

[Gr. *malakos,* soft, *phileein,* to love.]

malaguetta

mal-ə-get'ə, n.

grains of paradise (also **malaguetta pepper**).

[Origin obscure.]

malander, mallander, mallender

mal'ən-dər, n.

an eruption of the skin behind a horse's knee — often pl.

[Fr. *malandre* — L. *malandria* (sing. or pl.).]

malax, malaxate

mal'aks, -āt, vs.t.

to soften by kneading, rubbing or mixing.
ns. **mal'axage; malaxā'tion; mal'axātor.**

[L.L. *malaxāre,* to soften.]

malemute

māl'ə-mūt, n.

an Eskimo dog. — Also **mal'amute.**

[From a tribe on the Alaskan coast.]

mali, mallee

mä'lē, n.

one of the gardener class in India.

[Hindi *mālī.*]

malicho

mal'i-chō, -kō, n.

mischief (Shak., *Hamlet,* III, ii, 146).

[Conjectured to be for Sp. *malhecho,* mischief.]

mallemaroking

mal'i-mə-rō'king, n.

carousing of seamen in icebound ships.

[Obs. Du. *mallemerok,* a romping woman — *mal,* foolish, *marok* — Fr. *marotte,* a favoured object.]

mallemuck

mal'i-muk, n.

the fulmar or similar bird.

[Du. *mallemok* — *mal,* foolish, *mok,* gull; Ger. *Mallemuck.*]

malm

mäm, n.

calcareous loam, earth specially good for brick: an artificial mixture of clay and chalk.

[O.E. *m(e)alm (-stān),* a soft (stone).]

malmag

mal'mag, n.

the tarsier.

[Philippine word.]

maltha

mal'thə, n.

a thick mineral pitch: an ancient cement: mineral tar.

[Gr.]

mamelon

mam'ə-lən, n.

a rounded hill or protuberance.

[Fr., nipple.]

mameluco

mam-e-lōō'kō, n.

in Brazil, the offspring of a person of European stock and an Indian: — pl. **mamelu'cos.**

[Port.]

mammee

mam-ē', n.

a fruit (also **mammee apple)** of the West Indies, etc., having a sweet taste and aromatic odour: the tree producing it (*Mammea americana*; family Guttiferae).

mammee'-sapo'ta the marmalade tree or its fruit.

[Sp. *mamey,* from Haitian.]

mammock

mam'ək, n.

a shapeless piece, shred (also **mumm'ock**).

v.t. (*Shak.*) to tear to pieces, to mangle.

[Origin obscure.]

mancando

mangk-an'dō, (*mus.*) adj. and adv.

fading away.

[It., lacking.]

manchet

man'chit, n.

the finest bread of wheat (*obs.*): a round loaf (*arch.* or *dial.*): a loaf of manchet.

[Origin obscure.]

manchineel

manch-i-nēl', n.

a tropical American tree (*Hippomane*) of the spurge family, with poisonous latex.

[Sp. *manzanilla,* dim. of *manzana,* apple.]

mancus

mang'kəs, (*hist.*) n.

an old English coin or its value, thirty pence: — pl. **manc'uses.**

[O.E. *mancus.*]

mandir, mandira

mun'dər, -ä, n.

a Hindu or Jain temple.

[Hind.]

mandrel, mandril

man'drəl, n.

a bar of iron fitted to a turning-lathe on which articles to be turned are fixed: the axle of a circular saw.

[Fr. *mandrin.*]

mangal

mang-gäl', n.

a brazier.

[Turk.]

mangonel

mang'gə-nel, n.

a mediaeval engine for throwing stones, etc.

[O.Fr., — L.L. *mangonum* — Gr. *manganon.*]

manilla

mə-nil'ə, n.

a West African bracelet, serving as money.

[Sp.,—L.L. *manilia*, a bracelet—L. *manus,* the hand, or L. *monīlia* (pl. of *monīle*), necklace, influenced by *manus.*]

manille

mə-nil', n.

in ombre and quadrille, the highest card but one.

[Sp. *malilla.*]

manito

man'i-tō, n.

a spirit or object of reverence among American Indians: — pl. **man'itos.** — Also **manitou** (*-tŌŌ*).

[Algonkin.]

manjack

man'jak, n.

a West Indian boraginaceous tree (*Cordia macrophylla*): its fruit.

manoao

mä'nō-ow, n.

a shrub of the heath group: — pl. **ma'noaos.**

[Maori.]

manuka

mä'nŌŌ-kä, n.

an Australian and New Zealand tree (*Leptospermum*) of the myrtle family, with hard wood, its leaves formerly a substitute for tea.

[Maori.]

manul

mä'nōōl, n.

a Central Asian wild cat.

[Mongolian.]

manzanita

man-zə-nē'tə, n.

bearberry of Californian species.

[Sp., dim. of *manzana*, apple.]

maqui

mä'kē, n.

a Chilean evergreen shrub (*Aristotelia maqui*; fam. *Elaeocarpaceae*) whose berry yields a medicinal wine.

[Araucan.]

mara

mə-rä', n.

the so-called Patagonian hare or Dolichotis.

maraging

mär'ā-jing, n.

a metallurgical process by which a metal alloy is slowly cooled in the air, becoming very strong and resistant to corrosion.

[From *mar*tensite and *aging*.]

marah

mä'rä, n.

bitterness: something bitter.

[Heb.]

marasmus

mə-raz'məs, n.

a wasting away of the body.

adj. **maras'mic**.

n. **Maras'mius** a common genus of toadstools, including the fairy-ring champignon, drying up in sunshine but recovering in damp.

[Latinised — Gr. *marasmos* — *marainein*, to decay.]

maravedi

mar-ə-vā'di, n.

an obsolete Spanish copper coin of little value.

[Sp. *maravedí* — Ar. *Murābitīn*, the dynasty of the Almoravides (11th and 12th cent.).]

marcella

mär-sel'ə, n.

a type of cotton or linen fabric, in twill weave.

[Anglicisation of *Marseilles*.]

marcescent

mär-ses'ənt, adj.

withering without falling off.

adj. **marcesc'ible**.

[L. *marcēscēns, -entis*, pr.p. of *marcēscĕre* — *marcēre*, to fade.]

maremma

mär-em'ə, n.

seaside marshland: an Italian sheepdog.

[It., — L. *maritima*, seaside.]

margay
mär′gä, n.
a spotted S. American tiger-cat.
[Fr. (or Sp.), — Tupí
mbaracaïa.]

margosa
mär-gō′sə, n.
the tree that yields nim-oil.
[Port. *amargosa* (fem.), bitter.]

marid
mar′id, mä-rēd′, n.
a jinni of the most powerful
class.
[Ar. *mārid, marīd*.]

markhor
mär′kör, n.
a wild goat (*Capra falconeri*) of
the mountains of Asia.
[Pers. *mārkhōr*.]

maror
mä-rōr′, -rör, n.
a dish of bitter herbs (esp.
horseradish) eaten during the
Jewish Passover, symbolising
the bitterness of the Egyptian
oppression of the Israelites.
[Heb.]

marrowsky
mar-ow′ski, n.
a spoonerism.
v.i. to utter a spoonerism.
[Said to be from the name of a
Polish count.]

martagon
mär′tə-gən, n.
the Turk's-cap lily.
[Turk. *martagān*, a kind of
turban.]

martenot
mär′tən-ō, n.
an electronic musical instrument
resembling a spinet in
appearance, invented by the
Frenchman Maurice *Martenot*
(born 1898).

mascon
mas′kon, n.
any of several mass
concentrations of dense
material, of uncertain origin,
lying beneath the moon's
surface.
[*mas*s *con*centration.]

masoolah, massoola, masula
mä-soo̅′lə, n.
a high many-oared Indian
surf-boat.
[Origin obscure.]

massaranduba
mas-ə-ran-doo̅′bə, n.
the Brazilian milk-tree
(*Mimusops elata*). — Also
**masseranduba,
maceranduba.**
[Port. *maçaranduba*, from Tupí
name.]

massé

mas'ā, n.

in billiards, a sharp stroke made with the cue vertical or nearly so.

[Fr.]

masseter

mas-ē'tər, n.

a muscle that raises the under jaw.

[Gr. *masētēr* (not *massētēr*), chewer — *masaesthai*, to chew.]

massicot

mas'i-kot, n.

yellow lead monoxide.

[Fr.]

massymore

mas-i-mōr', *-mör'*, (*Scott*) n.

a subterranean prison.

[Perh. Sp. *mazmorra*; cf. **mattamore**.]

matachin

mat-ə-chēn', *-shēn'*, (*arch*.) n.

a masked sword-dancer or sword-dance.

[Fr. (*obs*.) *matachin* and Sp. *matachín*, perh. — Ar. *mutawajjihīn*, masked.]

matamata

ma-tə-mä'tə, n.

a South American river-turtle.

[Port., from Tupí *matamatá*.]

matelassé

mat-lä-sä, adj. and n.

(a jacquard fabric) having a raised pattern as if quilted. — Also **matel(l)asse**.

[Fr., — *matelas*, a mattress.]

matfelon

mat'fel-ən, n.

the greater knapweed.

[O.Fr. *matefelon*.]

matico

mä-tē'kō, n.

a Peruvian pepper shrub, used as a styptic: — pl. **mati'cos**.

[Sp. dim. of *Mateo*, Matthew.]

matross

mə-tros', (*obs*.) n.

a gunner's assistant in artillery.

[Du. *matroos*, app. — Fr. *matelot*, a sailor.]

mattamore

mat-ə-mōr', *-mör'* or *mat'*, n.

a subterranean chamber.

[Fr. *matamore* — Ar. *matmūrah*.]

matzoon

mät-soon', **madzoon**
mäd-zoon', ns.
a food similar to yoghurt made
from fermented milk.
[Armenian.]

maud

möd, n.
a Scottish shepherd's woollen
plaid.
[Origin unknown.]

mawseed

mö'sēd, n.
poppy seed as cage-bird food,
etc.
[Ger. *Mahsaat* — *Mah*, poppy.]

maxixe

mä-shē'shä, n.
a Brazilian dance: a tune for it.
[Port.]

mazut, mazout

mə-zoot', n.
petroleum residue after
distillation.
[Russ. *mazat'*, to daub, smear.]

meatus

mi-ā'təs, (*anat.*) n.
an opening of a passage or
canal: — pl. **mea'tuses.**
adj. **mea'tal.**
[L. *meātus* (pl. *-ūs*) — *meāre*, to
go.]

mebos

mä'bos, (*S.Afr.*) n.
salted or sugared dried apricots.
[Perh. Jap. *umeboshi*, a kind of
plum.]

meconic

mi-kon'ik, adj.
denoting an acid obtained from
poppies.
ns. **meconate** (*mek'ən-āt*, or
mēk') a salt of meconic acid;
mec'onin a white, fusible,
neutral substance ($C_{10}H_{10}O_4$)
existing in opium; **mecō'nium**
the first faeces of a newborn
child, or of a newly emerged
insect imago: opium;
Meconops'is (Gr. *opsis*,
appearance) a genus of largely
Asiatic poppies: (without *cap.*) a
plant of this genus: — pl.
meconops'ēs.
[Gr. *mēkōn*, the poppy.]

medina

mə-dē'nə, n.
in North African cities, the
ancient, native quarter.
[Ar., town.]

meith

mēth, (*Scot.*) n.
a landmark: a boundary.
[Prob. O.N. *mith*, a fishing-bank
found by landmarks.]

melampode

mel-am'pōd, mel', (*Spens.*) n.
the black hellebore.
[Gr. *melampodion.*]

melder

mel'dər, (*Scot.*) n.
the quantity of meal ground at
one time.
[O.N. *meldr.*]

melilot

mel'i-lot, n.
a genus (*Melilotus*) of
clover-like plants with racemes
of white or yellow flowers and a
peculiar sweet odour.
[Gr. *melilōtos* — *meli*, honey,
lōtos, lotus.]

melinite

mel'in-īt, n.
an explosive made from picric
acid.
[Fr. *mélinite* — Gr. *mēlinos*,
quince yellow — *mēlon*,
quince.]

melocoton, melocotoon

mel-ō-kot-ōn', -ōōn', (*obs.*) ns.
a large kind of peach. — Also
malakatoone', melicott'on.
[Sp. *melocotón* — It.
melocotogna, quince, peach —
L.L. *mēlum cotōneum* — Gr.
mēlon Kȳdōnion, Cydonian
(Cretan) apple, quince.]

meltith

mel'tith, (*Scot.*) n.
a meal: a cow's yield at one
milking.

menhaden

men-hā'dn, n.
an oily fish (*Brevoortia
tyrannus*) of the herring family,
found off the east coast of the
United States.
[From an Indian name.]

menominee

mi-nom'i-nē, n.
a whitefish of N. American
lakes.
[From an Indian tribe.]

mercaptan

mər-kap'tan, n.
a substance analogous to an
alcohol, with sulphur instead of
oxygen.
n. **mercap'tide** a compound
in which a metal takes the place
of a hydrogen atom of a
mercaptan.
[L. *mercūrium captāns*, laying
hold of mercury, from the
readiness with which it forms
mercury mercaptide.]

merchet

mûr'chit, (*hist.*) n.
a fine paid to a lord for the
marriage of a daughter.
[A.Fr. *merchet.*]

merling

mûr'ling, (*obs.*) n.

the whiting.

[O.Fr. *merlanke* — L. *merula*, a sea-carp.]

merlon

mûr'lən, (*fort.*) n.

the part of a parapet between embrasures.

[Fr. *merlon* — It. *merlone* — *merlo*, battlement.]

mesail, mezail

mes', mez'āl, n.

a vizor, esp. one made in two parts.

[Fr. *mézail*.]

mesel, meazel

mēz'l, (*obs.*) n.

a leper: leprosy (*Shak.*).

adj. leprous.

adj. **mes'eled.**

[O.Fr. *mesel* — L. *misellus*, dim. of *miser*, wretched.]

messan

mes'ən, (*Scot.*) n.

a lap-dog: a cur.

[Perh. Gael. *measan*.]

métairie

mā-ter-ē', n.

a piece of land cultivated for a share of the produce.

[Fr.; see **métayer**.]

métayer

mā-tā-yā' or *mā'*, n.

a farmer who pays, instead of money rent, a fixed proportion of the crops.

n. **métayage** (*-yäzh'*, or *mā'*) this system.

[Fr., — L.L. *medietārius* — L. *medietās*, half — *medius*, middle.]

metheglin

meth-eg'lin, n.

a Welsh fermented liquor made from honey.

[W. *meddyglyn* — *meddyg*, medicinal (— L. *medicus*, physician), *llyn*, liquor.]

metic

met'ik, n.

a resident alien.

[Gr. *metoikos* — *meta*, indicating change, and *oikos*, a house.]

metopon

met'ō-pon, n.

a pain-relieving drug derived from opium but less habit-forming than morphine.

metopryl

met'ō-pril, n.

an anaesthetic related to ether, but more powerful and less disturbing in after-effects.

mhorr

mör, n.

a West African gazelle.

[Ar.]

mia-mia

mī'ə-mī'ə, n.

a native dwelling hut.

[Aboriginal.]

mico

mē'kō, n.

a marmoset, esp. the black-tailed: — pl. **mi'cos.**

[Port., — Carib *meku*, monkey.]

miliary

mil'i-ər-i, adj.

like a millet-seed: characterised by an eruption like millet-seeds. n. **miliaria** (*mil-i-ā'ri-ə*) prickly-heat.

[L. *miliārius* — *milium*, millet.]

milo

mī'lō, n.

any of several drought-resistant varieties of sorghum, orig. from Africa but introduced elsewhere, cultivated as a grain and fodder crop: — pl. **mī'los.** — Also **milo maize.**

[Sotho *maili*.]

mimbar

mim'bär, **minbar** *min'*, ns.

a mosque pulpit.

[Ar. *minbar*.]

minauderie

mēn-ō-də-rē', n.

a display of affectation.

[Fr.]

minivet

min'i-vet, n.

a brightly coloured shrike-like bird (*Pericrocotus* of several species) of India, etc.

[Etymology unknown.]

mino

mē'nō, n.

a raincoat of hemp, etc.: — pl. **mi'nos.**

[Jap.]

mirligoes

mûr'li-gōz, (*Scot.*) n.pl.

dizziness.

mirliton

mûr'li-tən, mēr-lē-tõ, n.

a toy reed-pipe.

[Fr.]

mishmee, mishmi

mish'mē, n.

the bitter tonic rootstock of an Assamese gold-thread (*Coptis teeta*).

[Said to be Assamese *mishmītīta*.]

mispickel

mis'pik-əl, n.

arsenical pyrites, a mineral composed of iron, arsenic, and sulphur.

[Ger.]

mistico

mis'ti-kō, n.

a small Mediterranean coaster, between a xebec and a felucca: — pl. **mis'ticos.**

[Sp. *místico*, prob. from Ar.]

mistigris

mis'ti-gris, -grē, n.

a variation of poker in which a joker or blank card can be given any value: the card so used.

[Fr. *mistigri*, knave of clubs.]

mobby, mobbie

mob'i, n.

a spirituous beverage made from sweet-potatoes (*West Indies*): fruit juice for brandy-making, or brandy made therefrom (*U.S. arch.*).

[Carib *mabi*.]

mockado

mok-ä'dō, (*obs.*) n.

an inferior cloth of Flemish origin: trumpery: — pl. **mocka'does.**

[Prob. It. *mocaiardo*, haircloth.]

mocock

*mō-kok', **mocuck** mō-kuk'*, ns.

an American Indian birch-bark box or basket.

[Orig. Algonquian.]

modena

mod'i-nə, n.

a shade of crimson.

[*Modena* in Italy.]

modillion

mod-il'yən, (*archit.*) n.

an ornamental bracket under a Corinthian or other cornice.

[It. *modiglione* — L. *modulus* — *modus*, a measure.]

modius

mō'di-əs, mod'i-ōōs, n.

a Roman dry measure, about a peck: a cylindrical head-dress of the gods: — pl. **mō'dii** (-*ī*).

[L. *mŏdius*.]

moellon

mō'ə-lon, n.

rubble in mason-work.

[Fr.]

mofette

mō-fet', n.

an opening in the earth giving out carbon dioxide with some nitrogen and oxygen — the last stage of volcanic activity.

[Fr., — It. *mofeta*, perh. L. *mephītis*, foul exhalation.]

mofussil

mō-fus'l, n.

in India, all outside the capital or great towns.
adj. provincial: rural.
[Hind. *mufassil* — Ar. *mufassal*, distinct, separate, pa.p. of *fassala*, to separate.]

moggan

mog'ən, (*Scot.*) n.

a footless stocking.
[Origin unknown.]

mohel

mō'(h)el, n.

an official Jewish circumciser.
[Heb.]

mohur

mō'hər, n.

a former Persian and Indian gold coin, in India fifteen rupees.
[Pers. *mohr*.]

moineau

moi'nō, n.

a small flat bastion to protect a fortification while being erected.
[Fr.]

moko

mō'kō, n.

a system of tattooing practised by the Maoris: a Maori tattoo: — pl. **mōkos.**
[Maori.]

mona

mō'nə, n.

a West African monkey, *Cercopithecus mona*.
[It., Sp., or Port. *mona*, monkey.]

monaul, monal

mon'öl, n.

a magnificent Himalayan pheasant (*Lophophorus*).
[Nepali *munāl*.]

monial

mōn'i-əl, n.

a mullion.
[O.Fr., of unknown origin.]

monotroch

mon'ō-trok, (*Scott, facet.*) n.

a wheelbarrow.
[Gr. *monos*, single, alone, *trochos*, wheel.]

montaria

mont-ä-rē'ə, n.

in Brazil, a light canoe made of one log.
[Port.]

monteith

mən-, mon-tēth', n.

a large 17th- or 18th-century bowl, usually of silver, fluted and scalloped, for cooling punch-glasses (said to be named from 'a fantastical Scot' who wore his cloak so scalloped): a cotton handkerchief with white spots on a coloured ground (from Glasgow manufacturers).

montero

mon-tā'rō, n.

a huntsman: a Spanish horseman's helmet-like cap with a flap. — Also **monte'ro-cap'**: — pl. **monte'ros.**

[Sp. *montero*, a huntsman — *monte* — L. *mōns, montis*, a mountain.]

mooi

mō'i, (*Afrik.*) adj.

fine — a general word of commendation.

[From Du.]

mopoke

mō'pōk, n.

the owl *Ninox novaeseelandiae*, of Australia and New Zealand: (*Austr.*) the tawny frogmouth (to which the call is wrongly attributed): a silly person. — Also **mope'hawk, more'-pork.**

[From the cry of the owl.]

morat

mō'rat, mö', n.

a drink made of honey and mulberry juice.

[L.L. *mōrātum* — *mōrum*, mulberry.]

morbilli

mör-bil'ī, n.pl.

measles.

adjs. **morbill'iform, morbill'ous.**

[L.L. dim. of L. *morbus*, disease.]

moreen

mo-rēn', n.

a stout corded fabric, woollen, cotton, or both, often watered.

[Poss. conn. with **moire.**]

morgay

mör'gā, n.

the small spotted dogfish or bounce.

[Cornish and Welsh *morgi* — *mōr*, sea, *ci*, dog.]

morkin

mör'kin, n.

a beast that has died by accident.

n. **mor'ling, mort'ling** a sheep dead of disease: its wool.

[A.Fr. *mortekine* — L. *morticīna* (fem. adj.), carrion — *mors*, death.]

mormaor

mör-mā'ər, (*hist.*) n.

a high steward.

[Gael. *mormaer*, now *mòrmhaor* — *mòr*, great, *maor*, steward.]

Mormops

mör'mops, n.

a genus of repulsive-looking American leaf-nosed bats.

[Gr. *mormō*, a bugbear, *ōps*, face.]

morrhua

mor'ōō-ə, n.

an old generic, now specific, name of the cod (*Gadus morrhua*).

[L.L. *morua*.]

morro

mor'ō, n.

a rounded hill or headland: — pl. **morr'os**.

[Sp.]

morwong

mör'wong, mō'wong, n.

an Australian and N.Z. food fish.

[Aboriginal.]

moshav

mō-shäv', n.

an agricultural settlement in Israel: (also **moshav ovdim** *ōv-dēm'*) a joint association of privately-owned farms, on which machinery and marketing are usually operated communally: — pl. **moshavim** (-*shə-vēm'*), **moshvei ovdim** (*mosh-vā '*). **moshav shitufi** (*shi-tōō-fē'*) an agricultural association in which land and all resources are held

in common, but the family unit is preserved, with its own house and garden: — pl. **moshavim' shitufim'**.

[Heb., dwelling.]

moslings

moz'lingz, n.pl.

the thin shavings taken off by the currier in dressing skins.

[Perh. *morsellings*, as if dim. of **morsel**.]

motser

mot'sər, **motza** *mot'zə*, (*Austr. coll.*) ns.

a large amount of money, esp. the proceeds from a gambling win.

motuca

mō-tōō'kə, **mutuca** *mōō-tōō'kə*, ns.

a large Brazilian biting fly of the Tabanidae.

[Tupí *mutuca* (Port. *motuca*).]

moucharaby

mōō-shar'ə-bi, n.

a balcony enclosed with lattice-work.

[Fr., — Ar. *mashrabiyyah*.]

mouchard

mōō-shär, (Fr.) n.

a police spy.

mournival

mōr′ni-vəl, mör′, n.

in gleek, a set of four aces, kings, etc.

[Fr. *mornifle.*]

mousmee, mousmé

mōōs′mā, n.

a Japanese girl, esp. a waitress.

[Jap. *musume.*]

moutan

mōō′tan, n.

a tree peony.

[Chin.]

mpret

bret, n.

a former title of the ruler of Albania.

[Albanian, — L. *imperātor*, emperor.]

muckender

muk′ən-dər, (*obs.*) n.

a handkerchief: a table-napkin.

[Apparently from some Languedocian dialect; cf. Fr. *mouchoir*, Sp. *mocador.*]

mucro

mū′krō, n.

a short stiff sharp point forming an abrupt end: — pl. **mūcrō′nes** (*-nēz*), **mū′cros.** adjs. **mu′cronate, -d** (*-krən-āt, -id*).

[L. *mūcrō, -ōnis*, a sharp point.]

mudir

mōō-dēr′, n.

a local governor.

n. **mudir′ieh, mudir′ia** a mudir's province or office.

[Ar. *mudīr.*]

muid

mü-ē, n.

an old French measure of capacity: a hogshead: a dry measure for corn, etc.: (*S.Afr.*; *mā′id*) a sack of 3 bushels.

[Fr., — L. *modius*; cf. Du. *mud.*]

mulga

mul′gə, n.

any of several acacias, esp. *A. aneura*, typically found in arid regions of Australia: (with *the*) the outback.

mulga wire (*Austr.*) bush telegraph.

[Native word.]

muller

mul′ər, n.

a pulverising tool.

[Perh. O.Fr. *moloir — moldre* (Fr. *moudre*), to grind.]

mumpsimus

mump′si-məs, n.

an error cherished after exposure: stubborn conservatism: an antiquated person.

[An ignorant priest's blunder (in

an old story) for L. *sūmpsimus,*
we have received, in the mass.]

mundic

mun'dik, n.

iron pyrites.

[From Cornish.]

mundungus

mun-dung'gəs, (*arch.*) n.

a rank-smelling tobacco.

[Sp. *mondongo,* black
pudding.]

mungo

mung'gō, n.

the waste produced in a
woollen-mill from hard spun or
felted cloth, or from tearing up
old clothes, used in making
cheap cloth: — pl. **mun'gos.**

[Origin obscure.]

muntin, munting

munt'in(g), ns.

the vertical framing piece
between door panels.

**muqaddam, mokaddam,
mocuddum**

mōō-kud'um, mō-, ns.

a head-man.

[Ar.]

murgeon

mûr'jən, (*Scot.*) n.

a grimace.

v.t. and v.i. to mock with
grimaces.

[Origin obscure.]

muricate

mūr'i-kāt, (*bot.*) adj.

rough or warty with short sharp
points. — Also **mur'icated.**

[L. *mūricātus* — *mūrex, -icis,* a
murex, a sharp stone.]

murl

mûrl, (*Scot.*) v.t. and v.i.

to crumble.

adj. **murl'y.**

[Origin obscure.]

murlain, murlan, murlin

mûr'lən, (*Scot.*) n.

a round, narrow-mouthed
basket.

[Gael. *mùrlan.*]

murra, murrha

mur'ə, n.

an unknown precious material
for vases, etc., first brought to
Rome by Pompey (61 B.C.) from
the East, conjectured to be
agate.

adjs. **murrhine, murrine**
(*mur'īn, -in*), **myrrhine** (*mir'īn,
-in*).

[L. *murra;* Gr. *morria* (pl.).]

185

murre

mûr, n.

a guillemot: a razorbill.
n. **murrelet** (*mûr'lit*) a name for various small birds akin to the guillemot.
[Origin obscure.]

murva, moorva

mōōr'və, n.

bowstring hemp.
[Sans. *mūrvā*.]

muscadin

müs-ka-dɛ̃, (*hist.*) n.

a fop or dandy: a middle-class moderate revolutionary.
[Fr.]

muscardine

mus'kär-din, -dēn, -dīn, n.

a silkworm disease caused by a fungus (*Botrytis*).
[Fr.]

muscarine

mus'kər-in, n.

an alkaloid poison found in certain fungi.
adj. **muscarin'ic** of, like, or producing effects similar to muscarine.
[L. *muscarius* — *musca*, a fly.]

musit

mū'zit, (*Shak.*) n.

a gap in a fence or thicket through which an animal passes.

muskellunge

mus'kə-lunj, n.

a large North American freshwater fish (*Esox masquinongy*) of the pike family. — Also **maskal(l)onge** (*mas'kə-lonj*), **maskinonge**, **maskanonge** (*mas'kə-nonj*).
[Algonquian.]

musrol

muz'rōl, (*obs.*) n.

the nose-band of a bridle.
[Fr. *muserolle* — It. *museruola* — *muso*, muzzle.]

mussitation

mus-i-tā'shən, n.

low muttering: speaking movement without sound.
v.t. **muss'itate** to mutter.
[L. *mussitāre*, freq. of *mussāre*, to mutter.]

mutessarif

mōō-təs-ä'rif, n.

the head of a Turkish sanjak.
n. **mutessa'rifat** his office or jurisdiction.
[Turk. *mutesarif* — Ar. *mutasarrif*.]

muu-muu

mōō'mōō, n.

a simple loose dress worn chiefly in Hawaii.

[Hawaiian *mu'u mu'u*.]

mvule

mvōō'le, n.

a huge tropical African timber tree (*Chlorophora excelsa*) of the mulberry family.

myalism

mī'əl-izm, n.

West Indian Negro witchcraft. adj. **my'al.**

[Prob. of West African origin.]

mydriasis

mi-drī'ə-sis, n.

morbid dilatation of the pupil of the eye.
adj. **mydriatic** (*mid-ri-at'ik*).
n. a drug causing the pupil to dilate.

[Gr. *mydriāsis.*]

mygale

mig'ə-lē, n.

an American bird-catching spider of the genus **Mygale.**

[Gr. *mȳgalē*, a field-mouse, a shrew — *mȳs*, mouse, *galeē*, weasel.]

myiasis

mī'i-ə-sis, mī-i-ā'sis, n.

disease caused by presence of flies or their larvae.

[Gr. *myīa*, fly.]

myringa

mir-ing'gə, n.

the eardrum.
ns. **myringitis** (*-in-jī'tis*) inflammation of the eardrum; **myringoscope** (*-ing'gə-skōp*) an instrument for viewing the eardrum; **myringotomy** (*-ing-got'əm-i*) incision of the eardrum.

[L.L. *miringa* — Gr. *mēninx*, membrane.]

myxoma

mik-sō'mə, n.

a tumour of jelly-like substance: — pl. **myxō'mata.**
adj. **myxō'matous.**
n. **myxomatō'sis** a contagious virus disease of rabbits.

[Gr. *myxa*, mucus.]

N

naam, nam
näm, (*hist.*; *law*) n.
distraint.
[O.E. *nām*, related to *niman*, to take.]

nabk
nabk, nubk, n.
the Christ's-thorn.
[Ar. *nebq.*]

nacarat
nak'ə-rat, n.
a bright orange-red: a fabric so coloured.
[Fr.]

nacket
nak'it, **nocket** *nok'it*, ns.
a snack, light lunch.
[Origin obscure.]

naga
nä'gə, n.
a snake, esp. the cobra (*Ind.*): a divine snake (*Hind. myth.*).
[Sans. *nāga.*]

nagana
nä-gä'nə, n.
a disease of horses and cattle caused by a trypanosome transmitted by tsetse flies.
[Zulu *nakane.*]

nagari
nä'gə-rē, n.
devanagari: the group of alphabets to which devanagari belongs.
[Sans. *nāgarī*, town-script — *nāgaran*, town (perh. referring to a particular town); addition of *deva-* to form *devanagari* was a later development.]

nagmaal
nähh'mäl, näk', n. (*South Africa*)
a Dutch Reformed Church Sacrament, the Lord's Supper.
[Earlier *nachtmaal*, night meal; from Du.]

nagor
nä'gör, n.
a West African antelope (*Redunca redunca*).
[Fr., arbitrarily formed by Buffon from earlier *nanguer.*]

naik
nä'ik, n.
a lord or governor: a corporal of Indian infantry.
[Urdu *nā'ik* — Sans. *nāyaka*, leader.]

nainsook

nān'sŏŏk, n.

a kind of muslin like jaconet.
[Hind. *nainsukh* — *nain*, eye,
sukh, pleasure.]

naira

nī'rə, n.

the standard unit of currency in
Nigeria.

naker

nā'kər, n.

a kettledrum.
[O.Fr. *nacre* — Ar. *naqāra*.]

nandine

nan'din, n.

a West African palm-civet.
[Prob. a native name.]

nandu, nandoo

nan'dŏŏ, n.

rami or China grass.
[Tupí *nandú*.]

napiform

nā'pi-förm, adj.

turnip-shaped.
[L. *nāpus*, a turnip.]

nare

nār, n. (*arch.*)

a nostril, esp. a hawk's.
n.pl. **nār'ēs** (L.; *anat.*) nostrils.
adjs. **nār'ial, nār'ine** (-*īn*).
n. **nār'icorn** a horny

termination of a bird's nostril.
[L. *nāris*, pl. -*ēs*, nostril.]

narghile

när'gil-i, n.

a hookah. — Also **nargile(h),
narg(h)il(l)y.**
[Pers. *nārgīleh* — *nārgīl*, a
coconut (from which it used to
be made).]

nartjie

(*orig.* **naartje**) *när'chi*, (*Afrik.*)
n. a small sweet orange like the
mandarin.
[Prob. conn. with **orange**.]

nasard

naz'ərd, n.

an organ mutation-stop.
[Fr.]

nashgab

nash'gab, näsh'gäb, (*Scot.*) n.

prattle: chatter: a pert chatterer.
— Also **gab'nash.**

nastalik, nasta'liq

nas-tə-lēk', n.

Persian cursive script, having
long horizontal strokes and
rounded characters.
[Ar. from *naskhi*, cursive script,
and *talik*, hanging.]

189

navette

na-vet', n.

in jewel-cutting, a pointed oval shape: a jewel cut in this shape.

[Fr., shuttle, dim. of *nef*, ship.]

navew

nā'vū, n.

a rape or coleseed with carrot-shaped root: a wild Swedish turnip.

[Fr. *naveau*, dim. — L. *nāpus*.]

nebel

nē'bəl, n.

a Hebrew instrument, apparently a harp.

[Heb. *nēbel*.]

nebris

neb'ris, n.

a fawn-skin worn by Bacchus and his votaries.

[Gr. *nebris*.]

nef

nef, n.

a church nave (*obs.*): a mediaeval, usually shiplike, piece of plate for a great lord's napkin, table utensils, etc.

[Fr. *nef*, ship, nave — L. *nāvis*.]

nekton

nek'ton, n.

the assemblage of actively swimming organisms in a sea, lake, etc.

[Gr. *nēkton* (neut.), swimming.]

nelis, nelies

nel'is, n.

a winter pear: — pl. **nel'is, nel'ies.**

[Fr. *nélis.*]

nelly

nel'i, n.

a large petrel.

[Perh. the woman's name.]

nene

nā'nā, n.

the Hawaiian goose, a rare bird of Hawaii, having grey-brown plumage, a black face and partially-webbed feet.

[Hawaiian.]

nephalism

nef'ə-lizm, n.

total abstinence from alcoholic drinks.

n. **neph'alist.**

[Gr. *nēphalios*, sober; *nēphein*, to be sober.]

nerka

nûr'kə, n.

the sockeye salmon.

[Origin unknown.]

neroli

ner'ə-lē, n.

an oil distilled from orange flowers — also **neroli oil**.

[Said to be named from its discoverer, an Italian princess.]

nesh

nesh, (*dial.*) adj.

soft, crumbly: tender: delicate in one's health: cowardly, afraid: lacking energy.

n. **nesh'ness.**

[O.E. *hnesce*.]

Neskhi, Neski

nes'ki, **Naskhi** *nas'ki*, ns.

Arabic cursive handwriting.

[Ar. *naskhī*.]

neuston

nū'ston, n.

minute organisms on the surface of water.

[Gr. neut. of *neustos*, swimming.]

ngaio

nī'ō, n.

a New Zealand tree with white wood: — pl. **ngaio's.**

[Maori.]

ngwee

ng-gwē', n.

the hundredth part of a Zambian kwacha (q.v.), or a coin of this

value: — pl. **ngwee.**

[Native word, bright.]

nidor

nī'dör, n.

a strong smell or fume, esp. of animal substances cooking or burning.

adv. **nī'dorous.**

[L. *nīdor*, *-ōris*.]

nife

nī'fi, n.

the earth's hypothetical core of nickel and iron.

[Chemical symbols *Ni* and *Fe*.]

niffnaff

nif-naf', (*dial.*) n.

a trifle: a diminutive person.

v.i. to trifle.

adjs. **niff-naff'y, niff'y-naff'y** fastidious.

nilgai

nēl' or *nil'gī*, **nilgau, nylghau** *-gow*, *-gö*, ns.

a large Indian antelope, the male slaty-grey, the female tawny.

[Pers. and Hind. *nīl*, blue, Hind. *gāī*, Pers. *gāw*, cow.]

ninon

nē-nõ', n.

a silk voile or other thin fabric.

[Fr. *Ninon*, a woman's name.]

Nipa

nē', nī'pə, n.

a low-growing East Indian palm of brackish water (*Nipa fruticans*): an alcoholic drink made from it.

[Malay *nīpah.*]

nipter

nip'tər, n.

the ecclesiastical ceremony of washing the feet — the same as *maundy.*

[Gr. *niptēr,* a basin — *niptein,* to wash.]

nirl

nirl, (*Scot.*) n.

a lump: a crumb: a stunted person.

v.t. to stunt: to shrink or shrivel: to pinch with cold.

adjs. **nirled, nirl'it; nirl'y, nirl'ie** knotty: stumpy: stunted: niggardly.

[Perh. conn. Icel. *nyrfill,* niggard.]

nisus

nī'səs, n.

effort: striving: impulse.

[L. *nīsus,* pl. -*ūs.*]

nocake

nō'kāk, n.

meal made of parched Indian corn.

[Amer. Ind. word *nookik,* etc.]

noctule

nok'tūl, n.

the great bat, the largest British species.

[Fr., — It. *nottola,* L. *nox, noctis,* night.]

noils

noilz, n.pl.

short pieces of wool or other fibre separated from the longer fibres e.g. by combing. — Also n.sing. **noil** the wool or other fibre so separated.

[Origin unknown.]

noma

nō'mə, n.

a destructive ulceration of the cheek, esp. that affecting debilitated children.

[L. *nomē,* ulcer — Gr. *nomē,* ulcer, feeding — *nemein,* to feed, consume.]

nombril

nom'bril, (*her.*) n.

a point a little below the centre of a shield.

[Fr., navel.]

nomic

nom'ik, adj.

customary: conventional, esp. of spelling.

[Gr. *nomikos* — *nomos,* custom.]

nong

nong, (*Austr. slang*) n.

a fool, idiot.

[Origin uncertain.]

noria

nō'ri-ə, nö', n.

an endless chain of buckets on a wheel for water-raising.

[Sp. *noria* — Ar. *nā'ūrah*.]

norimon

nor'i-mon, n.

a Japanese palanquin.

[Jap. *nori*, to ride, *mono*, thing.]

norman

nör'mən, (*naut.*) n.

a bar inserted in a windlass on which to fasten or veer a rope or cable.

nosocomial

nos-ō-kō'mi-əl, adj.

relating to a hospital.

[Gr. *nosokomeion*, hospital — *nosos*, sickness, *komeein*, to tend.]

nostology

nos-tol'ə-ji, n.

the study of senility or return to childish characteristics.

adjs. **nostologic** (*-ə-loj'*), **-al**.

[Gr. *nostos*, return, *logos*, discourse.]

nostomania

nos-tō-mā'ni-ə, n.

an abnormal desire to go back to familiar places.

[Gr. *nostos*, return, **mania**.]

nostopathy

nos-top'ə-thi, n.

an abnormal fear of going back to familiar places.

[Gr. *nostos*, return, *pathos*, suffering.]

nostos

nos'tos, (Gr.) n.

a poem describing a return or a return journey.

notchel, nochel

noch'l, n. (*coll.*)

notice that one will not be responsible for another's debts. v.t. to repudiate the debts of (someone).

[Origin unknown.]

notour

nō'tər, (*Scot.*; now only *legal*) adj.

well known, notorious.

[L.L. *nōtōrius*.]

noup

nōōp, nŏŏp, (*obs.* Shetland; *Scott*) n.

a crag: a steep headland.

[O.N. *gnūpr*.]

novalia

nō-vā'li-ə, (*Scots law*) n.pl.
waste lands newly reclaimed.
[L. *novālia*.]

novercal

nō-vûr'kl, adj.
pertaining to or befitting a
stepmother.
[L. *novercālis — noverca*, a
stepmother.]

novum

nō'vəm, (*Shak.*) n.
a game at dice in which the
chief throws were nine and five.
[Poss. L. *novem*, nine.]

nowed

nowd, (*her.*) adj.
knotted.
[Fr. *noué*.]

nowy

nō'i, now'i, (*her.*) adj.
having a convex curvature near
the middle.
[O.Fr. *noé* (Fr. *noué*) — L.
nōdātus, knotted.]

nubecula

nū-bek'ū-lə, n.
a cloudiness: — pl.
nūbec'ulae (*-lē*) the
Magellanic Clouds.
[L. *nūbēcula*, dim. of *nūbēs*,
cloud.]

nucha

nū'kə, n.
the nape of the neck.
adj. **nū'chal.**
[L.L. *nucha* — Ar. *nukhā'*,
spinal marrow.]

nulla-nulla

nul'ə-nul'ə, n.
an Australian Aborigine's
hard-wood club. — Also
null'a.
[Aboriginal.]

nullipore

nul'i-pōr, -pör, n.
a coralline seaweed.
[L. *nūllus*, none, *porus*, a
passage, pore.]

numbat

num'bat, n.
a small Australian marsupial
(*Myrmecobius fasciatus*) which
feeds on termites.
[Aboriginal.]

numdah

num'dä, n.
an embroidered felt rug made in
India.
[Cf. **numnah.**]

numnah

num'nə, n.
a felt or, now usu., sheepskin,

cloth or pad placed under a saddle to prevent chafing.
[Hind. *namdā*.]

nunatak

nōō'na-tak, n.

a point of rock appearing above the surface of land-ice: — pl. **nu'nataks,** or (Sw.) **nu'nataker.**
[Eskimo.]

nuncupate

nung'kū-pāt, v.t.

to utter as a vow: to declare orally.
n. **nuncūpā'tion.**
adjs. **nunc'ūpātive** (of a will) oral: designative;
nunc'ūpatory (*-pə-tə-ri*; *obs.*) nuncupative: dedicatory.
[L. *nuncupāre*, to call by name — prob. from *nōmen*, name, *capěre*, to take.]

nundine

nun'dīn, *-din*, n.

the ancient Roman market-day, every eighth day (ninth by Roman reckoning, counting both days).
adj. **nun'dinal** (*-din-*) pertaining to a fair or market.
[L. *nūndinae*, market-day — *novem*, nine, *diēs*, a day.]

nuraghe

nōō-rä'gā, **nurhag** *nōō-räg'*, ns.

a broch-like Sardinian round tower, probably of the Bronze Age: — pls. **nuraghi** (*-gē*), **nurhags.**
adj. **nuragh'ic** relating to, found in, etc., nuraghi.
[Sardinian dialect.]

nutria

nū'tri-ə, n.

the coypu: its fur.
[Sp. *nutria*, otter — L. *lutra*.]

nuzzer

nuz'ər, n.

a present to a superior.
[Hind. *nazr*, gift.]

nyctalopia

nik-tə-lō'pi-ə, n.

properly, night-blindness, abnormal difficulty in seeing in a faint light: by confusion sometimes, day-blindness.
adj. **nyctalōp'ic.**
n. **nyc'talops** (*-lops*) one affected with nyctalopia: — pl. **nyctalō'pes.**
[Gr. *nyktalōps*, night-blind, day-blind — *nyx, nyktos*, night, *alaos*, blind, *ōps*, eye, face.]

nyctinasty

nik'ti-nas-ti, n.

sleep-movement in plants, joint
effect of changes in light and
temperature.
adj. **nyctinas'tic.**

[Gr. *nyx, nyktos,* night, *nastos,*
pressed.]

O

obang
ō'bang, n.
an old Japanese oblong gold coin.
[Jap. *ōban*.]

obeche
ō-bē'chē, n.
a large West African tree or its whitish wood.
[Nigerian name.]

obsidional
ob-sid'i-ən-əl, adj.
pertaining to a siege. — Also **obsid'ionary**.
[L. *obsidiō*, *-ōnis*, a siege.]

oca
ō'kə, n.
a South American wood-sorrel with edible tubers.
[Sp. from Quechua.]

ocker
ok'ər, (*Austr. coll.*) n.
an oafish uncultured Australian. adj. boorish, uncultured: Australian. — Also with *cap.* n. **ock'erism, Ock'erism** boorishness in Australians.
[After a character in a television programme; a form of *Oscar*.]

octapla
ok'tə-plə, n. sing.
a book of eight (esp. Biblical) parallel texts.
[Gr. *oktaplā* (contracted pl.), eightfold.]

octroi
ok'trwä or *ok-trwa'*, n.
formerly, and still in some European countries, a commercial privilege, as of exclusive trade: a toll or tax levied at the gates of a city on articles brought in: the place where, or officials to whom, it is paid: payment for passage of car on a road.
[Fr., — *octroyer*, to grant, from some such L.L. form as *auctōrizāre*, to authorise — L. *auctor*, author.]

oecist
ē'sist, **oikist** *oi'kist*, (*hist.*) ns.
the founder of a colony.
[Gr. *oikistēs* — *oikos*, a house.]

ogdoad
og'dō-ad, n.
a set of eight.
[Gr. *ogdoas*, *-ados* — *oktō*, eight.]

olitory

ol'i-tə-ri, adj.

pertaining to kitchen vegetables.

n. a kitchen-garden: a pot-herb.

[L. (*h*)*olitor*, gardener — (*h*)*olus*, (*h*)*oleris*, a pot-herb, vegetable.]

oliver

ol'i-vər, n.

a forge-hammer worked by foot.

[Origin unknown.]

ollav, ollamh

ol'äv, n.

a doctor or master among the ancient Irish.

[Ir. *ollamh.*]

olm

olm, ōlm, n.

a European, blind, cave-dwelling, eel-like salamander (*Proteus anguinus*).

[Ger.]

olpe

ol'pē, n.

a Greek jug.

[Gr. *olpē.*]

olykoek, olycook

ol'i-kōōk, (*U.S.*) n.

a kind of doughnut.

[Du. *oliekoek*, lit. oil-cake.]

omadhaun

om'ə-dön, n.

a fool.

[Ir. *amadan.*]

omer

ō'mər, n.

a Hebrew dry measure containing about 2¼ litres, 1/10 ephah.

[Heb. '*ōmer.*]

omlah

om'lä, n.

a staff of officials in India.

[Ar. '*umalā.*]

omophagia

ō-mō-fāj'yə, -i-ə, n.

the eating of raw flesh, esp. as a religious observance. — Also **omophagy** (*ō-mof'ə-ji*).

adjs. **omophagic** (*-faj'ik*), **omophagous** (*-mof'ə-gəs*).

[Gr. *ōmophagiā* — *ōmos*, raw, *phagein*, to eat.]

omophorion

ō-mō-fō'ri-on, -för', n.

an Eastern bishop's vestment like the pallium.

[Gr. *ōmophŏrion* — *ōmos*, shoulder, *pherein*, to carry.]

omrah

om'rä, n.

a Muslim lord.

[Hindi *umrā*, orig. pl. of Ar. *amīr*.]

onchocerciasis

ong-kō-sər-kī'-ə-sis, n.

a disease of man, also known as river blindness, common in tropical regions of America and Africa, caused by infestation by a filarial worm (*Onchocerca volvulus*) which is transmitted by various species of black fly, and characterised by subcutaneous nodules and very often blindness.

[Gr. *onkos*, a hook, *kerkos*, a tail.]

ondatra

on-dat'rə, n.

the musquash.

[Huron Indian.]

Oniscus

on-is'kəs, n.

a genus of woodlice.

adj. **onis'coid** of the family of Oniscus: like a woodlouse.

[Gr. *oniskos*, dim. of *onos*, an ass.]

onkus, oncus

ong'kəs, (*Austr. coll.*) adj.

disordered: bad.

oof

ōōf, (*slang*) n.

money — orig. **oof'tish**.

[Yiddish — Ger. *auf* (*dem*) *Tische*, on the table.]

oont

ōōnt, n.

in India, a camel.

[Hindi *ṭ.*]

opah

ō'pə, n.

the kingfish (*Lampris*), a large sea-fish with laterally flattened body, constituting a family of uncertain affinities.

[West African origin.]

opinicus

o-pin'i-kəs, (*her.*) n.

a half-lion, half-dragon.

[Origin unknown.]

opodeldoc

op-ō-del'dok, n.

a name given by Paracelsus to various local applications: soap-liniment.

[Derivation unknown, apparently Gr. *opos*, juice.]

oporice
ō-por'i-sē, n.
a medicine prepared from
quinces, pomegranates, etc.
[Gr. *opōrikē — opōrā*, late
summer, summer fruits.]

oppignorate, oppignerate
op-ig'nə-rāt, (*obs.*) v.t.
to pawn.
n. **oppignorā'tion.**
[L. *oppīgnorāre, oppīgnerāre —
ob*, against, *pīgnus, -oris, -eris*,
a pledge.]

oppilate
op'il-āt, v.t.
to block up, stop up.
n. **oppilā'tion.**
adj. **opp'ilātive.**
[L. *oppīlāre, -ātum — ob*, in the
way, *pīlāre*, to ram down.]

opsimath
op'si-math, n.
one who learns late in life.
n. **opsim'athy** learning
obtained late in life.
[Gr. *opsimathēs — opse*, late,
mathē, learning.]

opsonium
op-sō'ni-əm, n.
anything eaten with bread as a
relish, esp. fish.
ns. **opsomā'nia** any morbid
love for some special kind of
food; **opsomā'niac.**

adj. **opsonic** (*op-son'ik*) relating
to opsonin.
n. **op'sonin** a constituent of
blood-serum which makes
bacteria more readily consumed
by phagocytes.
[Latinised from Gr. *opsōnion —
opson*, cooked food, relish.]

orant
ō'rənt, ö', n.
a worshipping figure in ancient
Greek and early Christian art.
[L. *ōrāns, -antis*, pr.p. of *ōrāre*,
to pray.]

orarian
ō-, ö-rā'ri-ən, adj.
coastal.
n. a coast-dweller.
[L. *ōrārius — ōra*, shore.]

ord
örd, (*obs.*) n.
a point, e.g. of a weapon: a
beginning.
[O.E. *ord*.]

oread
ör'i-ad, ō'ri-ad, (*myth.*) n.
a mountain nymph: — pl.
o'reads, or **orē'adēs.**
[L. *ŏrēas, -adis —* Gr. *oreias,
oreiados — oros*, a mountain.]

orfe

örf, n.

a golden-yellow semi-domesticated variety of id. [Ger. *Orfe* — Gr. *orphōs*, the great sea-perch.]

orgeat

ör'ji-at, -zhat, or-zhä, n.

a syrup or drink made from almonds, sugar, etc., formerly from barley. [Fr. *orge* — L. *hordeum*, barley.]

oribi

or'i-bi, n.

a small South African antelope, the palebuck. [Afrik., app. from some native language.]

orichalc

or'i-kalk, (*Spens.* **oricalche**) n.

a gold-coloured alloy: brass. adj. **orichalceous** (*-kal'si-əs*). [Gr. *oreichalkos* — *oros*, a mountain, *chalkos*, copper; sense influenced by association with L. *aurum*, gold.]

orillion

o-ril'yən, n.

a semicircular projection at the shoulder of a bastion intended to cover the guns and defenders on the flank.

[Fr. *orillon* — *oreille*, an ear — L. *auricula*, dim. of *auris*, ear.]

orle

örl, (*her.*) n.

a border within a shield at a short distance from the edge: a number of small charges set as a border. [O.Fr., border, from a dim. formed from L. *ōra*, border.]

oropesa

or-ō-pē'zə, -pä'sə, n.

a fish-shaped float used in marine mine-sweeping to support the sweeping wire. [From the name of a trawler.]

orpharion

ör-fa-rī'ən, ör-fā'ri-ən, n.

a large lute-like instrument with six to nine pairs of metal strings. — Also **orpheŏ'reon**. [*Orpheus, Arīōn*, mythical musicians.]

orphrey

ör'fri, n.

gold or other rich embroidery, esp. bordering a vestment. [O.Fr. *orfreis* — L. *auriphrygium*, Phrygian gold.]

orthros

ör'thros, n.

one of the Greek canonical hours, corresponding to the

Western lauds.

[Gr. *orthros*, dawn.]

oscitancy

os'i-tən-si, n.

yawning: sleepiness: stupidity.

adj. **osc'itant.**

adv. **osc'itantly.**

v.i. **osc'itate** to yawn.

n. **oscitā'tion** yawning:
sleepiness.

[L. *ōscitāre*, to yawn.]

oshac

ō'shak, n.

the ammoniac plant.

[Ar. *ushshaq*.]

osmidrosis

os-mi-drō'sis, or *oz-*, n.

the secretion of ill-smelling
sweat.

[Gr. *osmē*, smell, *hidrōs*,
sweat.]

osseter

os-et'ər, n.

a species of sturgeon.

[Russ. *osetr*.]

ossifrage

os'i-frāj, n.

the lammergeier: the osprey.

n. **ossifraga** (*os-if'rə-gə*) the
giant fulmar.

[L. *ossifraga*, prob. the
lammergeier — *os, ossis*, bone,
and the root of *frangĕre*, to
break.]

otary

ō'tə-ri, n.

a sea-lion or sea-bear, a seal
with external ears: — pl.
o'taries.

adj. **ot'arine.**

[Gr. *ōtaros*, large-eared — *ous,
ōtos*, ear.]

oustiti

ōo-sti-tē', n.

a lock-opening tool.

[Fr., marmoset.]

outfangthief

owt'fang-thēf, n.

the right of judging and fining
thieves taken outside of one's
own jurisdiction.

[O.E. *ūtfangene-thēof* — *ūt*, out,
the root of *fōn*, to take, *thēof*,
thief.]

outroop

owt'rōop, (*obs.*) n.

an auction sale.

n. **out'rooper** (*obs.*) an
auctioneer: the Common Crier
of the City of London.

[Du. *uitroepen*, to cry out,
proclaim.]

ouvirandra

ōo-vi-ran'drə, n.

the lattice-leaf of Madagascar.

[From the Malagasy name.]

ovibos

ōv'i-bos, ov'i-bōs, n.
the musk-ox.
adj. **ovibō'vīne.**
[L. *ŏvis,* sheep, *bōs, bovis,* ox.]

owelty

ō'əl-ti, (*law*) n.
equality.
[A.Fr. *owelté* — L. *aequālitās,
-ātis.*]

ozaena

ō-zē'nə, n.
a fetid discharge from the
nostrils.
[Gr. *ozaina,* a fetid polypus of
the nose — *ozein,* to smell.]

ozeki

ō-zē'ki, n.
a champion sumo wrestler.
[Jap. *ōzeki.*]

ozokerite

ō-zō'kər-īt, -kēr'īt, **ozocerite**
ō-zos'ər-īt, ō-zō-sēr'īt, ns.
a waxy natural paraffin.
[Gr. *ozein,* to smell, *kēros,*
wax.]

P

pabouche

pə-bōōsh′, n.

a slipper.

[See **babouche.**]

paca

pä′kə, n.

the so-called spotted cavy of South America, akin to the agouti.

[Sp. and Port., — Tupí *paca.*]

paco

pä′kō, n.

an alpaca: — pl. **pa′cos.**

[Sp., — Quechua *paco.*]

padauk, padouk

pä-dowk′, n.

a Burmese timber tree of the red-sanders genus.

[Burmese.]

pademelon, paddymelon, padymelon

pad′i-mel′ən, n.

any of several small wallabies.

[Aboriginal.]

padma

pud′mə, n.

the sacred lotus.

[Sans.]

paenula

pē′nū-lə, n.

a Roman travelling cloak: a chasuble, esp. in its older form.

[L. *paenula.*]

paigle, pagle

pā′gl, (*arch.* and *dial.*) n.

the cowslip, sometimes also the oxlip.

[Origin unknown.]

paillette

pal-yet′, *pä-*, n.

a spangle.

n. **paillon** (*pal′yən*, *pä-yõ*) a piece of foil, to show through enamel, etc.

[Fr.]

pais

pā, (*arch.*) n.

the people from whom a jury is drawn.

[O.Fr.]

pakeha

pä'kə-hä, pä'kē-hä, (*N.Z.*) n.

a white man: a non-Polynesian citizen.

[Maori.]

paktong

pak'tong, n.

nickel-silver. — Also (erron.) **pack'fong, pak'fong.**

[Chin. *pak,* white, *t'ung,* copper.]

palafitte

pal'ə-fit, n.

a prehistoric lake dwelling.

[It. *palafitta* — *palo* (— L. *pālus*), a stake, *fitto,* pa.p. of *figgere* (— L. *figĕre*), to fix.]

palama

pal'ə-mə, n.

the webbing of a water-bird's foot: — pl. **pal'amae** (*-mē*). adj. **pal'amate.**

[Latinised from Gr. *palamē,* palm.]

palampore, palempore

pal'əm-pōr, -pör, n.

a flowered chintz bedcover common in the East.

[From *Palampur,* N. India, place of manufacture.]

palas

pal-äs', -äsh', n.

the dhak tree.

[Hind. *palāś.*]

palay

pa-lā', pä-lī', -lā', n.

the ivory-tree, a small S. Indian tree (*Wrightia*) of the dogbane family, with hard white wood.

[Tamil.]

palisander

pal-i-san'dər, n.

jacaranda or other rosewood.

[Fr. *palissandre,* from a name used in Guiana.]

palki, palkee

päl'kē, n.

a palanquin.

[Hind. *pālkī.*]

palla

pal'ə, n.

a Roman woman's mantle: — pl. **pall'ae** (*-ē*).

[L. *palla.*]

pallah

pal'ə, n.

the impala.

[Tswana *phala.*]

pallone

päl-lō'nā, n.

an Italian game in which a ball is struck with a gauntlet or armguard.

[It., augmentative of *palla*, ball.]

palolo

pa-lō'lō, n.

an edible sea-worm that burrows in coral-reefs, remarkable for its breeding swarms at a certain phase of the moon, the head remaining behind to regenerate: — pl. **palo'los**. — Also **palolo worm**.

[Samoan.]

palpebral

palp'i-brəl, adj.

of or pertaining to the eyelid.

[L. *palpebra*, the eyelid.]

paludament

pə-lū', -lōō', -də-mənt, n.

a Roman general's or high military officer's cloak. — Also **paludament'um**.

[L. *palūdāmentum*.]

panada

pə-nä'də, n.

a dish made by boiling bread to a pulp in water, and flavouring: a thick binding sauce of breadcrumbs or flour and seasoning.

[Sp. *pan* (L. *pānis*), bread.]

panchayat

pun-chä'yət, n.

a village or town council.

[Hindi *pañcāyat* — Sans. *pañca*, five.]

pand

pand, (*Scot.*) n.

the valance of a bed.

[Cf. O.Fr. *pandre*, to hang.]

pandiculation

pan-dik-ū-lā'shən, n.

the act of stretching and yawning.

[L. *pandiculārī, -ātus*, to stretch oneself.]

pandore

pan'dōr, -dör, n.

an esteemed variety of oysters formerly got at Prestonpans on the Firth of Forth.

[Said to be from the *doors* of the salt-*pans*, where they were found.]

pandour

pan'dōōr, n.

an 18th-century Croatian foot-soldier in the Austrian service: a robber. — Also **pan'door**.

[Fr., — Serbo-Croat *pàndūr* — L.L. *banderius*, follower of a banner.]

pandowdy

pan-dow'di, (U.S.) n.

a kind of apple pie or pudding.

[Origin unknown.]

panisk, panisc

pan'isk, n.

an inferior god, attendant on Pan.

[Gr. *Pāniskos,* dim. of *Pān.*]

panne

pan, n.

a fabric resembling velvet, with a long nap.

[Fr.]

pannose

pan'ōs, (bot.) adj.

like felt.

[L. *pannōsus — pannus,* cloth.]

panocha

pä-nō'chə, n.

a Mexican coarse sugar.

[Sp.]

pantaleon

pan-tal'i-on, n.

a very large dulcimer invented about 1700 by *Pantaleon* Hebenstreit.

pantine

pan'tēn, (obs.) n.

a pasteboard jumping-jack, fashionable in the 18th century.

[Fr. *pantine,* afterwards *pantin.*]

pantler

pant'lər, (Shak.) n.

the officer in a great family who had charge of the bread and other provisions. — Also **pant'er.**

[Fr. *panetier* — L. *pānis,* bread.]

paolo

pä'ō-lō, n.

an obsolete papal silver coin: — pl. **pa'oli** (-*lē*).

[It. *Paolo,* Paul, i.e. Pope Paul V.]

parablepsis

par-ə-blep'sis, n.

false vision: oversight. — Also **par'ablepsy.** adj. **parablep'tic.**

[Gr., looking askance — *para,* beside, beyond, *blepein,* to see.]

parabolanus

par-ə-bō-lā'nəs, n.

in the early Eastern Church, a layman who tended the sick.

[Gr. *parabolos,* venturesome, exposing oneself.]

paracentesis

par-ə-sen-tē'sis, (surg.) n.

tapping.

[Gr. *parakentēsis — para,* beside, beyond, *kenteein,* to pierce.]

paracme

pər-ak'mē, n.

the stage of decline or senescence after the culmination of development.

[Gr. *para*, beside, beyond, *akmē*, a point.]

paracusis

par-ə-kū'sis, n.

disordered hearing.

[Gr. *para*, beside, beyond, *akousis*, hearing.]

paradiddle

par'ə-did-l, n.

a drum roll in which the principal beats are struck by the left and right sticks in succession.

paradoxure

par-ə-dok'sūr, n.

a civet-like carnivore of Southern Asia and Malaysia, the palm-cat of India. adj. **paradoxū'rine.**

[Gr. *paradoxos*, paradoxical — *para*, beside, beyond, and *ourā*, tail.]

paramatta, parramatta

par-ə-mat'ə, n.

a fabric like merino made of worsted and cotton.

[App. from *Parramatta* in New South Wales.]

parament

par'ə-mənt, (*obs.*) n.

a rich decoration, hanging, or robe.

[L. *parāre*, to prepare.]

paramo

pä'rä-mō, n.

a bare wind-swept elevated plain in South America: — pl. **par'amos.**

[Sp. *páramo.*]

parang

pär'ang, n.

a heavy Malay knife.

[Malay.]

paraph

par'af, n.

a mark or flourish under one's signature.

v.t. to append a paraph to, to sign with initials.

[Fr. *paraphe.*]

parasang

par'ə-sang, n.

an old Persian measure of length, reckoned at 30 stadia, or between 3 and 4 miles.

[Gr. *parasangēs*, from O.Pers. (mod. Pers. *farsang*).]

paravail

par-ə-vāl', adj.

inferior: lowest, said of a feudal tenant: of least account — opp. to *paramount*.

[O.Fr. *par aval*, below — L. *per*, through, *ad*, to, *vallem*, accus. of *vallis*, valley.]

parbreak

pär'brāk, (*arch*.) n.

a vomit.

v.t. and v.i. (*pär'* or *-brāk'*) to vomit: — pa.p. **parbreaked**.

[M.E. *brake*, to vomit; cf. Du. *braken*; the pfx. may be Fr. *par*-.]

parcener

pär'sən-ər, n.

a co-heir.

n. **par'cenary** (*-ə-ri*), co-heirship.

[A.Fr. *parcener* — L.L. *partōnārius* — *pars*, part.]

parclose

pär'klōz, n.

a screen or railing in a church enclosing an altar or tomb, or separating a chapel or other portion from the main body of the church.

[O.Fr. pa.p. (fem.) of *parclore* — L. *per*, through, *claudĕre*, *clausum*, to close.]

parfleche

pär-flesh', n.

a dried skin, usu. of buffalo: an article made of it.

[App. Canadian Fr.]

pargana, pergunnah

pər-gun'ə, -ä, n.

a division of a zillah in India.

[Hind. and Pers. *parganah*.]

parison

par'i-sən, n.

a lump of glass before it is moulded into its final shape.

[Fr. *paraison* — *parer*, to prepare — L. *parāre*.]

parpen

pär'pən, n.

a stone passing through a wall from face to face: a wall of such stones: a partition: a bridge parapet. — Also **par'pane**, **par'pend**, **par'pent**, **par'point**, **per'pend**, **per'pent**.

ns. **par'pen-stone**; **par'pen-wall**.

[O.Fr. *parpain*.]

parrel, parral

par'əl, n.

a band by which a yard is fastened to a mast.

parrel truck a wooden ball strung on a parrel.

[Cf. O.Fr. *parail*, rigging.]

parrhesia

pa-rē'syə, -zyə, n.
boldness of speech.
[Gr. *parrēsiā — para,* beside,
beyond, *rhēsis,* speech.]

partan

pär'tn, (*Scot.*) n.
the edible crab.
[Gael.]

partlet

pärt'lit, (*obs.*) n.
a neck-covering: a ruff: a kind of
shirt.
[App. O.Fr. *patelette,* a band.]

parulis

pə-rōō'lis, (*med.*) n.
a gumboil.
[Gr. *para,* beside, *oulon,* the
gum.]

pashm

push'əm, n.
the fine underfleece of the goats
of Northern India, used for
making rugs, shawls, etc. —
Also **pashim** (*push'ēm*),
pashmina (*push-mē'nə*).
[Pers., wool.]

patamar

pat'ə-mär, n.
a vessel, on the Bombay coast,
with arched keel and great stem
and stern rake.
[Port., — Konkani *pātamāri.*]

patibulary

pə-tib'ū-lə-ri, adj.
of or pertaining to a gibbet or
gallows.
[L. *patibulum,* a gibbet.]

patte

pat, pät, n.
a narrow band keeping a belt or
sash in its place.
[Fr.]

paua

pä'wə, pow'ə, n.
the New Zealand name for the
abalone. — Also **paw'a.**
[Maori.]

pavid

pav'id, adj.
timid.
[L. *pavidus,* afraid — *pavēre,* to
be frightened.]

pavis, pavise

pav'is, n.
a shield for the whole body.
[O.Fr. *pavais* — It. *pavese,*
prob. from *Pavia* in Italy.]

pawl

pöl, n.
a catch engaging with the teeth
of a ratchet wheel to prevent
backward movement.
[Origin obscure; poss. conn.
with Du. or Fr. *pal,* L. *pālus,*
stake.]

paxwax

paks'waks, n.

the strong tendon in an animal's neck.

[Orig. *fax-wax* — O.E. (Anglian) *fæx* (W.S. *feax*), hair, *weaxan*, to grow.]

peavey, peavy

pē'vi, (*U.S.*) n.

a lumberman's spiked and hooked lever.

[Joseph *Peavey*, its inventor.]

peba

pē'bə, n.

a South American armadillo.

[Tupí.]

pébrine

pā-brēn', n.

a destructive protozoan disease of silkworms.

[Fr.]

peeoy, pioy, pioye

pē-ō'i, (*Scot.*) n.

a home-made firework, a cone of damp gunpowder.

peetweet

pēt'wēt, (*U.S.*) n.

the spotted sandpiper.

[Imit.]

peirastic

pī-ras'tik, adj.

experimental: tentative.

adv. **peiras'tically.**

[Gr. *peirastikos* — *peira*, a trial.]

pekan

pek'ən, n.

the wood-shock, a large North American marten.

[Canadian Fr. *pékan* — Algonquin *pékané*.]

pela

pā'lä, n.

white wax from a scale-insect.

[Chin. *peh-la*, white wax.]

pelham

pel'əm, (often with *cap.*) n.

on a horse's bridle, a type of bit, a combination of the curb and snaffle designs.

[Perh. name *Pelham*.]

pelite

pē'līt, n.

any rock derived from clay or mud.

adj. **pēlitic** (*-lit'ik*).

ns. **pē'loid** any naturally produced medium used in medical practice as a cataplasm; **pēlol'ogy**; **pēlother'apy** treatment by mud baths and the like.

[Gr. *pēlos*, clay, mud.]

pellock, pellack

pel'ək, **pellach** *pel'əhh, (Scot.)*
ns.

a porpoise.

[Origin unknown.]

pelma

pel'mə, n.

the sole of the foot.

adj. **pelmatic** (*-mat'ik*).

n.pl. **Pelmatozō'a** a division of
the Echinodermata, typically
stalked, including crinoids and
the fossil blastoids and cystoids.

[Gr. *pelma, -atos,* sole, stalk.]

pelorus

pel-ōr'əs, -ör', n.

a kind of compass from which
bearings can be taken.

[Perh. *Pelorus,* Hannibal's
pilot.]

pelta

pel'tə, (ant.) n.

a light buckler.

n. **peltast** (*pelt'ast*) a
light-armed Greek soldier with a
pelta.

adj. **pelt'ate** (*bot.*) having the
stalk attached not to the edge
but near the middle of the
under-surface.

[L., — Gr. *peltē.*]

penistone

pen'i-stən, n.

a cloth, a coarse frieze, formerly
made at *Penistone* in Yorkshire.

pennal

pen'əl, pen-äl', n.

formerly, a name for a freshman
at a German university.

n. **penn'alism** a system of
fagging once in vogue at
German universities.

[Ger. *Pennal* — L. *pennāle,*
pen-case.]

penneeck, penneech

pen-ēk', (Scott) n.

an old card game with a new
trump for every trick.

pennill

pen'il, W. *pen·'ihl,* n.

lit. a verse or stanza: — pl.
pennill'ion.

n. **pennill'ion-singing** a form
of Welsh verse-singing in which
the singer improvises an
independent melody and verse
arrangement against an
accompaniment (usu. on the
harp) consisting of a traditional
Welsh melody repeated: a
modern, modified form of
pennillion-singing involving one
or more singers and allowing
advance preparation.

[Welsh.]

pensil, pensel, pencel

pen'sl, n.

a small pennon.

[A.Fr. *pencel*, dim. of *penon*, pennon.]

penstock

pen'stok, n.

a sluice.

pensum

pen'səm, n.

a task: a school imposition (*U.S.*).

[L. *pēnsum*.]

pentimento

pen-ti-men'tō, n.

something painted out of a picture which later becomes visible again: — pl. **-ti** *-tē*.

[It. — *pentirsi*, to repent.]

pepo

pē'pō, n.

the type of fruit found in the melon and cucumber family, a large many-seeded berry formed from an inferior ovary, usually with hard epicarp: — pl. **pē'pos.**

[L. *pĕpō, -ŏnis* — Gr. (*sikyos*) *pepōn*, (a melon eaten) ripe, distinguished from a cucumber eaten unripe.]

percoct

pər-kokt', adj.

well-cooked: overdone: hackneyed.

[L. *percoctus* — *percoquĕre*, to cook thoroughly.]

percolin

pûr'kə-lin, n.

a small bird, a cross between a partridge and a quail.

perduellion

pər-dū-el'yən, (*arch.*) n.

treason.

[L. *perduelliō, -ōnis*.]

periaktos

per-i-ak'tos, n.

in the ancient Greek theatre, a tall revolving prism at the side of the stage, giving change of scene.

[Gr., revolving.]

periapt

per'i-apt, (*Shak.*) n.

an amulet.

[Gr. *periapton*, something hung round — *peri*, *haptein*, to fasten.]

periclase

per'i-klāz, -klās, n.

native magnesia.

[Gr. pfx. *peri-*, very, *klasis*, fracture (from its perfect cleavage).]

pericope

pər-ik'o-pē, n.

an extract, passage, esp. one selected for reading in church.

[Gr. *perikopē — peri, koptein,* to cut.]

peridot

per'i-dot, **peridote** *-dōt,* ns.

olivine: a green olivine used in jewellery.

adj. **peridŏt'ic.**

n. **peridotite** (*-dō'tīt*) a coarse-grained igneous rock mainly composed of olivine, usually with other ferro-magnesian minerals but little or no feldspar.

[Fr. *péridot,* origin unknown.]

perissology

per-is-ol'ə-ji, n.

verbiage: pleonasm.

[Gr. *perissologiā — perissos,* excessive, *logos,* speech.]

pern

pûrn, n.

a honey-buzzard (*Pernis*).

[Cuvier's mistake for Gr. *pternis,* a kind of hawk.]

pernancy

pûr'nən-si, (*law*) n.

receiving.

[A.Fr. *pernance* (O.Fr. *prenance*).]

perrier

per'i-ər, (*obs.*) n.

a machine or gun for discharging stones.

[O.Fr.]

persico, persicot

pûr'si-kō, n.

a cordial flavoured with kernels of peaches and apricots.

[Fr. *persico* (now *persicot*) — It. *persico* — L. *persicum,* a peach.]

pertuse

pər-tūs', adj.

punched: pierced: slit. — Also **pertūs'ate** (or *pûr'*), **pertused** (*-tūst'*).

n. **pertusion** (*-tū'zhən*).

[L. *pertundĕre, -tūsum — per, tundĕre,* to strike.]

pesade

pə-zäd', -säd', -zād', n.

dressage manoeuvre in which a horse rears up on its hindlegs without forward movement.

[Fr.; from It.]

pesewa

pə-soo'a, -sā'wa, -ə, n.

a Ghanaian unit of currency: — pl. **-a, -as.** — See **cedi.**

peshwa

pāsh'wa, n.

the chief minister of the Mahrattas, later the real sovereign. — Also **peish'wa(h).**

[Pers. *pēshwā*, chief.]

petara

pi-tä'rə, n.

a travelling box or basket for clothes. — Also **pita'ra(h).**

[Hind. *pitārāh, petārāh.*]

petary

pē'tər-i, n.

a peat-bog.

[Mediaeval L. *petāria* — root of **peat.**]

petasus

pet'ə-səs, n.

a low broad hat worn by the Greeks in antiquity: either the broad petasus that Hermes is represented as wearing in early Greek art or, by association, the winged hat he wears in later art.

[Latinised from Gr. *petasos.*]

petaurist

pe-tö'rist, n.

a flying-phalanger.

adj. **petaur'ine.**

[Gr. *petauristēs*, an acrobat.]

petchary

pech'ə-ri, n.

the grey king-bird.

[Imit.]

petcock

pet'kok, n.

a small tap or valve for draining condensed steam from steam-engine cylinders, or for testing the water-level in a boiler.

[Poss. obs. *pet*, to fart, or *petty*, and *cock*, a tap.]

petechia

pe-tē'ki-ə, n.

a small red or purple spot on the skin: — pl. **pete'chiae** (*-ē*).

adj. **petech'ial.**

[Latinised from It. *petecchia.*]

petersham

pē'tər-shəm, n.

a heavy greatcoat designed by Lord *Petersham*: rough-napped cloth generally dark blue of which it was made: a heavy corded ribbon used for belts, hat-bands, etc.

petrary

pet'rə-ri, n.

an engine for hurling stones.

[L.L. *petrāria* — L. *petra* — Gr. *petrā*, rock.]

petrissage

pā-trēs-äzh′, n.

massage by longitudinal rubbing and lateral squeezing. [Fr., — *pétrir*, to knead.]

petronel

pet′rə-nel, n.

a large horse pistol.

[Fr. *petrinal* — L. *pectus, pectoris*, the chest, whence fired, or L. *petra*, stone, i.e. gun-flint.]

pettichaps, petty-chaps

pet′i-chaps, n.

the garden or other warbler. [N. of England.]

petuntse

pe-toōnt′si, n.

a feldspathic rock used in making Chinese porcelain. — Also **petuntze.**

[Chin. *pai-tun-tse*, little white brick.]

phaeic

fē′ik, adj.

dusky.

n. **phae′ism** duskiness, incomplete melanism (in butterflies).

[Gr. *phaios*, dusky.]

phellem

fel′əm, (*bot.*) n.

cork.

ns. **phell′oderm** (Gr. *derma*, skin) a layer of secondary cortex formed by the phellogen on its inner side; **phellogen** (*fel′ō-jen*) a layer of meristem that forms cork without, otherwise cork-cambium.

adjs. **phellogenetic** (-ji-net′ik); **phell′oid** cork-like and formed like cork, but not, or very slightly, suberised.

n. **phelloplas′tic** a model in cork.

n.sing. **phelloplas′tics** the making of models in cork.

[Gr. *phellos*, cork.]

phelonion, phaelonion

fi-lō′ni-on, n.

an Eastern vestment like a chasuble.

[Late Gr. *phailŏnion, phĕlŏnion*, dim. of *phailonēs, phelonēs*, for *phainolēs* — L. *paenula*, a cloak.]

phengite

fen′jīt, n.

a transparent stone used by the ancients for windows, prob. selenite: sometimes applied to kinds of mica. — Also **phengites** (*fen-jī′tēz*).

[Gr. *phengītēs* — *phengos*, light.]

pheon

fē'on, (*her.*) n.

the barbed head of a dart or arrow, esp. as a heraldic bearing.

[Ety. dub.]

phillumeny

fil-o͞o'mən-i, n.

a fantastic word for collecting matchbox labels.
n. **phillu'menist.**

[L. *lūmen, -inis,* light.]

pholidosis

fol-id-ō'sis, n.

arrangement of scales, as in fishes and reptiles.

[Gr. *pholis, -idos,* scale.]

phorminx

för'mingks, n.

a kind of cithara: — pl. **phormin'ges** (*-jēz*).

[Gr.]

phrontistery

fron'tis-tə-ri, n.

a thinking-place.

[Gr. *phrontistērion —
phrontistēs,* a thinker —
phroneein, to think; applied by Aristophanes to the school of Socrates.]

piacular

pī-ak'ū-lər, adj.

expiatory: requiring expiation: atrociously bad.
n. **piacularity** (*-lar'i-ti*).

[L. *piāculum,* sacrifice — *piāre,* to expiate — *pius,* pious.]

piaffe

pi-af', pyaf, v.i.

in horsemanship, to advance at a piaffer.
n. **piaff'er** a gait in which the feet are lifted in the same succession as a trot, but more slowly. — Also *Spanish-walk.*

[Fr. *piaffer.*]

piassava

pē-əs-ä'və, **piassaba** *-bə,* ns.

a coarse stiff fibre used for making brooms, etc., got from Brazilian palms, *Attalea* (coquilla) and *Leopoldinia* (chiquichiqui): the tree yielding it.

[Port. from Tupí.]

picamar

pik'ə-mär, n.

a bitter oily liquid got from tar.

[L. *pix, picis,* pitch, *amārus,* bitter.]

pichiciago

pich-i-si-ä'gō, or *-ä'gō,* n.

a small burrowing South American armadillo: — pl.

pichicia'gos.
[Amer. Indian.]

pichurim
pich'ōō-rim, n.
a S. American tree (*Nectandra puchury*) of the laurel family: its aromatic kernel (also **pichurim bean).**
[Port. *pichurim* — Tupí *puchury*.]

pickeer
pi-kēr', v.i.
to forage (*obs.*): to skirmish: to scout: to flirt (*obs.*).
n. **pickeer'er.**
[Ety. dub.]

pickmaw
pik'mö, (*Scot.*) n.
the black-headed gull.
[Perh. **pick** (pitch), **maw** (mew).]

picotee
pik-ə-tē', n.
a florists' variety of carnation, orig. speckled, now edged with a different colour.
[Fr. *picoté*, prickled.]

pictarnie
pik-tär'ni, (*Scott*) n.
a tern.
[Origin unknown.]

picul
pik'ul, n.
a Chinese weight, about 60 kg.
[Malay *pikul*, a man's load.]

piend
pēnd, n.
a salient angle.
[Origin unknown.]

piepowder
pī'pow-dər, (*obs.*) n.
a wayfarer, itinerant.
Court of Piepowder(s) an ancient court held in fairs and markets to administer justice in a rough-and-ready way to all comers — also *Court of Dusty Feet.*
[O.Fr. *piedpoudreux* — *pied* (L. *pēs, pedis*), foot, *poudre* (L. *pulvis*), dust.]

piffero
pif'ə-rō, n.
a fife: an Italian bagpipe: a crude oboe: — pl. **piff'eros.**
n. **pifferaro** (*-ä'rō*) a piffero-player: — pl. **pifferari** (*-rē*).
[It., — O.H.G. *pfīfari*, piper.]

piggin
pig'in, n.
a small pail or bowl of staves and hoops, one stave usually prolonged as a handle: a vessel of various other kinds.

pightle

pī'tl, n.

a small enclosure: a croft.

[Ety. dub.]

pignorate, pignerate

pig'nər-āt, (*arch.*) v.t.

to give or take in pledge or pawn.

n. **pignorā'tion**.

[L. *pignus, -eris* or *-oris*, a pledge.]

pilch

pilch, (*arch.*) n.

an outer garment, orig. a fur cloak, later a coarse leather or woollen cloak: a rug for a saddle: a light saddle: a flannel cloth for wrapping a child.

n. **pilch'er** a scabbard (*Shak.*).

[O.E. *pyl(e)ce* — L.L. *pellicea* — L. *pellis*, skin.]

pilcrow

pil'krō, n.

a paragraph-mark.

[Origin obscure.]

pilliwinks

pil'i-wingks, n.pl.

an instrument of torture for crushing the fingers.

[Origin unknown.]

pindari, pindaree

pin-dä'rē, n.

a mercenary freebooter troublesome in India till 1817.

[Hind. *pindārī*.]

pinnock

pin'ək, (*dial.*) n.

the hedge-sparrow: the blue tit.

[M.E. *pynnuc*.]

pinole

pē-nō'lā, n.

parched Indian corn or other seeds ground and eaten with milk: a mixture of vanilla and aromatic substances in chocolate.

[Sp., — Aztec *pinolli*.]

piolet

pyo-lā', pyō-lā', n.

an ice-axe, spiked staff for climbing or (*obs.*) skiing.

[Fr., — Piedmontese dialect *piola*.]

piou-piou

pū-pū, n.

a French private soldier.

[Fr. slang; perh. *pion*.]

piragua

pi-ra'gwə, -rä', n.

a South American dugout canoe, or a craft with a single trunk as foundation, often a

schooner-rigged barge. — Also **periά'guα,** or (Fr.) **pirogue** (*pi-rōg'*).
[Sp. *piragua* — Carib *piraqua.*]

pirlicue, purlicue
pir', pûr'li-kū, (*Scot.*) n.
a peroration: a résumé in conclusion.
v.t. and v.i. to summarise in conclusion.
[Origin unknown.]

pirn
pûrn, (*Scot.*) *pirn,* n.
a reel, bobbin, or spool.
wind someone α bonny pirn
to set a fine problem for someone, involve someone in difficulties.
[Origin unknown.]

pirnie
pir'ni, (*Scot.*) adj.
unevenly wrought: striped.
n. (*Scot.*) a striped woollen nightcap.
adj. **pirn'it** (*Scot.*) interwoven with different colours: striped.
[App. conn. with **pirn.**]

pirozhki
pē-rozh'ke, **piroshke**
pē-rosh'kē, ns.pl.
small, triangular pastries with meat, fish, vegetable, etc. fillings.
[Russ., little pies.]

pistareen
pis-tə-rēn', n.
an old Spanish two-real piece formerly current in the United States.

pithos
pith'os, n.
a large Greek storage-jar.
[Gr.]

pium
pi-ōōm', n.
a small but very troublesome Brazilian biting fly.
[Tupí.]

placer
plas'ər, plās'ər, n.
a superficial deposit from which gold or other mineral can be washed.
plac'er-gold.
[Sp. *placer,* sandbank — *plaza,* place.]

plack
plak, n.
an old Scottish copper coin worth a third part of an English penny of the same period.
adj. **plack'less.**
[Prob. Flem. *placke,* an old Flemish coin, orig. a flat disc.]

plagium

plā'ji-əm, n.

the crime of kidnapping.

[L. *plăgium — plăga,* a net.]

planxty

plangks'ti, n.

an Irish dance or dance-tune, like a jig but slower.

[Origin unknown; not native Irish.]

plateasm

plat'i-azm, n.

pronunciation with a wide mouth-opening, as in Doric Greek.

[Gr. *plateiasmos — platys,* broad.]

platysma

plat-iz'mə, n.

a broad sheet of muscle in the neck.

[Gr. *platysma,* a flat piece.]

playa

plä'yə, n.

a basin which becomes a shallow lake after heavy rainfall and dries out again in hot weather.

[Sp.]

pledget

plej'it, n.

a wad of lint, cotton, etc., as for a wound or sore: an oakum string used in caulking.

[Origin unknown.]

pliskie

plis'ki, (*Scot.*) n.

condition or plight: a mischievous trick.

[Origin unknown.]

pluteus

plōō'ti-əs, n.

a sea-urchin or brittle-star larva, shaped like a many-legged easel.

adj. **plu'teal.**

[L. *pluteus,* a shed, boarding, desk.]

poaka

pō-ä'kə, (*Maori*) n.

a N.Z. bird, one of the stilts.

pochoir

posh'wär, n.

a form of colour stencilling, by hand, on to a printed illustration.

[Fr., stencil.]

podagra

pod-ag'rə, also *po',* n.

gout, properly in the feet.

adjs. **podag'ral, podag'ric, -al, podag'rous** gouty.

[Gr. *podagrā* — *pous, podos,* foot, *agrā,* a catching.]

podley
pod'li, (*Scot.*) n.
a young coalfish.

podsol, podzol
pod-zol', pod'-, n.
any of a group of soils characterised by a greyish-white leached and infertile topsoil and a brown subsoil, typical of regions with a subpolar climate.
adj. **podsol'ic.**
[Russ., — *pod,* under, *zola,* ash.]

pogge
pog, n.
the armed bullhead (*Agonus cataphractus*), a bony-plated fish.
[Origin unknown.]

pogonotomy
pō-gō-not'ə-mi, n.
shaving.
[Gr. *pōgōn, pōgōnos,* beard, *tomē,* a cutting.]

poi
pō'ē, n.
a Hawaiian dish, a paste of fermented taro root.
[Hawaiian.]

poitrel
poi'trəl, n.
armour for a horse's breast.
[O.Fr. *poitral* — L. *pectorāle,* a breastplate — *pectus, -oris,* the breast.]

pokal
pō-käl', n.
an ornamental drinking-vessel.
[Ger., — It. *boccale* — Gr. *baukălis,* a vessel for cooling wine, etc.]

polacca
po-lak'ə, n.
a three-masted Mediterranean vessel, with fore and main masts each in one piece (also **polacre** *po-lä'kər*): a polonaise, or composition in the manner of a polonaise.
[It. *polacca, polacra,* Polish (fem.); Fr. *polacre*: application to the vessel not explained.]

poley
pō'li, (*Austr.*) adj.
hornless. — Also n.

poleyn
pō'lān, n.
a piece of armour protecting the knee.
[M.E., — O.Fr. *polain.*]

pollan

pol'ən, n.

an Irish whitefish, esp. that (*Coregonus pollan*) found in Lough Neagh.

[Perh. Ir. *poll*, lake; cf. **powan**.]

pollent

pol'ənt, adj.

strong.

[L. *pollēns, -entis*, pr.p. of *pollēre*, to be strong.]

pollex

pol'eks, n.

the thumb or its analogue: — pl. **pollices** (*pol'i-sēz*).
adj. **poll'ical.**

[L. *pollex, -icis.*]

pollicitation

pol-is-i-tā'shən, n.

a promise: a promise which has not yet been accepted.

[L. *pollicitātiō, -ōnis.*]

polverine

pol'vər-ēn, (*obs.*) n.

glass-makers' potash.

[It. *polverino* — L. *pulvis, pulvĕris*, dust.]

polynia, polynya

pol-in'i-ə, -in'yə, n.

open water among sea ice, esp. Arctic.

[Russ. *polyn'ya.*]

pomace

pum'is, n.

crushed apples for cider-making, or the residue after pressing: anything crushed to pulp, esp. after oil has been expressed.

pom'ace-fly a fruit-fly (Drosophila).

[App. L.L. *pōmācium*, cider — L. *pōmum*, apple, etc.]

Pomak

pō-mäk', n.

a Bulgarian Muslim.

pombe

pom'be, n.

any of various Central and East African alcoholic drinks.

[Swahili.]

pomfret

pom'frit, n.

any of several fishes, including an East Indian fish valued as food.

[Earlier *pamflet* — Fr. *pample* — Port. *pampo.*]

pomoerium

pō-mē'ri-əm, n.

an open space around a town, within and without the walls.

[L. *pōmoerium*, app. for *postmoerium* — *post* and *moiros*, old form of *mūrus*, wall.]

pongee
pun-, pon-jē′, n.
a soft silk, made from cocoons
of a wild silkworm: a fine cotton.
[Perh. Chin. *pun-chī*, own
loom.]

poon
pōōn, n.
an Indian tree, *Calophyllum
inophyllum*, or other species of
the genus (family Guttiferae).
poon′-oil an oil expressed
from its seeds; **poon′-wood**.
[Sinh. *pūna*.]

poonac
pōō′nak, n.
coconut oil-cake.
[Sinh. *punakku*.]

poort
pōrt, pōōrt, (S.Afr.) n.
a mountain pass.
[Du., — L. *porta*, gate.]

poorwill
pōōr′wil, n.
a Western North American
nightjar (*Phalaenoptilus*),
smaller than the whippoorwill.
[From its note.]

popliteal
pop-lit′i-əl,
often *pop-lit-ē′əl*, adj. of the
back of the knee. — Also

poplit′ic.
[L. *poples, -itis.*]

poppering
pop′ər-ing, **poperin** *-in*, ns.
a variety of pear. — Also
poppering pear (*Shak.*
pop′rin).
[*Poperinghe* in Belgium.]

porosis
pō-rō′sis, pö-, n.
formation of callus, the knitting
together of broken bones: — pl.
poro′ses.
[Gr. *pōrōsis* — *pōros*, callus.]

porraceous
por-ā′shəs, adj.
leek-green.
[L. *porrāceus* — *porrum*, a
leek.]

porrigo
por-ī′gō, n.
scalp disease of various kinds:
— pl. **porri′gos**.
adj. **porriginous** (*-ij′*).
[L. *porrīgō, -inis*, dandruff.]

portlast
pōrt′, pört′ləst, (obs. naut.) n.
probably the gunwale. — Also
portoise (*pōrt′, pört′iz*) and
wrongly **port′land**.
yards down a portlast with
yards down on or near the
deck.
[Origin unknown.]

portolano

pör-tə-lä′nō, n.

in the Middle Ages, a navigation manual giving sailing directions and illustrated with charts showing ports, coastal features, etc.: — pl. **portola′nos, -ni** (*-nē*). — Also **portolan, portulan (chart)** (*por′tə-lən, -tū-*).

[It., navigation manual, harbour-master.]

posaune

pō-zow′nə, n.

the trombone.

[Ger.]

posnet

pos′nit, n.

a small cooking-pot with feet and handle.

[O.Fr. *pocenet*.]

posteen

pos-tēn′, n.

an Afghan greatcoat, generally of sheepskin with the fleece on. — Also (*erron.*) **poshteen′**.

[Pers. *postī*, leather.]

posticous

pos-tī′kəs, (*bot.*) adj.

posterior: outward, extrorse.

[L. *postīcus*, hinder — *post*.]

postil

pos′til, n.

a marginal note, esp. in the Bible: a commentary: a homily: a book of homilies.

v.t. and v.i. to gloss.

v.t. and v.i. **pos′tillate**.

ns. **postillā′tion; pos′tillātor; pos′tiller**.

[O.Fr. *postille* (It. *postilla*) — L.L. *postilla*, possibly — L. *post illa* (*verba*), after those (words).]

postliminy

pōst-lim′i-ni, n.

the right of a returned exile, prisoner, etc., to resume his former status: the right by which persons or things taken in war are restored to their former status.

adj. **postlimin′iary**.

[L. *postlīminium*, lit. return behind the threshold — *līmen, -inis*, threshold.]

potiche

po-tēsh′, n.

an Oriental vase rounded or polygonal in shape, narrowing at the neck.

n. **potichomania**

(*-shō-mā′ni-ə*) a craze for imitating Oriental porcelain by lining glass vessels with paper designs, etc.

[Fr. *potiche, potichomanie*.]

potin

pot-ɛ̃', n.

an old alloy of copper, zinc, lead, and tin.

[Fr.]

potoroo

pōt-ə-rōō', *pot-*, n.

a small marsupial akin to the kangaroo, a rat-kangaroo.

[Aboriginal.]

potto

pot'ō, n.

a member of a West African genus (Perodicticus) of lemurs: also applied to the kinkajou: — pl. **pott'os.**

[Said to be a West African name.]

poulaine

pōō-lān', n.

a long, pointed shoe-toe.

[O.Fr. (*à la*) *Poulaine*, (in the fashion of) Poland.]

poulp, poulpe

pōōlp, n.

the octopus.

[Fr. *poulpe* — L. *pōlypus* — Doric Gr. *pōlypos = polypous*.]

pourpoint

pōōr'point, n.

a mediaeval quilted doublet.

[Fr.]

poussette

pōōs-et', n.

a figure in country-dancing in which couples hold both hands and move up or down the set, changing places with the next couple.

v.i. to perform a poussette.

[Fr., dim. of *pousse*, push.]

powan

pow'ən, *pō'ən*, n.

a species of whitefish (Coregonus) found in Loch Lomond and Loch Eck.

[Scots form of **pollan.**]

powsowdy

pow-sow'di, (*Scot.*) n.

any mixture of heterogeneous kinds of food. — Also **pousow'die.**

[Origin unknown.]

prad

prad, (*slang*) n.

a horse.

[Du. *paard* — L.L. *paraverēdus*.]

praedial, predial

prē'di-əl, adj.

pertaining to, connected with, or derived from, the land: landed: rural: agrarian: attached to the land.

n. a praedial slave.

[L.L. *praediālis* — *praedium*, an estate.]

prase

prāz, n.

a leek-green quartz.

[Gr. *prason*, leek.]

pratincole

prat'ing-kōl, n.

a bird akin to the plovers, with swallow-like wings and tail.

[L. *prātum*, meadow, *incola*, an inhabitant.]

prau

prä'ōō, prow, **prahu** *prä'(h)ōō*, **proa** *prō'ə*, ns.

a Malay sailing- or rowing-boat, esp. a fast sailing-vessel with both ends alike, and a flat side with an outrigger kept to leeward.

[Malay *prāū*.]

premorse

pri-mörs', adj.

ending abruptly, as if bitten off.

[L. *praemorsus*, bitten in front — *prae*, *mordēre*, *morsum*, to bite.]

primage

prīm'ij, n.

a payment, in addition to freight, made by shippers for loading, originally a gratuity to captain and crew, afterwards made to owners.

[Anglo-L. *primāgium*.]

primero

pri-mā'rō, n.

an old card-game.

[Sp. *primera*.]

prisage

prī'zij, n.

the former right of the English kings to two tuns of wine from every ship importing twenty tuns or more.

[O.Fr. *prise*, taking.]

proairesis

prō-ā'ri-sis, or -ī', n.

the act of choosing.

[Gr. *proairesis*.]

probang

prō'bang, n.

an instrument for pushing obstructions down the oesophagus.

[Called *provang* by its inventor, the Welsh judge, Walter Rumsey (1584–1660); origin unknown; prob. influenced by **probe**.]

probouleutic

prō-bōō-lū'tik, adj.

for preliminary deliberation.

[Gr. *probouleusis*, preliminary deliberation.]

procoelous

prō-sē'ləs, adj.

cupped in front.

[Gr. *pro*, before, *koilos*, hollow.]

progeria

prō-jer'i-ə, n.

a rare disease causing premature ageing in children.

[Gr. *pro*, before, *gēras*, old age.]

prolonge

prō-lonj', n.

a rope for a gun-carriage.

[Fr.]

pronaos

prō-nā'os, n.

the vestibule in front of a temple: — pl. **prona'oi.**

[Gr. *prŏnāos* — *pro*, before, *nāos*, a temple.]

propine

prə-pīn', (chiefly *Scot.*, *arch.*) v.t.

to pledge in drinking: to present, offer.

n. a tip: a gift.

[L. *propīnāre* — Gr. *propīnein*, to drink first — *pro*, before, *pīnein*, to drink.]

propolis

prop'ə-lis, n.

bee-glue, a brown sticky resinous substance gathered by bees from trees and used by them as cement and varnish.

[Gr. *propolis*.]

prore

prōr, *prör*, (*poet.*) n.

a prow: a ship.

[Obs. Fr., — L. *prōra*, prow — Gr. *prōiră*.]

proseuche, -cha

pros-ū'kē, *-kə*, ns.

a place of prayer, oratory: — pl. **proseu'chae** (*-kē*).

[Gr. *proseuchē*, prayer, place of prayer — *pros*, to, *euchē*, prayer.]

proslambanomenos

pros-lam-ban-om'e-nos, (*anc. Gr. mus.*) n.

an additional note at the bottom of the scale.

[Gr., pr.p. pass. of *proslambanein*, to take in addition — pfx. *pros-*, *lambanein*, to take.]

protanopia

prō-tən-op'i-ə, n.

a form of colour-blindness in which red and green are confused because the retina does not respond to red.

n. **prō′tanope** a sufferer from protanopia.
adj. **prōtanop′ic** colour-blind to red.
[Mod. L. *protanopia*.]

protervity
prō-tûr′vi-ti, n.
peevishness: perversity: wantonness.
[L. *prōtervus, prŏtervus*.]

proveditor
prō-ved′i-tər, **provedor(e), providor** *prov-i-dōr′, -dör′*, ns.
a high official, governor, inspector, commissioner: a purveyor.
[It. *provveditore*, Port. *provedor*, Sp. *proveedor*.]

prozymite
proz′i-mīt, n.
one who uses leavened bread in the eucharist — opp. to *azymite*.
[Gr. *prozȳmia*, ferments.]

pruina
prōō-ī′nə, (*bot.*) n.
a powdery bloom or waxy secretion.
adj. **pruinose** (*prōō′i-nōs*) covered with pruina: having a frosted look.
[L. *pruīna*, hoar-frost.]

prunt
prunt, n.
a moulded glass ornament on glass: a tool for making it.
adj. **prunt′ed.**
[Origin uncertain.]

pryse
prīz, (*Scott*) n.
a horn-blast at the taking or killing of a deer.
[O.Fr. *pris*, taken.]

prytaneum
prit-an-ē′əm, (*ant.*) n.
the town-hall of an ancient Greek city: — pl. **prytanē′a.**
[Latinised from Gr. *prytaneion* — *prytanis*, a presiding magistrate.]

psammite
sam′īt, (*rare*) n.
any rock composed of sandgrains.
adj. **psammitic** (*-it′ik*).
n. **psamm′ophil(e)** a sand-loving plant.
adj. **psammoph′ilous.**
n. **psamm′ophyte** (*-ō-fīt*) a plant that grows only on sand.
adj. **psammophytic** (*-fit′ik*).
[Gr. *psammos*, sand.]

psoas
(p)sō′əs, n.
a muscle of the loins and pelvis: the tenderloin.

[Gr. (pl.) *psoai*, the accus. *psoās* being mistaken for a nom. sing.]

psychrophilic

sī-krō-fil'ik, (*bot.*) adj.
growing best at low temperatures.
[Gr. *psȳchros*, cold, *phileein*, to love.]

ptarmic

(p)tär'mik, n.
a substance that causes sneezing.
[Gr. *ptarmos*, a sneeze.]

pterin

(p)ter'in, n.
any of a group of substances occurring as pigments in butterfly wings, important in biochemistry.
ns. **pteroic** ((*p*) *ter-ō'ik*) **acid** the original folic acid found in spinach; **pteroylglutamic** ((*p*)*ter'ō-il-glōō-tam'ik*) **acid** the folic acid that is therapeutically active in pernicious anaemia.
[Gr. *pteron*, a wing.]

ptilosis

til-ō'sis, n.
plumage or mode of feathering.
[Gr. *ptĭlōsis* — *ptilon,* a down feather.]

ptochocracy

(p)tō-kok'rə-si, n.
the rule of beggars or paupers — wholesale pauperisation.
[Gr. *ptōchos*, a beggar, *kratos*, power.]

ptosis

(p)tō'sis, n.
downward displacement: drooping of the upper eyelid: — pl. **ptō'ses** (*-sēz*).
[Gr. *ptōsis* — *piptein*, to fall.]

puccoon

puk-ōōn', n.
bloodroot: extended to species of gromwell and other American plants yielding pigments.
[Virginian Indian name.]

puja

pōō'jə, n.
worship: reverential observance: a festival.
[Sans. *pūjā*, worship.]

pulka

pul'kə, n.
a Laplander's boat-shaped sledge. — Also **pulk, pulk'ha**.
[Finnish *pulkka*, Lappish *pulkke, bulkke*.]

pulque

pōōl'kā, -kē, n.

a fermented drink made in Mexico from agave sap.

[Amer. Sp.]

pultun, pultan, pulton, pultoon

pul'tun, -tən, -tōōn, ns.

an Indian infantry regiment.

[Hind. *pultan* — Eng. **battalion.**]

pulu

pōō'lōō, n.

a silky fibre from the Hawaiian tree-fern leaf-bases.

[Hawaiian.]

pulvil

pul'vil, n.

perfumed powder: extended to snuff and other powders. — Also **pulvil'io, pulvill'io** (pl. **pulvil(l)'ios), pulville'.**
v.t. **pul'vil** to powder or scent with pulvil: — pa.t. and pa.p. **pul'villed.**
adj. **pul'vilised, -ized.**

[It. *polviglio* — *polve*, powder — L. *pulvis*.]

pulwar

pul'wär, n.

a light keelless boat used on the Ganges.

[Hind. *palwār*.]

puna

pōōn'ə, n.

bleak tableland in the Andes: cold wind there: mountain sickness.

[Amer. Sp., — Quechua.]

punalua

pōō-nə-lōō'ə, n.

a system of group marriage, sisters (by blood or tribal reckoning) having their husbands in common, or brothers their wives, or both. adj. **punalu'an.**

[Hawaiian.]

pundigrion

pun-dig'ri-on, (obs.) n.

a pun.

[Origin unknown; It. *puntiglio* is only a conjecture.]

pundonor

pōōn-dō-nōr', -nör', n.

point of honour: — pl. **pundonor'es** (*-ās*).

[Sp., — *punto de honor.*]

punty, puntee, pontie, ponty

pun'ti, **pontil** *pon'til*, ns.

an iron rod used in holding and manipulating glassware during the process of making.

[Prob. Fr. *pontil*, app. — It. *pontello, puntello*, dim. of *punto*, point.]

pupunha

pōō-pōōn'yə, n.

the peach-palm: its fruit.

[Port. from Tupí.]

purdonium

pûr-dō'ni-əm, n.

a kind of coal-scuttle introduced by one *Purdon.*

purfle

pûr'fl, v.t.

to ornament the edge of, as with embroidery or inlay.

n. a decorated border: a profile (*obs.*).

n. **pur'fling** a purfle, esp. around the edges of a fiddle.

[O.Fr. *pourfiler* — L. *prō*, before, *fīlum*, a thread.]

purpresture

pûr-pres'chər, n.

encroachment upon public property.

[O.Fr. *purpresture* — *pour*, for (L. *pro*), *prendre* — L. *praehendĕre*, to take.]

puteli

put'e-lē, n.

a flat-bottomed Ganges craft.

[Hindi *paṭelī*.]

putlog

put'log, **putlock** *-lok*, ns.

a cross-piece in a scaffolding, the inner end resting in a hole left in the wall.

[Origin obscure; **putlock** seems to be the older form.]

putois

pü-twä', n.

a brush of polecat's hair, or substitute, for painting pottery.

[Fr.]

puttock

put'ək, n.

a kite (*Shak.*): a buzzard: a kite-like person.

[M.E. *puttok*, perh. conn. with O.E. *pyttel*, kite.]

puture

pū'tyər, **pulture** *pul'*, (*hist.*) ns.

the claim of foresters, etc., to food for man, horse, and dog within the bounds of a forest.

[A.Fr. *puture*, Old Northern Fr. *pulture* — L.L. *pu(l)tūra*, app. — L. *puls*, *pultis*, porridge.]

pyot, pyat, pyet, piet

pī"ət, (*Scot.*) n.

a magpie.

adj. pied.

adj. **pi'oted.**

pyroballogy

pī-rō-bal'ə-ji, (*Sterne*) n.

the science of artillery.

[Gr. *pȳr*, fire, *ballein*, to throw, *logos*, discourse.]

pyrrhous

pir'əs, adj.

reddish.

[Gr. *pyrros*, flame-coloured —
pȳr, fire.]

pythogenic

pī-thō-jen'ik, adj.

produced by filth.

[Gr. *pȳthein*, to rot, root of
gignesthai, to become.]

Q

qanat
kä-nät', n.
an underground tunnel for carrying irrigation water.
[Ar. *qanāt,* pipe.]

qintar
kin-tär', n.
an Albanian unit of currency equal to one hundredth of a lek.
[Albanian.]

quagga
kwag'ə, n.
an extinct S. African wild ass (*Equus quagga*), less fully striped than the zebras, to which it was related.
[Perh. Hottentot *quacha*.]

quandong
kwan' or *kwon'dong,* n.
a small Australian tree (*Santalum acuminatum*) of the sandalwood family; its edible drupe (*native peach*) or edible kernel (**quan'dong-nut**): an Australian tree (*Elaeocarpus grandis*) (**silver, blue** or **brush quandong**): a disreputable person (*Austr. coll.*). — Also **quan'dang, quan'tong.**
[Aboriginal.]

quannet
kwon'it, n.
a file mounted like a plane.
[Origin unknown.]

quant
kwant, n.
a punting or jumping pole, with a flat cap.
v.t. to punt.
[Poss. conn. with L. *contus*, Gr. *kontos.*]

quarrender, quarender
kwor'ən-dər, **quarantine, quarenden, quarrington**
-ən-tin, -dən, -ing-tən, (*S.W. England*) ns.
a kind of red apple.
[Origin unknown.]

quat
kwot, n.
a pimple: an insignificant person (*Shak.*).
[Origin unknown.]

queach
kwēch, (*obs.*) n.
a thicket.
adj. **queach'y, queech'y**
forming a thicket: boggy: sickly.
[Origin obscure.]

quebracho

kā-brä′chō, n.

name of several S. American
trees yielding very hard wood
(*white quebracho*,
Aspidosperma — fam.
Apocynaceae; *red quebracho*,
Schinopsis — fam.
Anacardiaceae): their wood or
bark: — pl. **quebra′chos.**

[Sp., — *quebrar*, to break,
hacha, axe.]

quersprung

kver′shprōōng, n.

in skiing, a jump-turn at right
angles.

[Ger.]

quey

kwā, (*Scot.*) n.

a heifer: a young cow that has
not yet had a calf.

[O.N. *kvīga*; Dan. *kvie.*]

quiddany

kwid′ə-ni, n.

a confection of quince-juice and
sugar.

[L. *cotōnea*, quince —
cydōnia.]

quiddle

kwid′l, (*dial.*) v.i.

to trifle.

ns. **quidd′le** a fastidious
person; **quidd′ler.**

qui-hi, -hye

kwī′-hī′, n.

an Englishman in India, esp. in
Bengal, in colonial days.

[Hind. *koī hai*, the call for a
servant, Is anyone there? —
koī, anyone, *hai*, is.]

quillai

ki-lī′, n.

the soap-bark tree.

n. **Quillaja, Quillaia** *(ki-lī′ə,
-lē′ə)* a genus of S. American
rosaceous trees whose bark
has soaplike properties:
(without *cap.*) a tree of this
genus, a quillai.

[Amer. Sp.]

quillon

kē-yō̄, n.

either arm of the cross-guard of
a sword-handle.

[Fr.]

quinnat

kwin′ət, n.

the king-salmon.

[From an Amer. Ind. name.]

quokka

kwok′ə, n.

a small marsupial, *Setonix
brachyurus*, found in W.
Australia.

[Aboriginal.]

quoll
kwol, n.
a small Australian marsupial
(*Dasyurus macrurus*).
[Aboriginal.]

quop
kwop, (*obs.* or *dial*) v.i.
to throb.
[M.E. *quappe*; imit.]

R

rabanna
rə-ban'ə, n.
a Madagascan raffia fabric.
[Malagasy.]

rabbet
rab'it, n.
a groove cut to receive an edge.
v.t. to groove: to join by a rabbet: — pr.p. **rabb'eting;** pa.t. and pa.p. **rabb'eted.**
rabb'eting-machine',
-plane, -saw; rabb'et-joint.
[Fr. *rabat — rabattre,* to beat back.]

rabi
rub'ē, n.
the spring grain harvest in India, Pakistan, etc.
[Ar. *rabī',* spring.]

raca
rä'kə, (B.) adj.
worthless.
[Chaldee *rēkā* (a term of reproach).]

rac(c)ahout
rak'ə-hōōt, n.
acorn meal.
[Fr., — Ar. *rāqaut.*]

rache,
also **rach, ratch,** *rach,* n.
a dog that hunts by scent.
[O.E. *racc,* setter; O.N. *rakki.*]

racon
rā'kon, n.
a radar beacon.
[*ra*dar, bea*con.*]

rafale
rä-fäl', n.
a burst of artillery in quick rounds.
[Fr., gust of wind.]

raggle
rag'l, (Scot.) n.
a groove in masonry, esp. to receive the edge of a roof.
v.t. to make a raggle in.
[Origin obscure.]

ragi, ra(g)gee, raggy
rä'gē, rag'i, n.
a millet (*Eleusine coracana*) much grown in India, Africa, etc.
[Hind. (and Sans.) *rāgī.*]

raguly
rag'ū-li, (*her.*) adj.
with projections like oblique
stubs of branches. — Also
rag'ūled.
[Origin obscure.]

raik
rāk, n.
course, journey: range: pasture.
v.i. to go: to range.
[O.N. *reik* (n.), *reika* (vb.) walk.]

rakshas, rakshasa
räk'shəs, -ə, (*Hindu myth.*) ns.
an evil spirit.
[Sans *rākṣasa.*]

rambutan
ram-bōō'tən, n.
a lofty Malayan tree (*Nephelium
lappaceum*), akin to the longan:
its hairy edible fruit.
[Malay *rambūtan* — *rambut,*
hair.]

ramfeezle
ram-fē'zl, (*Scot.*) v.t.
to weary out.

rampick
ram'pik, **rampike** *-pīk,* (*arch.
and U.S.*) ns.
a dead tree, or one decayed at
the top, broken off, or partly
burned.
adjs. **ram'pick, -ed.**
[Origin obscure.]

random
ran'dəm, n., adj., and adv.
tandem with three horses.

ranzel
ran'zl, **rancel, -sel** *-sl,* ns.
formerly in Orkney and
Shetland a search for stolen
goods.
ran'zelman, etc. (*Scott
Ran'zellaar*) an official who
did this.
[O.Scot. *ransell;* O.N.
rannsaka.]

raploch
rap'lohh, (*Scot.*) n. and adj.
homespun.
[Origin unknown.]

rapparee
rap-ər-ē', n.
a wild Irish plunderer, orig. of
the late 17th. cent.
[Ir. *rapaire,* half-pike, robber.]

rappee
ra-pē', n.
a coarse, strong-flavoured
snuff.
[Fr. *râpé,* rasped, grated —
râper, to rasp.]

rasse
ras'(ə), n.
a small civet, *Viverricula indica.*
[Jav. *rase.*]

238

rastrum

ras'trəm, n.

a music-pen.

[L. *rāstrum,* rake.]

ratine, ratteen

rat-ēn', n.

a rough, open dress-fabric. — Also **rat'iné** (*-i-nā*; Fr. *ratiner,* to frieze, put a nap on).

[Fr. *ratine.*]

ratoon

rat-, rət-ōōn', n.

a new shoot from the ground after cropping, esp. of sugar-cane or cotton.

v.i. to send up ratoons.

v.t. to cut down so as to obtain ratoons.

n. **ratoon'er** a plant that ratoons.

[Sp. *retoño,* shoot.]

rayah

rī'a, n.

a non-Muslim subject of Turkey.

[Ar. *ra'īyah — ra'ā,* to pasture.]

razee

rā-zē', n.

a ship cut down by reducing the number of decks.

v.t. to remove the upper deck(s) of.

[Fr. *rasé,* cut down.]

razzia

raz'ya, n.

a pillaging incursion.

[Fr., — Algerian Ar. *ghāzīah.*]

reate

rēt, n.

water-crowfoot.

[Origin obscure.]

rebato

rə-bä'tō, (*Shak.*) n.

a stiff collar or support for a ruff: — pl. **reba'toes.** — Also **reba'ter, raba'to** (pl. **raba'toes**).

[Fr. *rabat.*]

recheat

ri-chēt', **rechate** *ri-chāt',* (*Shak.*) ns.

a horn-call to assemble hounds.

v.i. to sound the recheat.

[O.Fr. *racheter, rachater,* to reassemble.]

reckling

rek'ling, n.

the weakest, smallest, or youngest of a litter or family.

adj. puny.

[Origin obscure; poss. from O.N. *reklingr,* an outcast.]

239

redan

ri-dan', (*fort.*) n.

a fieldwork of two faces forming a salient.

[O.Fr. *redan* — L. *re-*, *dēns*, *dentis*, a tooth.]

redargue

ri-där'gū, (*obs.* or *Scot.*) v.t.

to refute: to confute.

[L. *redarguēre* — *re(d)-*, again, *arguĕre*, argue.]

redowa

red'ō-va, n.

a Bohemian dance: music for it, usually in quick triple time.

[Ger. or Fr., — Czech *rejdovák*.]

redshort

red'shört, adj.

brittle at red-heat. — Also **red'sear, -share, -shire**.

[Sw. *rödskör* — *röd*, red, *skör*, brittle.]

refel

ri-fel', (*obs.*) v.t.

to refute: to disprove: to confute: to repulse: — pr.p. **refell'ing**; pa.t. and pa.p. **refelled'**.

[L. *refellĕre* — *fallĕre*, to deceive.]

refocillate

ri-fos'il-āt, (*obs.*) v.t.

to refresh, cherish.

n. **refocillā'tion**.

[L. *refocillāre*, *-ātum*, to cherish — *focus*, a hearth.]

regrate

ri-grāt', (*hist.*) v.t.

to buy and sell again in or near the same market, thus raising the price — once a criminal offence in England.

ns. **regrā'ter, -tor** one who regrates (*hist.*): a middleman (*S.W. England*); **regrā'ting**.

[O.Fr. *regrater*, of doubtful origin.]

regur, regar

rā', *rē'gər*, n.

the rich black cotton soil of India, full of organic matter.

[Hind. *regar*.]

reh

rā, n.

an efflorescence of sodium salts on the soil in India.

[Hindustani.]

reim-kennar

rīm'ken-ər, n.

an enchanter, enchantress.

[App. invented by Scott — Ger. *Reim*, rhyme, *Kenner*, knower.]

remblai

rã-ble, n.

earth used to form a rampart, embankment, etc.: stowage in a mine.

[Fr.]

remuda

ri-mū'də, rã-mōō'dha, n.

a supply of remounts.

[Sp., exchange.]

repechage

rep'ə-shäzh, Fr. *rə-pesh-äzh,* (*rowing, fencing*, etc.) adj.

pertaining to a supplementary competition in which second-bests in earlier eliminating competitions get a second chance to go on to the final.

[Fr. *repêchage,* a fishing out again.]

reptation

rep-tā'shən, n.

squirming along, or up, a smooth-walled narrow passage. adj. **rep'tant** (*biol.*)

[L. reptāre, to creep.]

reremouse, rearmouse

rēr'mows, n.

a bat: — pl. **rere'-, rear'mice.**

[O.E. *hrēremūs,* app. — *hrēran,* to move, *mūs,* a mouse.]

retree

ri-trē', n.

slightly damaged paper.

[Perh. Fr. *retret, retrait.*]

retund

ri-tund', v.t.

to blunt.

[L. *retundĕre,* to blunt.]

revalenta

rev-ə-len'tə, n.

lentil-meal. — Earlier **ervalen'ta.**

[*Ervum lens,* Linnaean name of the lentil — L. *ervum,* bitter vetch, *lēns, lentis,* lentil.]

rhapontic

ra-pon'tik, n.

ordinary kitchen-garden rhubarb.

[L.L. *rhā ponticum,* Pontic rhubarb.]

rhexis

reks'is, n.

rupture, esp. of a blood-vessel.

[Gr. *rhēxis,* breach.]

rhipidate

rip'i-dāt, adj.

fan-shaped.

ns. **rhipid'ion** in the Greek Church, the eucharistic fan or flabellum; **rhipid'ium** a fan-shaped cymose

inflorescence. — *ns.pl.*
Rhipip'tera, Rhipidop'tera
the Strepsiptera.
[Gr. *rhīpis, rhīpidos,* a fan.]

rhodora

rō-dō'rə, -dö', n.

a handsome N. American
species of Rhododendron, or
separate kindred genus.
[L. *rhodōra,* meadow-sweet,
said to be a Gallic plant-name.]

rhopalic

rō-pal'ik, adj.

of a verse, having each word a
syllable longer than the one
before.
n. **rhō'palism.**

[Gr. *rhopalikos,* club-like,
rhopalon, a club.]

rhyton

rī'ton, n.

a drinking-cup or pottery horn
(Greek, etc.) with a hole in the
point to drink by: — pl. **rhy'ta.**
[Gr. *rhўton,* neut. of *rhўtos,*
flowing.]

ria

rē'ə, (*geol.*) n.

a normal drowned valley.
[Sp. *ría,* river-mouth.]

ricin

rī'sin, ris', n.

a highly toxic albumin found in
the beans of the castor-oil plant.

ricker

rik'ər, n.

a spar or young tree-trunk.
[Perh. Ger. *Rick,* pole.]

ridotto

ri-dot'ō, n.

a public dancing-party: — pl.
ridott'os.
[It.]

riel

rē'əl, n.

the basic monetary unit of
Kampuchea.

riem

rēm, n.

a raw-hide thong.
n. **riempie** (*rēm'pē;* dim. of
riem) a long riem about the
width of a shoe-lace, used as
string, for the weaving of
chair-backs and seats, etc.
[Afrik.]

riffler

rif'lər, n.

a small file with curved ends
used by sculptors, wood- or
metal-workers, etc., for intricate
work.
[Fr. *rifloir,* from *rifler,* to scrape,
file.]

rigol, rigoll

rig'əl, n.

a gutter or water-channel: a groove, esp. an encircling groove: a circlet (*Shak.*).

[Fr. *rigole*, gutter, groove.]

rimu

rē'mōō, n.

a coniferous tree of New Zealand, *Dacrydium cupressinum.*

[Maori.]

ringent

rin'jənt, adj.

gaping.

[L. *ringēns, -entis*, pr.p. of *ringī*.]

ringgit

ring'git, n.

the unit of currency of Malaysia, comprising 100 sen.

[Malay.]

ringhals

ring'hals, **rinkhals** *ringk'(h)als*, ns.

a Southern African snake, *Haemachatus haemachatus,* which spits or sprays its venom at its victims.

[Afrik. *ring*, a ring, *hals*, a neck.]

rip-rap, riprap

rip'rap, n.

loose broken stones, used to form a foundation on soft ground or under water, or in the construction of revetments and embankments: a foundation formed of these.

[From an obs. word imit. of the sound of repeated blows.]

rispetto

rēs-pet'ō, n.

a type of Italian folk-song with eight-line stanzas, or a piece of music written in the same style: — pl. **rispet'ti** (*-tē*).

[It.]

robalo

rob'ə-lō, n.

an American pike-like fish (*Centropomus*), of a family akin to the sea-perches: — pl. **rob'alos.**

[Sp. *róbalo*, bass.]

roberdsman

rob'ərdz-man, (*obs.*) n.

a stout robber. — Also **rob'ertsman.**

[App. from *Robert*; allusion unknown.]

roborant

rob'ər-ənt, n.

a strengthening drug or tonic. — Also adj.

[L. *rōborāns, -antis*, pr.p. of
rōborāre, to strengthen,
invigorate.]

rocambole

rok'əm-bōl, n.

a plant close akin to garlic.

[Fr.]

rochet

roch'it, n.

a mantle (*obs.*): a close-fitting
surplice-like vestment proper to
bishops and abbots.

[O.Fr., of Gmc. origin; cf. Ger.
Rock, O.E. *rocc*.]

rockaway

rok'ə-wā, n.

an American four-wheeled
pleasure carriage, formerly
made at *Rockaway,* New
Jersey.

roke

rōk, n.

a vapour: steam: mist: small
rain: smoke.
v.t. and v.i. to steam: to smoke.
adj. **rōk'y.**

[Perh. Scand.]

rokelay, rocklay

rok'(ə)-lā, (*Scot.*) ns.

a woman's short cloak, worn in
the 18th century.

[Fr. *roquelaire*; see
roquelaure.]

roker

rōk'ər, n.

any ray other than skate, esp.
the thornback.

[Perh. Dan. *rokke*, Sw. *rocka*,
ray.]

romal

rō-mäl', **rumal** *rōō-mäl'*, ns.

a handkerchief: a head-cloth.

[Pers. *rūmāl*.]

rondavel

ron-dav'əl, ron', n.

in S. Africa, a round hut, usu.
with grass roof: a more
sophisticated building of similar
shape, used e.g. as guest
house.

[Afrik. *rondawel*.]

roon

rōōn, **rund** *run(d), rōōn(d),
røn(d),* (*Scot.*) ns.

a list or selvage: a strip or
thread of cloth. — Also (*Galt*)
royne (*roin*).

[Origin obscure.]

roose

rōōz, (*Scot.*) *rüz*, (*dial.*) v.t.

to praise.

[M.E. *rosen* — O.N. *hrōsa*, to
praise.]

roquelaure

rok'ə-lōr, -lör, n.

a man's knee-length cloak worn in the 18th and early 19th century.

[Fr., after the Duc de *Roquelaure* (1656–1738).]

roric

*rō'rik, rö', * **rorid** *rō'rid, rö', * **roral** *rō'rəl, rö', * adjs.

dewy.

[L. *rōs, rōris,* dew.]

rosalia

rō-zä'lyä, (mus.) n.

a series of repetitions of the same passage, each a tone higher.

[Said to be from an Italian folksong, *Rosalia cara mia.*]

roscid

ros'id, adj.

dewy.

[L. *rōscidus* — *rōs,* dew.]

rosella

rō-zel'ə, n.

a handsome Australian parakeet, first observed at Rose Hill near Sydney.

[For *rosehiller.*]

roselle, rozelle

rō-zel', n.

an East Indian hibiscus.

rosolio, rosoglio

rō-zō'lyō, n.

a sweet cordial made with raisins (formerly, it is said, with sundew).

[It. *rosolio* — L. *rōs sōlis,* dew of the sun.]

rotch, rotche, roch

roch, n.

the little auk. — Also **rotch'ie.**

[Cf. Du. *rotje,* petrel; Fris. *rotgies,* pl. of *rotgoes,* brent-goose.]

rother

rodh'ər, (Shak., emendation) n.

an ox, cow.
roth'er-beast.

[O.E. *hrȳther,* an ox, a cow; cf. Ger. pl. *Rinder,* horned cattle.]

rotl

rot'l, n.

a variable Levantine weight: — pl. **rot'ls, ar'tal.**

[Ar. *ratl.*]

roturier

ro-tü-ryā, n.

a plebeian.

[Fr., prob. — L.L. *ruptūra,* ground broken by the plough

— L. *rumpĕre*, *ruptum*, to break.]

rounce

rowns, n.

in a hand printing-press, the apparatus, or its handle, for moving the carriage.

[Du. *ronse*.]

rounceval

rown'si-vl, n.

a giant (*obs.*): a great bouncing woman (*obs.*): a marrow-fat pea.

adj. gigantic.

[Poss. *Roncesvalles*, in the Pyrenees.]

rouncy

rown'si, (*arch.*) n.

a riding-horse: a nag.

[O.Fr. *ronci*.]

routh, rowth

rowth, (*Scot.*) n.

abundance.

adj. plentiful.

adj. **routh'ie**.

[Origin obscure.]

roynish

roin'ish, (*Shak.*) adj.

scurvy, mangy: mean.

[O.Fr. *roigne*, mange.]

rubiginous

rōō-bij'i-nəs, adj.

rusty-coloured. — Also **rubig'inose** (*-nōs*).

[L. *rūbīgō* or *rōbīgō*, *-inis*, rust.]

rudas

rōō'dəs, (*Scot.*) n.

a foul-mouthed old woman: a randy, a hag.

adj. coarse.

[Origin obscure.]

ruderal

rōō'dər-əl, (*bot.*) n. and adj.

(a plant) growing in waste places or among rubbish.

[L. *rūdus*, *-eris*, rubbish.]

ruelle

rü-el', n.

the space between a bed and the wall: a bed-chamber where great French ladies held receptions in the morning in the 17th and 18th centuries: a morning reception: a narrow lane.

[Fr., dim. of *rue*, street.]

rullion

rul'yən, (*Scot.*) n.

a raw-hide shoe.

[O.E. *rifeling*.]

runch

runsh, (*Scot.*) n.

charlock: wild radish.

[Origin obscure.]

rundle

run'dl, n.

a round, a ladder-rung: a ring, circle, disc, or ball.

adj. **run'dled.**

[**roundel.**]

rupestrian

rōō-pes'tri-ən, adj.

composed of rock: inscribed on rock.

[L. *rūpēs*, rock.]

rupia

rōō'pi-ə, n.

a skin ulcer covered by crusts of dried secretion and dead tissue.

[Gr. *rhypos*, filth.]

rupicoline

rōō-pik'ō-līn, **rupicolous** *-ləs*, adjs.

rock-dwelling.

[L. *rūpēs*, a rock, *colĕre*, to inhabit.]

rusa, roosa

rōō'sə, n.

an Indian grass (**rusa grass**) from which an aromatic oil (**rusa oil**) is distilled.

[Hind. *rūsā.*]

rusalka

rōō-sal'kə, n.

a Russian water-nymph.

[Russ.]

rusma

ruz'mə, n.

a depilatory of lime and orpiment.

[App. Turk. *khirisma* — Gr. *chrīsma*, ointment.]

russel

rus'l, n.

a ribbed cotton and woollen material.

russ'el-cord a kind of rep made of cotton and wool.

[Poss. Flem. *Rijssel*, Lille.]

rutilant

rōō'ti-lənt, (*rare*) adj.

shining: glowing ruddily.

[L. *rutilāns, -antis*, pr.p. of *rutilāre*, to be reddish.]

rutter

rut'ər, (*obs.*) n.

a mercenary horse-soldier.

[M.Du. *rutter* — O.Fr. *routier.*]

rybat

rib'ət, n.

a dressed stone at the side of a door, window, etc.

ryot, raiyat

rī'ət, n.

an Indian peasant.

n. **ry'otwari, raiy'atwari**
(-*wä-rē*) a system of land-tenure
by which each peasant holds
directly of the state.

[Hind. *raiyat, raiyatwārī* — Ar.
ra'īyah, a subject.]

rype

rü'pə, n.

a ptarmigan: — pl. **ry'per.**
[Dan.]

S

sabra

sä'brə, n.

a native-born Israeli, not an immigrant.

[Mod. Hebrew *sābrāh*, type of cactus.]

saburra

sə-bur'ə, n.

a granular deposit, as in the stomach.

adj. **saburr'al.**

n. **saburrā'tion** (*med.*) application of hot sand.

[L. *saburra*, sand.]

sacellum

sə-sel'əm, n.

a god's unroofed sanctuary: a little chapel: a tomb or monument in the form of a chapel within a church: — pl. **sacell'a.**

[L. dim. of *sacrum*, a holy place — *sacer*, consecrated.]

saeter

set'ər, sāt', n.

in Norway, an upland meadow which provides summer pasture for cattle, and where butter and cheese are made: a hut on a saeter providing shelter for those looking after the animals.

[Norw.]

safrole

saf'rōl, n.

a usu. colourless oily liquid obtained from sassafras and used in perfumes, soaps and insecticides.

[*sassafras, -ol.*]

sagathy

sag'ə-thi, n.

a woollen stuff.

[Origin unknown; cf. Fr. *sagatis*, Sp. *sagatí*.]

saggar, saggard, sagger, seggar

sag', seg'ər(d), ns.

a clay box in which pottery is packed for baking.

[Perh. **safeguard.**]

saginate

saj'i-nāt, v.t.

to fatten.

n. **saginā'tion.**

[L. *sagīnāre*, to fatten.]

saguaro

sä-(g)wä'rō, n.

the giant cactus: — pl. **sagua'ros.**

[From an American Indian language.]

saguin, sagoin, sagouin

sag'win, sag-oin', n.

a titi monkey.

[Fr. *sago(u)in* — Port. *saguim* — Tupí *saguin*.]

sagum

sā'gəm, (L. *sag'ōōm*) n.

a Roman military cloak: — pl. **sa'ga.**

[L. *săgum*; prob. Gaulish.]

sai

sä'i, n.

the capuchin monkey.

[Tupí, monkey.]

saibling

zīp'ling, n.

the char.

[Ger. dial.]

saic, saick, saique

sä-ēk', sā'ik, n.

a Levantine vessel like a ketch.

[Fr. *saïque* — Turk. *shāīqā*.]

saiga

sī'gə, n.

a West Asian antelope.

[Russ.]

saimiri

sī-mē'rē, n.

a squirrel-monkey.

[Tupí *sai*, monkey, *miri*, little.]

sajou

sä-zhōō', -jōō', n.

a capuchin monkey.

[Fr., — Tupí *sai*, monkey and augmentative *-uassu*.]

saker

sā'kər, n.

a species of falcon (*Falco sacer*) used in hawking, esp. the female: an obsolete small cannon.

n. **sa'keret** the male saker.

[Fr. *sacre*, prob. — Ar. *saqr*, confounded with L. *sacer*, sacred.]

sakieh, sakiyeh, sakia

sä'ki-(y)ə, n.

an Eastern water-wheel.

[Ar. *sāqiyah*.]

sakkos

sak'os, n.

an Eastern bishop's vestment like an alb or a dalmatic. — Also **sacc'os.**

[Gr. *sakkos*, a bag.]

salangane

sal'əng-gān, n.

a swiftlet (*Collocalia*) that builds edible nests.

[Tagálog *salangan*.]

salchow

sal'kō, -kov, n.

in ice-skating, a jump in which the skater takes off from the inside back edge of one skate, spins in the air and lands on the outside back edge of the other skate.

[From Ulrich *Salchow*, 20th cent. Swedish skater.]

salep

sal'ep, n.

dried Orchis tubers: a food or drug prepared from them.

[Turk. *sālep*, from Ar.]

saligot

sal'i-got, n.

the water-chestnut.

[Fr.]

sallenders

sal'ən-dərz, n.

a skin disease affecting the hocks of horses.

[Cf. Fr. *solandre*.]

saloop

sə-lōōp', n.

salep: a drink made from salep, later from sassafras.

[**salep**.]

salse

sals, n.

a mud volcano.

[*Salsa*, name of one near Modena.]

saltern

sölt'ərn, n.

a salt-works.

[O.E. *s*(*e*)*altern* — *s*(*e*)*alt*, salt, *ærn*, house.]

sambar, sambur

sam'bər, n.

a large Indian deer.

[Hindi *sbar*.]

sambuca

sam-bū'kə, n.

an ancient musical instrument like a harp.

[L. *sambūca* — Gr. *sambȳkē*, prob. an Asiatic word; cf. Aramaic *sabbekā*.]

samel

sam'l, adj.

underburnt (as a brick).

[App. O.E. pfx. *sam-*, half, *æled*, burned.]

samfoo, samfu

sam'foo, n.

an outfit worn by Chinese women, consisting of a jacket and trousers.

[Cantonese.]

samiel

sā'mi-əl, n.

the simoom.

[Ar. *samm,* poison, Turk. *yel,* wind.]

samp

samp, (*U.S.*) n.

a coarsely ground maize: porridge made from it.

[From an American Indian word.]

samshoo, samshu

sam'shoo, n.

Chinese rice spirit.

[Pidgin; origin doubtful.]

sanbenito

san-be-nē'tō, n.

a garment worn by Inquisition victims at public recantation or execution: — pl. **sanbeni'tos.**

[Sp. *San Benito,* St Benedict, from its resemblance to St Benedict's scapular.]

sancho, sanko

sang'kō, n.

a West African guitar: — pl. **san'chos, -kos.**

[Ashanti *osanku.*]

sander, zander

san', zan'dər, n.

a pike-perch.

[Ger.]

sangar, sungar

sung'gər, n.

a stone breastwork: a look-out post.

[Pushtu *sangar.*]

sangaree

sang-gə-rē', n.

a West Indian drink of wine, diluted, sweetened, spiced, etc. — Also **sangria** (*sang-grē'ə*) a similar Spanish drink.

[Sp. *sangría.*]

sanies

sā'ni-ēz, n.

a thin discharge from wounds or sores.

adj. **sa'nious.**

[L. *saniēs.*]

sanjak

san'jak, n.

formerly, a subdivision of a Turkish vilayet or eyalet.

[Turk. *sancak,* flag, sanjak.]

sannup

san'əp, n.

the husband of a squaw: a brave.

[Amer. Ind. word.]

sannyasi

sun-yä'si, n.

a Hindu religious hermit who lives by begging. — Also **sannya'sin**

[Hindi, — Sans. *samnyāsin*, casting aside.]

santir

san-tēr', **santur, santour** *-tōōr'*, ns.

an Eastern dulcimer.

[Ar. *santīr*, Pers. and Turk. *sāntūr*.]

santon

san'ton, n.

an Eastern dervish or saint.

[Sp. *santón* — *santo*, holy — L. *sanctus*, holy.]

sapajou

sap'ə-jōō, n.

a capuchin monkey: a spider monkey (*obs.*).

[Fr. from a Tupí name.]

sappan, sapan

sap'an, -ən, n.

brazil-wood (*Caesalpinia sappan*) — usu.

sap(p)'an-wood.

[Malay *sapang*.]

sapperment

sap-ər-ment', interj.

a German oath.

[Ger. *Sakrament*, sacrament.]

sapsago

sap-sā'gō, sap'sə-gō, n.

a hard green cheese made from skim milk and melilot: — pl. **sapsagos.**

[Ger. *Schabziger*.]

sarafan

sar-ə-fan', or *sar'*, n.

a Russian peasant woman's cloak.

[Russ.]

sarangi

sä'rung-gē, n.

an Indian fiddle.

[Hind.]

sarbacane

sär'bə-kān, n.

a blowpipe (weapon).

[Fr.]

sarcocolla

sär-kō-kol'ə, n.

a Persian gum from Astragalus or other plants, reputed to heal wounds.

[Gr. *sarkokolla* — *kolla*, glue.]

sardel

sär-del', **sardelle** *-del(-ə)*, ns.
a small fish related to the sardine.

sarrasin, sarrazin

sär'ə-zin, n.
buckwheat.
[Fr. (*blé*) *sarrasin*, Saracen (corn).]

sarus

sä'rəs, sā'rəs, n.
an Indian crane. — Also **sarus crane.**
[Hind. *sāras*.]

sasin

sas'in, n.
the common Indian antelope.
[Nepalese.]

sassaby

sə-sā'bi, n.
the bastard hartebeest, a large S. African antelope.
[Tswana *tsessébe.*]

satara

sä-tä'rə, sat'ə-rə, n.
a ribbed, hot-pressed and lustred woollen cloth.
[*Sátára* in India.]

satyagraha

sut'yə-gru-hə, or *-grä'*, n.
orig. Mahatma Gandhi's policy of passive resistance to British rule in India, now any non-violent campaign for reform.
[Sans., reliance on truth.]

sauba

sä-ōō'bə, sö'bə, n.
a S. American leaf-carrying ant. — Also **sau'ba-ant.**
[Tupí.]

sauger

sö'gər, n.
a small American pike-perch.

saulie

sö'li, (*Scot.*) n.
a hired mourner.
[Origin obscure.]

saurel

sō-rel', sör'əl, n.
the horse-mackerel, scad.
[Fr.]

saury

sö'ri, n.
a sharp-beaked fish (*Scombresox saurus*) akin to the garfish.
[Perh. Gr. *sauros*, lizard.]

savate

sä-vät′, n.

boxing with the use of the feet.

[Fr.]

saxatile

sak′sǝ-tīl, -til, adj.

rock-dwelling.

[L. *saxātilis — saxum*, a rock.]

saxaul, saksaul

sak′söl, n.

a low, thick, grotesquely contorted tree (*Haloxylon*) of the goosefoot family, found on the salt steppes of Asia.

saxicavous

sak-sik′ǝ-vǝs, adj.

rock-boring.

n. **Saxic′ava** a genus of rock-boring lamellibranchs.

[L. *saxum*, a rock, *cavāre*, to hollow.]

saxicolous

sak-sik′ǝ-lǝs, adj.

living or growing among rocks.

n. **Saxic′ola** the wheatear genus.

adj. **saxic′oline**.

[L. *saxum*, a rock, *colĕre*, to inhabit.]

sazhen

sä-zhen′, n.

a Russian measure, about 2 metres.

[Russ.]

sbirro

zbir′rō, n.

an Italian police officer: — pl.

sbirri (*-rē*).

[It.]

scaglia

skal′yǝ, n.

an Italian limestone, usu. reddish.

n. **scagliŏ′la** an imitation stone of cement and chips. — Also adj.

[It. *scaglia*, scale, dim. *scagliuola*.]

scaldino

skal-, skäl-dē′nō, n.

an Italian earthenware brazier: — pl. **scaldi′ni** (*-nē*).

[It. *scaldare*, to warm.]

scall

sköl, n. (*B*.)

scabbiness, esp. of the scalp.

adj. (*Shak.*) scurvy: mean.

adj. **scalled**.

[O.N. *skalli*, bald head.]

scandent

skan′dǝnt, adj.

climbing.

[L. *scandēns, -entis*.]

scapple

skap'l, **scabble** *skab'l*, vs.t.

to work without finishing, as stone before leaving the quarry.

[O.Fr. *escapeler*, to dress timber.]

scatch

skach, n.

a stilt.

[O.N.Fr. *escache* (Fr. *échasse*).]

scaturient

skat-ū'ri-ənt, adj.

gushing.

[L. *scatūriēns, -entis — scatūrīre*, to gush out.]

scauper

skö'pər, n.

a tool with semicircular face, used by engravers.

sceat, sceatt

shat, (*hist.*) n.

a small silver (or gold) coin of Old English times: — pl. **sceatt'as.**

[O.E.]

sceuophylax

s(k)ū-of'i-laks, (*Greek Church*) n.

a sacristan.

n. **sceuophylacium** (*-lā'si-əm*) a sacristy.

[Gr. *skeuos*, a vessel, *phylax*, a watcher.]

schappe

shap'ə, n.

a fabric of waste silk with gum, etc., partly removed by fermentation.

v.t. to subject to this process.

[Swiss Ger.]

schiavone

skyä-vō'nā, n.

a 17th-century basket-hilted broadsword used by the Doge's bodyguard of Slavs.

[It. *Schiavoni*, Slavs.]

schiedam

skē'dam, or *-dam'*, n.

Holland gin, chiefly made at Schiedam (*s'hhē-däm'*), near Rotterdam.

schimmel

shim'l, n.

a roan horse.

[Ger., white horse; also Du.]

schläger

shlä'gər, n.

a German student's duelling-sword.

[Ger., — *schlagen*, to beat.]

schlich

shlihh, n.

the finer portions of crushed ore, separated by water.
[Ger.]

schmelz

shmelts, n.

glass used in decorative work.
[Ger. *Schmelz*, enamel.]

schout

skowt, n.

a municipal officer.
[Du.]

schuit, schuyt

skoit, n.

a Dutch flat-bottomed river-boat.
[Du.]

schuss

shōōs, n.

in skiing, a straight slope on which it is possible to make a fast run: such a run.
v.i. to make such a run.
[Ger.]

sciamachy

sī-am'ə-ki, **skiamachy**
skī-am'ə-ki, ns.

fighting with shadows: imaginary or useless fighting.
[Gr. *skiamakhia*.]

scissel

sis'l, n.

metal clippings: scrap left when blanks have been cut out. — Also **sciss'il**.

[O.Fr. *cisaille — ciseler — cisel*, a chisel .]

scolex

skō'leks, n.

a tapeworm head: — pl. **scoleces** (*skō-lē'sēz*; erroneously **scō'lices**).
adjs. **scō'lecid** (*-lə-sid*), **scōleciform** (*-les'i-förm*) like a scolex.
n.pl. **Scōleciform'ia** the lugworm order.
n. **scō'lecite** (*-sīt*) a member of the zeolite group of minerals.
adj. **scōlecoid** (*-lē'koid*) like a scolex.
[Gr. *skolēx, -ēkos*, a worm.]

scopa

skō'pə, n.

a bee's pollen-brush: — pl. **sco'pae** (*-pē*).
adj. **scō'pate** tufted.
n. **scopula** (*skop'ū-lə*) a little tuft of hairs.
adj. **scop'ulate**.
[L. *scōpae*, twigs, a broom.]

scopophobia

skop-ō-fō'bi-ə, n.

fear of being looked at.
[Gr. *skopeein*, to view, *phobos*, fear.]

scordato

skör-dä'tō, (*mus.*) adj.
put out of tune.
n. **scordatura** (*-tōō'rə*) a
temporary departure from
normal tuning.
[It.]

scoria

skō', skö'ri-ə, n.
dross or slag from
metal-smelting: a piece of lava
with steam-holes: — pl.
sco'riae (*-ri-ē*).
adjs. **sco'riac, scoriaceous**
(*-ri-ā'shəs*).
n. **scorifica'tion** reduction to
scoria: assaying by fusing with
lead and borax; **sco'rifier** a
dish used in assaying.
v.t. **sco'rify** to reduce to scoria:
to rid metals of (impurities) by
forming scoria.
adj. **sco'rious.**
[L., — Gr. *skōriā —skōr,* dung.]

scorper

skör'pər, n.
a gouging chisel.
[For **scauper.**]

scorzonera

skör-zō-nē'rə, n.
a plant like dandelion, with
edible root — *black salsify.*
[It.]

scotia

sko'ti-ə, -shi-ə, n.
a hollow moulding, esp. at the
base of a column.
[Gr. *skŏtiā — skotos,*
darkness.]

scran

skran, n.
provisions: broken victuals.
bad scran to you (*Ir.*) bad fare
to you.
[Ety. dub.]

scraw

skrö, (*arch.*) n.
a thin sod or turf.
[Ir. *sgrath.*]

scray, scraye

skrā, n.
the tern.
[Cf. W. *ysgräell.*]

scrieve

skrēv, (*Scot.*) v.i.
to glide swiftly along.
[Prob. O.N. *skrefa — skref,*
stride.]

scrimure

skrīm'yər, (*Shak.*) n.
a fencer.
[Fr. *escrimeur.*]

scrobe

skrōb, n.

a groove.

adj. **scrobic'ulate** (*skrob-*) pitted.

[L. *scrobis*, a ditch.]

scroddled

skrod'ld, adj.

(of pottery) made of clay scraps of different colours.

[Cf. L.G. *schrodel*, scrap.]

scroyle

skroil, (*Shak.*) n.

a wretch.

[Origin doubtful.]

scrunt

skrunt, (*Scot.*) n.

anything stunted (as an apple, a tree) or worn: a niggard.

adj. **scrunt'y.**

scruto

skrōō'tō, (*theat.*) n.

a kind of stage trap-door: — pl. **scru'tos.**

[Origin obscure.]

scumber

skum'bər, (*arch.*) v.t. and v.i.

to defecate (of dog or fox).

n. dung. — Also **skumm'er.**

[Prob. O.Fr. *descumbrer*, to disencumber.]

scuncheon, sconcheon, scontion

skun', skon'shən, n.

the inner part of a jamb.

[O.Fr. *escoinson.*]

scuppernong

skup'ər-nong, n.

a grape from the *Scuppernong* river, N. Carolina: wine from it.

scutch

skuch, v.t.

to dress (e.g. flax) by beating: to switch.

n. a tool for dressing flax, a swingle: a bricklayer's cutting tool.

ns. **scutch'er** a person, tool, or part of a machine that scutches: the striking part of a threshing-mill; **scutch'ing. scutch'-blade.**

[Prob. O.Fr. *escousser*, to shake off.]

scye

sī, n.

an opening for insertion of a sleeve.

[Origin obscure.]

scyphus

sīf'əs, n.

a large Greek drinking-cup (*ant.*): a cup-shaped structure: — pl. **scyph'ī.**

adj. **scyph'iform.**

n. **scyphis'toma** the segmenting polyp stage of a jellyfish (Gr. *stoma*, mouth): — pl. **scyphis'tomas, -stomae.** — *ns.pl.* **scyphomedū'sae, Scyphozō'a** the jellyfishes as a class.

[Gr. *skyphos*, cup.]

scytale

sit'ə-lē, n.

a Spartan secret writing on a strip wound about a stick, unreadable without a stick of like thickness.

[Gr. *skytalē*, a staff.]

seacunny

sē'kun-i, n.

a lascar steersman or quartermaster.

[App. Pers. *sukkānī* — Ar. *sukkān*, rudder, confused with **sea** and **con.**]

seannachie

sen'ə-hhē, n.

Highland or Irish genealogist and transmitter of family lore. — Also **seann'achy, senn'achie.**

[Gael. *seanachaidh*.]

searce

sûrs, **search** *sûrch*, (*obs.*) vs.t. to sift.

ns. (*obs.*) a sieve.

[O.Fr. *saas*; *r* unexplained.]

sebundy

si-bun'di, n.

Indian irregular soldiery or soldier.

[Urdu *sibandī*.]

seckel

sek'l, n.

a variety of pear.

[Owner's name.]

securiform

si-kū'ri-förm, adj.

axe-shaped.

[L. *secūris*, axe — *secāre*, to cut, *förma*, form.]

seecatch

sē'kach, n.

an adult male Aleutian fur seal: — pl. **see'catchie.**

[Russ. *sekach*, prob. from Aleutian Indian.]

sei

sā, n.

a kind of rorqual (*Balaenoptera borealis*) — also **sei whale.**

[Norw. *sejhval*, sei whale.]

seiche

sāsh, sesh, n.

a periodic fluctuation from side to side of the surface of lakes.

[Swiss Fr.]

sekos

sē'kos, n.

a sacred enclosure.

[Gr. *sēkos.*]

selachian

si-lā'ki-ən, n.

any fish of the shark class. —
Also adj.

[Gr. *selachos.*]

selictar

se-lik'tär, n.

a sword-bearer.

[Turk. *silihdār* — Pers. *silahdār*
— Ar. *silh*, weapon.]

selva

sel'və, n. (usu. in pl. **selvas)**

wet forest in the Amazon basin.

[Sp., Port. — L. *silva*, wood.]

semantron

sem-an'tron, n.

a wooden or metal bar used
instead of a bell in Orthodox
churches and in mosques: — pl.
seman'tra.

[Gr. *sēmantron*, sign, signal.]

semis

sē'mis, sā'mis, n.

a bronze coin of the ancient
Roman republic, half an as.

[L. *sēmis, sēmissis.*]

semsem

sem'sem, n.

sesame.

[Ar. *simsim.*]

semuncia

si-mun'sh(y)ə, n.

a Roman half-ounce: a bronze
coin, an as in its ultimate value.
adj. **semun'cial.**

[L. *sēmuncia* — *sēmi-*, half,
uncia, a twelfth.]

sen

sen, n.

a Japanese monetary unit, the
hundredth part of a yen: a
former Japanese coin, of the
value of this: — pl. **sen.**

[Jap.]

sengreen

sen'grēn, n.

the house-leek.

[O.E. *singrēne*, evergreen,
house-leek, periwinkle — pfx.
sin-, one, always (cf. L. *semel*,
once), *grēne*, green; cf. Ger.
Sin(n)grüne, periwinkle.]

sennit

sen'it, **sinnet** *sin'it*, ns.

a flat braid of rope yarn.

[Origin uncertain.]

senvy

sen'vi, (*obs.*) n.

mustard (plant or seed).

[O.Fr. *senevé* — L. *sināpi* —
Gr. *sināpi*, mustard.]

sephen

sef'en, n.

a sting-ray.

[Ar. *safan*, shagreen.]

sepiment

sep'i-mənt, n.

a hedge, a fence.

[L. *saepīmentum*, a hedge.]

sérac, serac

sā-rak', sā'rak, n.

one of the cuboidal or pillar-like
masses into which a glacier
breaks on a steep incline.

[Swiss Fr., originally a kind of
cheese.]

serang

se-rang', n.

a lascar boatswain.

[Pers. *sarhang*, a commander.]

serape

se-rä'pā, n.

a Mexican riding-blanket.

[Sp. *sarape*.]

seraskier

ser-as-kēr', n.

a Turkish commander-in-chief
or war minister.

n. **seraskier'ate** the office of
seraskier.

[Turk. pron. of Pers. *ser'asker*
— *ser*, head, Ar. *'asker*, army.]

serdab

sər-däb', n.

an underground chamber: a
secret chamber in an Egyptian
tomb.

[Pers. *sard*, cold, *āb*, water.]

sericon

ser'i-kon, n.

conjectured to be a red (or
black) tincture in alchemy.

seriema

ser-i-ē'mə, -ā'mə, n.

either of two S. American birds
of the family *Cariamidae*,
related to the cranes and the
rails, somewhat like a small
crested crane in form. — Also,
now obsolescent, **caria'ma**.

[Tupí *çariama*.]

serkali

ser-käl'ē, n.

the Government: white rulers.

[Swahili.]

seron, seroon

si-rōn', -ron', -rōōn', (*arch.*) ns.

a crate or hamper: a bale wrapped in hide.

[Sp. *serón.*]

serow

ser'ō, n.

a Himalayan goat-antelope.

[Lepcha (Tibeto-Burman language) *sa-ro.*]

serpigo

sər-pī'gō, n. (*Shak.* **sapego,** or **suppeago**)

any spreading skin disease: — pl. **serpigines** (*-pij'in-ēz*), **serpī'goes.**

adj. **serpiginous** (*-pij'*).

[L.L. *serpīgō* — L. *serpĕre,* to creep.]

serval

sûr'vl, n.

a large, long-legged, short-tailed African cat or tiger-cat.

[Port. (*lobo*) *cerval,* lit. deer-wolf, transferred from another animal.]

seston

ses'ton, n.

a very small plankton organism.

[Gr. *seston* — *sethein* to strain, filter.]

seta

sē'tə, n.

a bristle: a bristle-like structure: the stalk of a moss capsule: — pl. **se'tae** (*-tē*).

adjs. **setaceous** (*si-tā'shəs*), **setose** (*sē'tōs, -tōs'*).

[L. *saeta* (*sēta*), bristle.]

seton

sē'tn, n.

a thread or the like passed through the skin as a counter-irritant and means of promoting drainage: an issue so obtained.

[L.L. *sētō, -ōnis,* app. — L. *sēta, saeta,* bristle.]

sewellel

si-wel'əl, n.

an American rodent linking beavers and squirrels.

[Chinook *shewallal,* a robe of its skin.]

sewin, sewen

sū'in, n.

a Welsh sea-trout grilse.

[Origin unknown.]

shabble

shab'l, (*Scot.*) n.

an old rusty sword.

[Cf. It. *sciabola,* Pol. *szabla,* and **sabre.**]

shabrack

shab'rak, n.

a trooper's housing or saddle-cloth.

[Ger. *Schabracke,* prob. — Turk. *çāprāq.*]

shaddock

shad'ək, n.

an Oriental citrus fruit like a very large orange, esp. the larger pear-shaped variety, distinguished from the finer grapefruit: the tree that bears it.

[Introduced to the W. Indies *c.* 1700 by Captain *Shaddock.*]

shagroon

shə-grōōn', n.

an original settler in New Zealand of other than English origin.

[Perh. Ir. *seachrān,* wandering.]

shalloon

shə-lōōn', n.

a light woollen stuff for coat-linings, etc.

[Perhaps made at *Châlons-sur-Marne.*]

shama

shä'mə, n.

an Indian songbird of the thrush family.

[Hindi *śāmā.*]

shamiana(h)

shä-mē-ä'nə, n.

a large tent or canopy.

[Hindi *shāmiyāna;* from Pers.]

shandry

shan'dri, (*N. England*) n.

a light cart on springs.

n. **shan'drydan** a shandry: an old-fashioned chaise: a rickety vehicle.

[Origin unknown.]

shanny

shan'i, n.

the smooth blenny.

[Origin obscure.]

sharn

shärn, (*dial.*) n.

cow-dung.

adj. **sharn'y.**

sharny peat a cake of cow-dung mixed with coal.

[O.E. *scearn;* cf. O.N. *skarn.*]

shaster

shas'tər, **shastra** *shäs'trä,* ns.

a holy writing.

[Sans. *śāstra* — *śās,* to teach.]

shchi, shtchi

shchē, n.

cabbage soup.

[Russ.]

sheading

shē'ding, n.

one of the six divisions or districts of the Isle of Man.

sheat-fish

shēt'-fish, **sheath-fish** *shēth',* ns.

a gigantic fish (*Silurus glanis,* the European catfish) of European rivers: any kindred fish.

[Ger. *Scheidfisch.*]

sheltie, shelty

shel'ti, n.

a Shetland pony or sheepdog.

[Perh. O.N. *Hjalti,* Shetlander.]

shewel

shoo'əl, n.

a scarecrow or mark to scare deer. — Also **sew'el.**

shicker

shik'ər, n.

strong drink.

adj. **shick'ered** drunk.

[Yiddish.]

shikar

shi-kär', n.

hunting, sport.

ns. **shikar'ee, shikar'i** a hunter.

[Urdu, from Pers. *shikār.*]

shilpit

shil'pit, (*Scot.*) adj.

sickly-looking: washy: puny: insipid: inferior.

[Ety. dub.]

shim

shim, n.

a slip of metal, wood, etc., used to fill in space or to adjust parts.

[Ety. dub.]

shippo

ship-ō', n.

Japanese cloisonné ware.

[Jap. *shippô,* seven precious things, hence something beautiful.]

shiralee

shir'ə-lē, (*Austr.*) n.

a swagman's bundle.

[Orig. unknown.]

shivoo

shə-voo', (*Austr. coll.*) n.

a (noisy) party.

[From N. Eng. dial. *sheevo,* a shindy; perh. conn. with Fr. *chez vous,* at your house.]

shoat, shote, shot(t)

shōt, n.

a young hog.

[From M.E.; conn. Flem. *shote.*]

shoji

shō'jē, n.

a screen of paper covering a wooden framework, forming a wall or sliding partition in Japanese homes.

[Jap., — *sho,* to separate, *ji,* a piece.]

shrieval

shrē'vl, adj.

pertaining to a sheriff.

n. **shriev'alty** the office, term of office, or area of jurisdiction, of a sheriff.

[*Shrieve,* obs. form of **sheriff.**]

shroff

shrof, n.

in the East, a banker, money-changer, or money-lender: an expert in detection of bad coin.

v.t. to examine with that view.

v.i. to practise money-changing.

n. **shroff'age** commission for such examination.

[Ar. *sarrāf.*]

sial

sī'al, -əl, n.

the lighter partial outer shell of the earth, rich in *si*lica and *al*umina. — Also **sal** (*sal*).

adj. **sial'ic.**

siamang

sē'ə-mang, syä'mang, n.

the largest of the gibbons, found in Sumatra and Malacca.

[Malay.]

sika

sē'kə, n.

a Japanese deer, small, spotted white in summer.

[Jap. *shika.*]

sile, seil

sīl, (*dial.*) v.t.

to strain.

v.i. to rain heavily.

n. a strainer (also **sī'ler**).

[Scand.; cf. Sw. and Norw. *sila,* to strain.]

silladar

sil'ə-där, n.

an irregular cavalryman.

[Urdu and Pers. *silāhdār.*]

sillock

sil'ək, (*N.Scot.*) n.

a young coalfish.

[Cf. O.N. *silungr,* a small salmon.]

sima

sī'mə, n.

the part of the earth's crust underlying the sial.

[From *si*licon and *ma*gnesium.]

similor

sim'i-lör, n.

a yellow alloy used for cheap jewellery.

[Fr., — L. *similis,* like, *aurum,* gold.]

simkin, simpkin

sim'kin, n.

an Urdu corruption of **champagne.**

simpai

sim'pī, n.

the black-crested langur of Sumatra.

[Malay.]

simurg(h)

si-mōōrg', -mûrg', **simorg** *-mörg',* ns.

a monstrous bird of Persian fable.

[Pers. *sīmurgh.*]

sinapism

sin'ə-pizm, n.

a mustard plaster.

[Gr. *sināpi.*]

sindon

sin'dən, (*arch.*) n.

fine (esp. linen) cloth, or a garment, etc., made from it: a shroud, esp. that preserved as Jesus's at Turin, Italy.

ns. **sindonol'ogy** the study of this shroud and its history;

sindonol'ogist;

sindonoph'any (Gr. *phainein,* to show) the periodic exhibiting of this shroud to the public.

[Gr. *sindōn,* fine cloth, winding sheet.]

singult

sing'gult, (*arch.*) n.

a sob.

n. **singult'us** (*med.*) hiccuping.

[L. *singultus,* a sob.]

sinopia

sin-ō'pi-ə, n.

a reddish-brown pigment used for one of the preparatory drawings of a fresco, obtained from **sin'opite,** an iron ore: the drawing. — Also **sinō'pis.**

[L. *sinopis,* sinopite.]

sircar, sirkar, circar

sər-kär', sûr', n.

government: the authorities: a province or district: an Indian clerk or factotum.

[Urdu *sarkār,* a superintendent — Pers. *sar,* head, *kār,* agent.]

sirgang

sûr'gang, n.

a green Asiatic jay-like bird.

[Prob. from native name.]

sirvente

sēr-vāt', n.

a troubadour's lay.

[Fr.]

sistrum

sis'trəm, n.

an ancient Egyptian wire rattle used in Isis-worship: — pl. **sis'tra.**

[L. *sīstrum* — Gr. *seistron*.]

situla

sit'ū-lə, (*ant.*) n.

a bucket: — pl. **sit'ūlae** (-ē).

[L.]

siwash

sī'wosh, (also with *cap.*; *north western U.S. derog. coll.*) n.

a N.W. American Indian. — Also adj.

[Chinook, — Fr. *sauvage*, wild.]

skart, scart

skärt, **scarth, skarth** *skärth*, (*Scot.*) ns.

a cormorant.

[O.N. *skarfr*.]

skaw, scaw

skö, n.

a low cape, ness (in place names).

[O.N. *skagi*.]

skeesicks

skē'ziks, (*U.S.*) n.

a rascal.

skeg

skeg, (*naut.*) n.

a brace between keel and rudder: a projection from, or in place of, a keel: a stabilising fin projecting from the underside of a surfboard.

[Du. *scheg*.]

skelder

skel'dər, v.i.

to beg: to swindle.

[Cant; of obscure origin.]

skelm

skelm, (*S.Afr.*) n.

a rascal.

[Du. *schelm*, Ger. *Schelm*.]

skilling

skil'ing, n.

an obsolete coin of Scandinavian countries, of small value.

[Dan.]

skillion

skil'yən, (*Austr.*) n.

an outhouse or lean-to, esp. one with a sloping roof. — Also **skill'ing.**

skillion roof a roof slanting out from the wall of a building.

[Eng. dial. *skilling*, an outhouse, lean-to.]

skimmington
skim'ing-tən, n.

a burlesque procession in ridicule of husband or wife in case of infidelity or other ill-treatment.
[Ety. unknown.]

skio, skeo
skyō, (*Orkney* and *Shetland*) n.

a hut: a shed: — pl. **skios, skeos.**
[Norw. *skjaa*.]

skippet
skip'it, n.

a flat box for protecting a seal (as of a document).
[Origin unknown.]

skirret
skir'it, n.

a water-parsnip with edible roots.
[M.E. *skirwhit*, as if *skire white*, pure white, but perh. altered from O.Fr. *eschervis*.]

skolion
skō'li-on, n.

a short drinking-song in ancient Greece, taken up by the guests in irregular succession: — pl. **skŏ'lia.**
[Gr. *skŏlion*.]

skudler, scuddaler, scudler
skud'lər, (*Shetland*) n.

the leader of a band of guisers: the conductor of a festival.
[Origin obscure.]

slammakin, slammerkin
slam'ə(r)-kin, (*obs.*) ns.

a loose gown: a slovenly-dressed woman: a slattern.
adj. slovenly.
[Origin obscure.]

slane
slān, n.

a turf-cutting spade.
[Ir. *sleaghan*.]

sleech
slēch, n.

slimy mud: a mud-flat.
adj. **sleech'y.**
[Origin uncertain.]

sley
slā, n.

a weaver's reed.
[O.E. *slege* — *slēan*, to strike.]

sloan
slōn, (*Scot.*) n.

a snub: a reproof.
[Ety. dub.]

sloyd, sloid

sloid, n.

a Swedish system of manual training by woodwork.

[Sw. *slöjd,* dexterity.]

sluit

slü'it, slo͞ot, (S.Afr.) n.

a narrow water-channel. — Also **sloot.**

[Du. *sloot,* ditch.]

slummock

slum'ək, v.i.

to move awkwardly.

smaik

smāk, (Scot.) n.

a contemptible fellow, rascal.

smallage

smöl'ij, n.

wild celery.

[**small,** Fr. *ache* — L. *apium,* parsley.]

smaragd

smar'agd, n.

the emerald.

adj. **smarag'dine** (*-din, -dēn, -dīn*) emerald green.

n. **smarag'dite** a green amphibole.

[L. *smaragdus* — Gr. *smaragdos.*]

smeddum

smed'əm, n.

fine powder: spirit, mettle (*Scot.*).

[O.E. *smed*(*e*)*ma, smeodoma,* fine flour.]

smew

smū, n.

a small species of merganser.

[Origin uncertain.]

smoot

smo͞ot, (slang) n.

a compositor who does odd jobs in various houses.

v.i. to work in this way.

[Origin obscure.]

smytrie

smīt'ri, (Scot.) n.

a collection of small things.

[Cf. Flem. *smite.*]

snapha(u)nce

snap'häns, -höns,

snaphaunch *-hönsh, (obs.)* ns.

a freebooter: a flintlock or a weapon with one: a spring catch or trap.

[Cf. Du. *snapshaan* — *snappen,* to snap, *haan,* a cock.]

snash

snash, (*Scot.*) n.

insolence, abusive language.
v.i. to talk impudently.
[Prob. imit.]

snaste

snāst, (now *dial.*) n.

a wick: a candle-snuff.
[Origin obscure.]

snath

snath, **snathe** *snādh*, **snead**
snēd, **sneath** *snēth*, **sned**
sned, ns.

the curved handle or shaft of a
scythe.

[O.E. *snǣd*, a scythe handle, a
slice.]

snig

snig, (*dial.*) n.

a river-eel, esp. an immature
(olive and yellow) eel.
v.t. to drag a load with chains or
ropes.
v.t. **snigg'er** to catch (salmon)
with a weighted hook.
v.i. **snigg'le** to fish for eels by
thrusting the bait into their
hiding places: to fish for salmon,
etc., by striking with a hook.
v.t. to catch thus.
n. a baited hook.
ns. **snigg'ler; snigg'ling.**
[Origin obscure.]

snirt

snirt, snûrt, (*Scot.*) n.

a smothered laugh.
v.i. **snirt'le** to snicker.
[Imit.]

snool

snōōl, (*Scot.*) n.

one who submits tamely to
wrong or oppression.
v.t. to keep in subjection: to
snub.
v.i. to be tamely submissive.
[Ety. dub.]

snotter

snot'ər, n.

the lower support of the sprit.
[Origin obscure.]

sobole

sō'bōl, **soboles** *sob'ō-lēz*, (*bot.*)
ns.

a creeping underground stem
producing roots and buds: — pl.
sob'ōlēs,
adj. **sobolif'erous** having
soboles.

[L. *sobolēs, subolēs*, a shoot —
sub, under, and the root of
alĕre, to nourish, sustain.]

soc

sok, (*law*) n.

the right of holding a local court.
ns. **soc'age, socc'age** tenure
of lands by service fixed and
determinate in quality;

**soc'ager, soc'man,
sōke'man** a tenant by socage;
soke (*sōk*) soc: a district under
a particular jurisdiction;
soke'manry tenure by
socage; **sōk'en** a district under
a particular jurisdiction.
[O.E. *sōcn*, inquiry, jurisdiction.]

socle
sō'kl, sok'l, (*archit.*) n.
a plain face or plinth at the foot
of a wall, column, etc.
[Fr., — It. *zoccolo* — L.
socculus, dim. of *soccus*, a
shoe.]

soffioni
sof-yō'nē, n.pl.
volcanic steam-holes.
[It.]

soffit
sof'it, n.
a ceiling, now generally
restricted to the ornamented
underside of a stair,
entablature, archway, etc.
[It. *soffitto* — L. *suffixus*, pa.p.
of *suffigĕre*, to fasten beneath
— *sub*, under, *figĕre*, to fix.]

softa
sof'tə, n.
a Muslim theological student,
attached to a mosque.
[Turk. *sōfta*.]

solan
sō'lən, n.
the gannet. — Also **soland
(goose), solan goose.**
[O.N. *sūla*.]

solander
sō-lan'dər, n.
a box in the form of a book,
invented by the Swedish
botanist Daniel *Solander*
(1736–82).

solano
sō-lä'nō, n.
a hot south-east wind in Spain:
— pl. **sola'nos.**
[Sp., — L. *sōlānus* (*ventus*), the
east wind — *sōl*, the sun.]

solfatara
sol-fä-tä'rə, n.
a volcanic vent emitting only
gases, esp. one emitting acid
gases (hydrochloric acid and
sulphur dioxide): — pl.
solfata'ras.
adj. **solfata'ric.**
[From the *Solfatara* (lit.
sulphur-mine, sulphur-hole)
near Naples — It. *solfo*,
sulphur.]

soliped
sol'i-ped, n.
an animal with uncloven hoofs.
adjs. **sol'iped, solip'edous.**
[L. *sōlus*, alone, *pēs, pedis*, a
foot.]

solive

so-lēv′, n.

a joist or beam of secondary importance.

[Fr., — L. *sublevāre*, to support.]

solleret

sol′ər-et, n.

a jointed steel shoe.

[O.Fr., dim. of *soler*, slipper.]

solum

sō′ləm, n.

ground, soil: a piece of ground.

[L. *sŏlum*, the ground.]

sombrerite

som-brā′rīt, n.

rock-guano.

[*Sombrero* in the West Indies.]

sonde

sond, n.

any device for obtaining information about atmospheric and weather conditions at high altitudes.

[Fr.]

sondeli

son′de-li, n.

the Indian musk-shrew.

[Kanarese *sundili*.]

soneri

son′, sōn′ə-rē, n.

cloth of gold.

[Hind. *sonā*, gold.]

sontag

son′tag, zōn′tähh, n.

a woman's knitted cape, tied down round the waist.

[From the famous German singer Henriette *Sontag* (1806–1854).]

sopherim

sō′fə-rim, n.pl.

the scribes, the expounders of the Jewish oral law.

adj. **sopheric** (*-fer′ik*).

[Heb. *sōferīm*.]

sopite

sō-pīt′, v.t.

to dull, lull, put to sleep: to put an end to.

[L. *sōpītus*, pa.p. of *sōpīre*, to put to sleep, calm, settle.]

sora

sō′rə, sö′, n.

a N. American short-billed rail. — Also **so′ree**.

[Indian name.]

sorehon

sōr′hon, sör′, n.

an ancient Irish exaction of free accommodation by a lord from a

freeholder or tenant.
[See **sorn**.]

sorn

sörn, (*Scot.*) v.i.

to obtrude oneself as an
uninvited guest.

ns. **sor'ner; sorn'ing.**

[Obs. Ir. *sorthan*, free quarters.]

soroban

sör'ə-bän, n.

a Japanese abacus.

[From Jap. — Chin. words
meaning 'calculating board'.]

soroche

so-rō'chä, n.

mountain sickness.

[Sp. — Quechua *surúcht*,
antimony (present in the Andes
and formerly believed to cause
the sickness).]

souari, saouari

sow-ä'ri, n.

a tree (Caryocar) of Guiana
yielding a durable timber and
edible butternuts.
s(a)oua'ri-nut.

[Fr. *saouari*, from Galibi.]

soum, sowm

sōōm, (*Scot.*) n.

the proportion of sheep or cattle
suitable for any pasture: pasture
for one cow or its equivalent in
sheep, etc.

v.t. and v.i. to determine in
terms of soums.

n. **soum'ing.**

souming and rouming the
determination of the number of
soums appropriate to a
common pasture, and their
apportionment (according to
ability to supply fodder through
winter) to the various rooms or
holdings.

[Form of **sum**.]

sounder

sown'dər, n.

a herd of swine: a young boar.

[O.Fr. *sundre*; of Gmc. origin;
cf. O.E. *sunor*.]

sourdeline

sōōr'də-lēn, n.

a small bagpipe.

[Fr.]

sourock

sōō'rək, (*Scot.*) n.

sorrel.

[**sour**.]

soutache

sōō-täsh', n.

a narrow braid.

[Fr.]

souter

sōō'tər, (*Scot.*) n.

a shoemaker, a cobbler. — Also
sow'ter, sou'tar.

adj. **sou'terly.**
souter's clod (*Scott*) a brown wheaten roll.
[O.F. *sūtere* (O.N. *sūtari*) — L. *sūtor* — *suĕre*, to sew.]

sowens, sowans
sō'ənz, (*Scot.*) n.pl.
a dish made from the farina remaining among the husks of oats, flummery.
[Supposed to be from Gael. *sùghan*, the liquid of sowens — *sùgh*, juice.]

spadassin
spad'ə-sin, n.
a swordsman, a bravo.
[Fr., — It. *spadaccino* — *spada*, a sword.]

spadroon
spə-drōōn', (*hist.*) n.
a cut-and-thrust sword: swordplay with it.
[Fr. (Genevan dialect) *espadron*.]

spagyric, -al
spə-jir'ik, -əl, adjs.
alchemical.
ns. **spagyr'ic, spagyrist**
(*spaj'ər-ist*) an alchemist. —
Also **spagir'ic, spager'ic,** etc.
[Prob. coined by Paracelsus.]

spancel
span'sl, n.
a hobble, esp. for a cow.
v.t. to hobble.
adj. **span'celled.**
[Du. or L.G. *spansel*.]

spane, spain, spean
spān, (*Scot.*) v.t.
to wean.
[M.Du. or M.L.G. *spanen*, or O.Fr. *espanir*; cf. Ger. *spänen*.]

spaniolate
span'yō-lāt, **spaniolise, -ize**
-līz, vs.t.
to hispanicise.
[O.Fr. *Espaignol*, a Spaniard.]

sparable
spar'ə-bl, n.
a small headless nail used by shoemakers.

sparling
spär'ling, **sperling, spirling**
spûr', spir'ling, (now *Scot.*) ns.
the smelt.
[Partly O.Fr. *esperlinge* (of Gmc. origin), partly M.L.G. *spirling* or M.Du. *spierling*.]

sparth(e)
spärth, (*arch.*) n.
a long battle-axe.
[O.N. *spartha*.]

spayad

spā'ad, **spayd, spade** *spād*,
spay *spā*, (*obs.*) ns.
a hart in his third year.
[Origin obscure.]

spekboom

spek'bōm, n.
a S. African succulent shrub of
the purslane family.
[Du., bacon tree.]

spelk

spelk, (*N. dial.*) n.
a splinter, of wood, etc.
[O.E. *spelc*.]

spelter

spel'tər, n.
zinc, esp. impure zinc.
[Cf. L.G. *spialter*.]

spence

spens, n.
a larder (*dial.*): a pantry (*dial.*):
an inner room, parlour (*Scot.*).
[O.Fr. *despense*, a buttery —
despendre — L. *dispendĕre*.]

speos

spē'os, n.
grotto-temple or tomb: — pl.
spe'oses.
[Gr., cave.]

spetch

spech, n.
a piece of skin used in making
glue.
[N. dial. *speck*, a patch of
leather or cloth.]

sphendone

sfen'do-nē, n.
an ancient Greek women's
head-band: an elliptical or
semi-elliptical auditorium.
[Gr. *sphendonē*, a sling.]

sphragistic

sfrə-jist'ik, adj.
pertaining to seals and signets.
n. sing. **sphragist'ics** the
study of seals.
[Gr. *sphrāgistikos* — *sphrāgis*,
a seal.]

spiccato

spik-kä'tō, adj. and adv.
half staccato.
n. spiccato playing or passage:
— pl. **spicca'tos.**
[It.]

spilite

spī'līt, n.
a very fine-grained basic
igneous rock.
adj. **spilitic** (*-it'ik*).
n. **spī'losite** a spotted slate,
formed by contact
metamorphism.
[Gr. *spilos*, a spot.]

spitchcock
spich'kok, n.
an eel split and broiled.
v.t. to split and broil, as an eel.
[Orig. unknown.]

spitcher
spit'chə, (*naval slang*) adj.
done for.
[Maltese *spiċċa*, pron. *spitch'a*,
finished, ended.]

spitz
spits, n.
a Pomeranian dog: a group of
breeds of dog generally having
long hair, pointed ears and a
tightly curled tail, incl. husky,
samoyed, Pomeranian, etc.
[Ger.]

spleuchan
splōōhh'ən, (*Scot.*) n.
a tobacco-pouch: a purse.
[Gael. *spliùc(h)an.*]

spoffish
spof'ish, (*arch.*) adj.
fussy, officious — also **spoff'y.**
[Origin obscure.]

spontoon
spon-tōōn', n.
a small-headed halberd
formerly carried by some
infantry officers.
[Fr. *sponton* — It. *spontone* —
punto — L. *punctum*, a point.]

spraint
sprānt, n.
otter's dung.
[O.Fr. *espraintes*, lit. pressed
out.]

spreagh
sprāhh, *sprehh*, n.
a prey: a foray.
n. **spreagh'ery, sprech'ery**
(*sprehh'*) cattle-lifting: petty
possessions, esp. plunder.
[Gael. *spréidh*, cattle.]

sprent
sprent, (*arch.*) adj.
sprinkled.
[Pa.p. of obs. *sprenge* — O.E.
sprengen, *sprengan*, causative
of *springan*, to spring.]

sprod
sprod, (*Northern*) n.
a second-year salmon.
[Origin obscure.]

spruit
sprāt, *sprü'it*, *sprīt*, (*S.Afr.*) n.
a small, deepish watercourse,
dry except during and after
rains.
[Du., sprout.]

squacco
skwak'ō, n.
a small crested heron: — pl.
squacc'os.
[It. dial. *sguacco.*]

squeteague

skwi-tēg', n.

an Atlantic American spiny-finned food-fish (*Cynoscion*), misnamed salmon or trout.

[Narragansett *pesukwiteaug*, they make glue.]

sraddha, shraddha

s(h)rä'dä, ns.

an offering to the manes of an ancestor.

[Sans. *śrāddha*.]

stacte

stak'tē, n.

a Jewish spice, liquid myrrh.

n. **stactom'eter** a pipette for counting drops.

[Gr. *staktos, -ē, -on,* dropping.]

stadda

stad'ə, n.

a comb-maker's double-bladed hand-saw.

[Origin unknown.]

staddle

stad'l, n.

a support, esp. for a stack of hay, etc.: the bottom of a stack: a small tree left unfelled: a stump left for coppice.

stadd'le-stone' a low mushroom-shaped arrangement of a conical and flat, circular stone, used as a support for a hay stack.

[O.E. *stathol*, foundation; Ger. *Stadel*.]

staffage

sta-fäzh', n.

accessories in a picture.

[Sham Fr., — Ger. *staffieren*, to garnish.]

staith(e)

stāth, (*N. England*) n.

a wharf: a structure for shipping coal: an embankment.

[O.E. *stæth*, bank, and O.N. *stöth*, landing-stage.]

stalko

stö'kō, (*Anglo-Ir.*) n.

a gentleman without fortune or occupation: — pl. **stalk'oes.**

[Perh. Ir. *stócach*, idler.]

stammel

stam'l, (*hist.*) n.

a kind of woollen cloth, usu. dyed red: red colour.

adj. of stammel: red.

[Fr. *estamel*, or independently formed M.E. *stamin* — O.Fr. *estamin*, both from L. *stāmina*, warp threads.]

stamnos

stam'nos, n.

an ancient Greek short-necked jar: — pl. **stam'noi.**

[Gr.]

standish

stan'dish, (*arch.*) n.

an inkstand.

[Poss. for *stand-dish*.]

staniel, stanyel

stan'yəl, **stannel** *stan'l* (*Shak.* **stallion** *stal'yən*), ns.

the kestrel.

[O.E. *stāngella*, lit. stone yeller.]

staragen

star'ə-gən, (*obs.*) n.

the tarragon plant.

[Cf. Sp. *estragón*, Fr. *estragon*, *tarragon*.]

staretz, starets

stär'ets, n.

in Russia, a holy man, a religious teacher.

[Russ. *starets*.]

starosta

stär'os-tə, (*hist.*) n.

a Russian village headman: a Polish noble holding a **star'osty** or domain by grant of life-estate from the crown.

[Russ. and Pol. *starosta*, elder.]

stavesacre

stāvz'ā-kər, n.

a tall larkspur whose seeds were formerly used against lice.

[O.Fr. *stavesaigre* — L.L. *staphisagria* — Gr. *staphis*, raisins, *agrios*, wild.]

steenkirk

stēn'kûrk, n.

a lace cravat loosely worn.

[From the battle of *Steenkerke*, 3 August 1692.]

stellion

stel'yən, or **stellio lizard** *stel'i-ō liz'ərd*, ns.

a Levantine lizard (*Agama stellio*) with starry spots.

n. **stell'ionate** a fraud that does not come under any specific head (*law*).

[L. *stēlliō, -ōnis*, a star-spotted lizard, a knave — *stēlla*, star.]

stempel, stemple

stem'pl, n.

a cross-timber in a shaft, as support or step.

[Cf. Ger. *Stempel*.]

stenlock

sten'lək, (*Scot.*) n.

a coalfish: an overgrown coalfish.

[Origin doubtful.]

stephane

stef'ə-nē, n.

an ancient Greek head-dress like a diadem.

[Gr. *stephanē* — *stephein*, to encircle.]

stepney

step'ni, n.

a spare wheel, often *fig.*: a mistress, esp. a white slaver's.

[Said to be from the name of a street where the wheels were made.]

sterlet

stûr'lit, n.

a small sturgeon.

[Russ. *sterlyad*.]

sternutation

stûr-nū-tā'shən, n.

sneezing.

adjs. **sternū'tative, sternū'tatory** that causes sneezing.

n. a substance that causes sneezing. — Also **ster'nūtātor**.

[L. *sternūtāre*, intens. of *sternuĕre*, to sneeze.]

sticcado

stik-ä'dō, **sticcato** *-tō*, ns.

a kind of xylophone: — pls. **-do(e)s, -to(e)s.**

[Perh. It. *steccato*, palisade.]

stillage

stil'ij, n.

a frame, stand, or stool for keeping things off the floor: a box-like container for transporting goods: a cask-stand.

ns. **still'ing, still'ion** a cask-stand.

[Prob. Du. *stellage, stelling* — *stellen*, to place.]

stithy

stidh'i, **stiddie** *stid'i*, ns.

an anvil: a smithy.

v.t. to forge on an anvil.

[O.N. *stethi*; Sw. *städ*, an anvil.]

stiver

stī'vər, n.

formerly, a Dutch penny: a very small coin or sum.

[Du. *stuiver*.]

stoccado

stok-ä'dō, **stoccata** *-tə*, ns.

a thrust in fencing: — pls. **-dos, -tas.**

[It. *stoccata*, thrust — *stocco*, rapier — Ger. *Stock*, stick.]

stonker

stong'kər (*slang*), v.t.

to kill, destroy, overthrow, thwart.

n. **stonk** (*stongk*; *mil. slang*; back-formation) intense bombardment.

[Ety. dub.]

storge

stör'gē, *-jē*, n.

parental affection.

[Gr.]

stornello

stör-nel'ō, n.

a short (usually three-lined) popular Italian verse-form: — pl. **stornell'i** (*-ē*).

[It.]

stouth

stōōth, (*obs. Scot.*) n.

theft.

ns. **stouth'rie, stouth'erie** theft: stolen goods: provision, furniture; **stouth'rief** (*Scots law*) theft with violence (later only in a dwelling-house). **stouth and routh** plenty, abundance.

[O.N. *stuldr*, theft.]

stradiot

strad'i-ot, (*hist.*) n.

a Venetian light horseman from Albania or Greece.

[It. *stradiotto* — Gr. *stratiōtēs*, soldier.]

stramazon, stramaçon

stram'ə-zon, -son, (*obs.*) ns.

a downward cut in fencing.

[It. *stramazzone*, and Fr. *estramaçon*.]

stramineous

strə-min'i-əs, adj.

strawy: light, worthless: straw-coloured.

[L. *strāmineus* — *strāmen*, straw.]

stramonium

strə-mō'ni-əm, n.

the thorn-apple: a drug like belladonna got from its seeds and leaves.

[Mod. L., poss. from a Tatar word.]

strass

stras, n.

paste for making false gems.

[Josef *Strasser*, its inventor.]

strelitz

strel'its, n.

a soldier of the Muscovite guards, abolished by Peter the Great: — pl. **strel'itzes, strel'itzi**.

[Russ. *strelets*, bowman.]

strig

strig, (*Southern*) n.

a stalk.

v.t. to remove the stalk from: — pr.p. **strigg'ing**.

[Origin obscure.]

stringhalt

string'hölt, n.

a catching up of a horse's legs, usu. of one or both hind-legs. — Also **spring'halt**.

stroud

strowd, n.

a blanket made for trading with American Indians.

n. **stroud'ing** its material,
coarse wool.

[Prob. made at *Stroud*,
Gloucestershire.]

stroup

strōōp, (*Scot.*) n.

a spout, nozzle.

[Cf. Sw. *strupe*, throat.]

strummel

strum'l, **strammel** *stram'l*, (*obs.
slang*) ns.

straw: hence, hair.

[Cf. L. *strāmen*, straw.]

studdle

stud'l, n.

a post: a prop.

[O.E. *stodla.*]

stull

stul, (*dial.*) n.

a horizontal prop in a mine.

n. **stulm** (*stulm*) an adit: a small
draining-shaft.

[Cf. Ger. *Stollen.*]

stummel

stum'l, n.

the bowl and adjacent part of a
pipe.

[Ger.]

stuprate

stū'prāt, v.t.

to ravish, violate.

n. **stuprā'tion.**

[L. *stuprāre, -ātum.*]

subah

sōō'bä, n.

a province of the Mogul empire:
a subahdar.

ns. **suba(h)dar'** the governor
of a subah: an Indian captain;
subahdar'y, su'bahship the
office of subahdar.

[Urdu.]

subdolous

sub'dō-ləs, (*rare*) adj.

crafty.

[L. pfx. *sub-*, in sense of
somewhat, *dolus*, a wile.]

subsecive

sub'si-siv, (*arch.*) adj.

remaining over: spare.

[L. *subsecīvus* — *sub, secāre*,
to cut.]

subtack

sub'tak', n.

an underlease in Scotland.

n. **sub'tack'sman** a holder
by subtack.

subtrist

sub-trist', (*arch.*) adj.

somewhat sad.

[L. *subtrīstis — sub, trīstis*, sad.]

subulate

sū'bū-lāt, adj.

awl-shaped.

[L. *sūbula*, an awl.]

succade

suk-ād', n.

fruit or vegetable candied or in syrup.

[A.Fr. *sukade*, perh. — L. *succus*, juice.]

sucre

sōō'krā, n.

the monetary unit of Ecuador.

[Named after Antonio José de *Sucre* (1795-1830).]

sucurujú

sōō-kōō-rōō-zhōō', n.

a S. American Indian name for the anaconda.

sudd

sud, n.

a mass of floating vegetable matter obstructing the White Nile: a temporary dam.

[Ar. *sudd*, obstruction.]

sudder

sud'ər, (in India) adj.

chief.

n. a supreme court.

[Ar. *çadr*, chief.]

suffete

suf'ēt, n.

one of the chief administrative officials of ancient Carthage.

[L. *sūfes, -etis*, from a Punic word.]

sulcus

sul'kəs, n.

a groove, furrow, fissure: a fissure between two convolutions of the brain: — pl. **sul'ci** (*-sī*).

adj. **sul'cal** (*-kl*) of a sulcus: grooved: furrowed: pronounced with sulcal tongue.

v.t. **sul'calise, -ize** to furrow.

adjs. **sul'cate, -d** furrowed, grooved: with parallel longitudinal furrows.

n. **sulcā'tion**.

[L. *sulcus*, a furrow.]

suovetaurilia

sū-ov-i-tö-ril'i-ə, L. *sōō-o-we-tow-rē'li-a*, n.pl.

a Roman sacrifice of a sheep, a pig, and an ox.

[L. *sūs*, pig, *ovis*, sheep, *taurus*, ox.]

supercherie
sü-per-shə-rē, n.
a taking at disadvantage: fraud.
[Fr.]

suppawn, supawn
sə-pön', n.
maize porridge.
[Natick *saupáun,* softened.]

sural
sū'rl, adj.
pertaining to the calf of the leg.
[L. *sūra,* the calf.]

surat
sōō-rat', or *sōō',* n.
coarse uncoloured cotton.
[*Surat,* in India.]

surculus
sûr'kū-ləs, (*bot.*) n.
a sucker.
adj. **sur'culose** having or
producing suckers.
[L. *sūrculus,* a twig.]

suricate
sū', sōō'ri-kāt, n.
a S. African animal of the civet
family.
[Origin unknown.]

surmullet
sər-mul'it, n.
a species of red mullet, admired
by the Romans for its

colour-changes as it died.
[Fr. *surmulet.*]

surquedry
sûr'kwi-dri, (*Spens.*) n.
arrogance. — Also (*obs.*)
sur'quedy.
[O.Fr. *surcuiderie — surcuidier
—* L. *super,* above, and
cōgitāre, -ātum, to think.]

surra
sōō'rə, n.
a trypanosome disease of
horses, etc., in Eastern Asia.
[Marathi *sūra,* wheezing.]

surturbrand, surtarbrand
sûr'tər-brand, n.
lignite found interbedded with
lavas in Iceland.
[Icel. *surtarbrandr — Surtar,*
gen. of *Surtr,* name of a
fire-giant, *brandr,* brand.]

surucucu
sōō-rōō-kōō-kōō', n.
a S. American Indian name for
the bushmaster.

sutile
sū', sōō'tīl, -til, (*rare*) adj.
done by stitching.
[L. *sūtilis — suĕre,* to sew.]

sutor

sū', sōō'tor, -tər, (*arch.*) n.

a cobbler.

adjs. **suto'rial, suto'rian**
relating to cobbling or to
sewing.

[**souter;** or directly from L.
sūtor, -ōris, cobbler.]

swaraj

swä-räj', (*Ind.*) n.

self-government, independence,
home-rule.

ns. **swaraj'ism** formerly, the
policy of Indian political
independence; **swaraj'ist** an
advocate of this.

[Sans. *svarājya* — *sva,* own,
rājya, rule.]

swats

swots, (*Scot.*) n.

new ale.

[O.E. *swatan* (pl.), beer.]

sweeny

swē'ni, n.

atrophy of the shoulder muscles
of a horse.

[O.E. *swindan,* to pine away,
disappear.]

swelchie

swelhh'i, (*Orkney*) n.

a whirlpool: a tidal race.

[O.N. *svelgr.*]

sweven

swev'n, (*obs.*) n.

a dream.

[O.E. *swefn.*]

swingle

swing'gl, n.

a scutching tool: the swipple of
a flail.

v.t. to scutch.

n. **swing'ling.**

swing'le-bar, swing'letree a
whippletree: a swing-stock;
swing'le-hand a scutching
tool; **swing'ling-stock** a
swing-stock.

[Cf. O.E. *swingell,* stroke,
scourge, rod, and M.Du.
swinghel.]

swipple

swip'l, n.

a swingle or striking part of a
flail.

swire

swīr, n.

a neck (*obs.*): in place names, a
hollow between two hills.

[O.E. *swēora* (Northern *swīra*),
neck.]

swissing

swis'ing, n.

ordinary calendering.

[Origin unknown.]

switchel

swich′l, n.

treacle-beer, molasses and water, etc.: in Newfoundland, cold tea.

[Origin unknown.]

sybotic

sī-bot′ik, adj.

pertaining to a swineherd.
n. **sybotism** (*sib′ə-tizm*).

[Gr. *sybōtēs*, swineherd — *sȳs*, swine, *boskein*, to feed, tend.]

sycamine

sik′ə-mīn, (*B.*) *n.*

the mulberry-tree.

[Gr. *sȳkamīnos*, of Semitic origin, influenced by *sȳkon*, a fig.]

sycee

sī-sē′, n.

silver ingots used as Chinese money. — Also **sycee silver.**

[Chin. *sí sz′.*]

syconium

sī-kō′ni-əm, n.

a multiple fruit in which the true fruits (the pips) are enclosed in a hollow fleshy receptacle — the fig.

[Gr. *sȳkon*, a fig.]

sycosis

sī-kō′sis, n.

inflammation of the hair follicles, esp. of the beard.

[Gr. *sȳkōsis*, a fig-shaped ulcer — *sȳkon*, a fig.]

symphile

sim′fīl, n.

an animal of another kind kept as a guest or domestic animal in an ants' or termites' nest.
ns. **sym′philism** (-*fil-izm*), **sym′phily.**
adj. **sym′philous.**

[Gr. *symphiliā*, mutual friendship — *syn, philos*, a friend.]

synaxis

si-nak′sis, n.

in the early Church, meeting for worship, esp. for the eucharist.
n. **synaxā′rion** (*Gr. Ch.*) a lection containing an account of a saint's life.

[Gr. *synaxis*, a bringing together — *syn*, together, *agein*, to lead.]

synd, sind

sīnd, v.t.

to rinse: to wash out or down.
n. a rinsing: a washing down with liquor.
n.pl. **synd′ings, sind′ings.** — Also **syne** (*Burns*).

[Origin obscure.]

syndesmosis

sin-des-mō'sis, n.

the connection of bones by ligaments: — pl. **-es** (*-ēz*).
adj. **syndesmotic** (*-mot'ik*).

[Gr. *syndesmos* — *syn, desmos,* a bond.]

synedrion

sin-ed'ri-on, n.

a judicial assembly: a sanhedrin. — Also
syned'rium: — pl. (of both)
syned'ria.
adj. **syned'rial.**

[Gr. *syn,* together, *hedrā,* seat.]

syntexis

sin-tek'sis, n.

liquefaction: melting: wasting.
adjs. **syntec'tic, -al.**

[Gr. *syntēxis* — *syn,* with, *tēkein,* to melt.]

syrtis

sûr'tis, (*Milt.*) n.

a quicksand: — pl. **syr'tes** (*-tēz*).

[L. *Syrtēs,* Gr. *Syrtides* (sing. of each *Syrtis*), name of two sandy bays of N. Africa — Gr. *sȳrein,* to draw, sweep along.]

syssarcosis

sis-är-kō'sis, n.

the connection of one bone with another by intervening muscle: — pl. **-oses** (*-ō'sēz*).

[Gr. *syn,* together, *sarx,* flesh.]

syssitia

si-sit'i-ə, or *-sish',* n.

the ancient Spartan custom of eating the chief meal together in public.

[Gr. *syssītiā* — *syn,* together, *sītos,* food.]

T

taal
täl, (*arch.*) n.
Afrikaans or Cape Dutch.
[Du., speech.]

tabaret
tab'ə-ret, n.
an upholsterer's silk stuff, with
alternate stripes of watered and
satin surface.
[Orig. tradename.]

tabellion
tə-bel'yən, n.
an official scrivener in the
Roman empire and elsewhere.
[L.L. *tabelliō, -ōnis* — L. *tabella*,
tablet, dim. of *tabula*, a board.]

tabes
tā'bēz, n.
wasting away.
n. **tabefaction** (*tab-i-fak'shən*)
wasting away, emaciation.
v.t. and v.i. **tab'efy**.
n. **tabescence** (*tab-es'əns*)
wasting: shrivelling.
adjs. **tabesc'ent; tabetic**
(*-bet'ik*); **tab'id**.
tabes dorsa'lis locomotor
ataxia.
[L. *tābēs, -is*.]

tacahout
tak'ə-howt, n.
a gall on the tamarisk, a source
of gallic acid.
[From Berber.]

tacamahac
tak'ə-mə-hak, n.
a gum-resin yielded by several
tropical trees: the balsam
poplar, or its resin.
[From Nahuatl.]

tach, tache
tach, (*B.*) n.
a fastening or clasp.
[O.Fr. *tache*.]

taconite
tak'ə-nīt, n.
a sedimentary rock containing
enough iron to make it a
low-grade iron ore.
[*Taconic* Mountains in N.E.
United States.]

tafia
taf'i-ə, n.
a variety of rum.
[Perh. a W. Indian name, but cf.
Malay *tāfiā*.]

taghairm

tə-gûrm', n.

in the Scottish Highlands, divination: esp. inspiration sought by lying in a bullock's hide behind a waterfall.

[Gael.]

taglioni

tal-yō'nē, n.

an early 19th-century overcoat.

[Named after a family of dancers.]

taha

tä'hä, n.

a S. African weaver-bird.

[Zulu *taka*.]

tahr, tehr

tär, n.

a beardless Himalayan wild goat (*Hemitragus jemlaicus*) that frequents forest precipices.

[App. its name in the W. Himalaya, confused with Nepali *thär*; see **thar**.]

tahsil

tä(hh)-sēl', n.

in India, a division for revenue and certain other purposes.

n. **tahsildar'** an officer of a tahsil.

[Hindi *tahsīl* — Ar.]

tai

tī, n.

a Japanese sea-bream.

taisch, taish

tīsh, n.

in the Scottish Highlands, an apparition or voice of one about to die: second-sight.

[Gael. *taibhis, taibhse*, apparition.]

taka

tä'kə, n.

the standard unit of currency in Bangladesh.

[Beng.]

takin

tä'kin, tä-kēn', n.

a large ungulate (*Budorcas taxicolor*) akin to the goats and antelopes.

[Tibetan.]

tala

tä'la, n.

a traditional rhythmic pattern in Indian music.

[Sans., hand-clapping.]

talapoin

tal'ə-poin, n.

a Buddhist monk, esp. of Pegu, in Burma: a small green W. African guenon monkey.

[Port. *talapão* — Old Peguan *tala pôi*, my lord.]

talayot

tä-lä′yot, n.

a prehistoric usually unchambered stone monument of the Balearic Islands.

[Balearic Sp. for Sp. *atalaya*, an outlook — Ar. *al talā'i*, the vanguard.]

talegalla

tal-i-gal′ə, n.

the brush-turkey.

[Malagasy *talèva*, the purple coot, and L. *gallus*, a cock.]

talipes

tal′i-pēz, n.

club-foot.

adj. **tal′iped** (*-ped*) having a club-foot. — Also n.

[L. *tālus*, ankle, *pēs*, foot.]

talipot, talipat

tal′i-pot, -pat, -put, ns.

an E. Asian fan-palm (Corypha).

[Sinh. *talapata* — Sans. *tālī*, palmyra palm, *pattra*, leaf.]

tallat, tallet, tallot

tal′ət, (*W. of England*) n.

a loft.

[W. *taflod* — L.L. *tabulāta*, flooring.]

talma

tal′mə, n.

a loose cloak or cape.

[From F. J. *Talma*, the actor (1763–1826).]

taluk

tä-lōōk′, n.

a tract of proprietary land: a subdivision of a district, a collectorate.

n. **taluk′dar** holder of a taluk.

[Hind. *ta'alluq*, estate.]

tamandua

tä-män′dū-ä, -dwä′, n.

a S. American ant-eater smaller than the ant-bear.

n. **tamanoir** (*tä-mä-nwär′*; Carib *tamanoa*, same root as *tamanduà*) the great ant-bear.

[Port. *tamanduá* — Sp. *tamándoa* — Tupí *tamanduà*.]

tamanu

täm′ä-nōō, n.

a lofty gamboge tree of the East Indies and Pacific Islands, its trunk yielding tacamahac.

[E. Ind.]

tamara

tam′ə-rə, n.

a mixture of cinnamon, cloves, coriander, etc.

tamarack

tam'ə-rak, n.

the American or black larch.
[Amer. Ind.]

tamari

ta-mä'ri, n.

a concentrated sauce made of
soya beans and salt.
[Jap.]

tamarin

tam'ə-rin, n.

a small S. American
squirrel-monkey (Midas).
[Fr., from Carib.]

tamasha

tə-mä'shä, (*Ind.*) n.

an entertainment, show: fuss.
[Ar. and Pers. *tamāshā.*]

tamin, tamine

tam'in, n.

a thin worsted stuff, highly
glazed.
[Fr. *étamine*; cf. **stammel.**]

tamis

tam'is, n.

cloth sieve.
n. **tamise** (*tä-mēz'*) name for
various thin woollen fabrics.
[Fr.]

tanaiste

tön'ish-tā, n.

the deputy prime minister of the
Republic of Ireland.

[Ir., second, next, deputy; cf.
tanist.]

tangelo

tan'ji-lō, n.

a hybrid between *Tang*erine
orange and pom*elo*: — pl.
tan'gelos.

[Portmanteau word.]

tanghin

tang'gin, n.

a Madagascan poison formerly
used for the judicial ordeal: the
apocynaceous tree yielding it.
n. **tangh'inin** its active
principle.

[Malagasy *tangèna.*]

tangie

tang'i, n.

an Orcadian water-spirit,
appearing as a seahorse, or
man covered with seaweed.

tangun

tang'gun, n.

the Tibetan piebald pony.
[Hindi *tāghan* — Tibetan
rtanān.]

tanist

tan'ist, n.

a Celtic chief's heir elect.
n. **tan'istry** the system of
succession by a previously
elected member of the family.
[Ir. *tánaiste,* Gael. *tànaiste,* heir,
successor.]

tanti

tan'tī, tan'tē, (L.) adj.
worth while.

tapa, tappa

tä'pə, n.

paper-mulberry bark.
[Polynesian generally.]

tapadera

tä-pä-dā'rə, **tapadero** *-rō* (pl.
tapade'ros), ns.

the guard in front of a Mexican
stirrup.
[Sp., lid, cover — *tapar,* to
cover.]

tapeti

tap'ə-ti, n.

the Brazilian rabbit.
[Tupí.]

tapotement

tä-pot-mã, tə-pōt'mənt, n.
percussion in massage.
[Fr.]

tarand

tar'ənd, (*obs.*) n.

a northern beast fabled to
change colour like the
chameleon: a reindeer.
[Gr. *tarand(r)os,* a reindeer, or
(prob.) elk.]

tarantas(s)

tä-rän-täs', n.

a four-wheeled Russian vehicle
mounted on poles.
[Russ. *tarantas.*]

tarlatan

tär'lə-tən, n.

an open, transparent muslin.
[Fr. *tarlatane;* origin doubtful.]

tarpan

tär'pan, n.

a small extinct wild horse of the
steppes of S. European Russia,
not identical with Przewalski's
horse.
[Tatar.]

tarrock

tar'ək, (*local*) n.

a sea-bird of various kinds.
[Origin obscure.]

tartana

tär-tä'nə, n.

a little covered wagon.
[Sp.]

tarwhine

tär'(h)wīn, n.

an Australian sea-bream.

[Aboriginal.]

tate, tait

tāt, (Scot.) n.

a small portion, pinch, tuft.

tath

täth, (dial.) n.

cattle dung: coarse tufted grass
that grows where it has fallen.

v.t. to manure.

v.i. to drop dung.

[O.N. *tath.*]

tatou

ta'tōō, or -tōō', n.

an armadillo, esp. the giant
armadillo.

[Tupí *tatú.*]

taube

tow'bə, n.

a German monoplane with
recurved wings (1914–18 war).

[Ger., dove.]

tautog

tö-tog', n.

a labroid fish of the North
American Atlantic coast.

[Narragansett *tautauog.*]

tawpie, taupie

tö'pi, (Scot.) n.

a clumsy, heedless, or
inefficient girl.

[Cf. Norw. *taap*, a half-wit.]

tayra, taira

tī'rə, n.

a large South American species
of the weasel family.

[Tupí *taira.*]

teagle

tē'gl, (dial.) n.

a hoist or lift: a baited line for
catching birds.

v.t. to hoist or catch with a
teagle.

teapoy

tē'poi, n.

a small table or tripod: (by
confusion with **tea**) a tea-caddy.

[Hind. *tīn, tīr-*, three, Pers. *pāi*,
foot.]

tebbad

teb'ad, n.

a sandstorm.

[Cf. Pers. *tab*, fever, *bād*, wind.]

teckel

tek'l, n.

a dachshund.

[Ger.]

tectrix

tek'triks, n.

a feather covering the
quill-bases on a bird's wings
and tail (also called **covert**): —
pl. **tectrices** (-*trī'sēz*).
adj. **tectricial** (-*trish'l*).
[L. *tēctrīx, -īcis,* fem. of *tēctor,
-ōris,* a coverer, plasterer —
tegĕre, to cover.]

teer

tēr, v.t.

to plaster: to daub: to spread.
[O.Fr. *terer* — *terre,* earth.]

tef, teff

tef, n.

an Ethiopian cereal grass,
Eragrostis abyssinica.
[Amharic *têf.*]

teg, tegg

teg, n.

a sheep (or *obs.* a doe) in its
second year.
[Perh. Scand.]

teguexin

te-gwek'sin, n.

a large black and yellow South
American lizard.
[Aztec *tecoixin.*]

294

teil

tēl, n.

the linden or lime tree.
teil tree the lime: the terebinth
(*B.*).
[O.Fr. *teil* — L. *tilia.*]

telamon

tel'ə-mən, (*archit.*) n.

a man's figure as a pillar: — pl.
telamones (-*mō'nēz*).
[Gr. mythological hero,
Telamōn — *tlēnai,* to endure,
bear.]

teledu

tel'ə-dōō, n.

the stinking badger of Java. —
Also **stinkard, stinking
badger.**
[Javanese.]

telega

tel-eg'ə, tel-yeg'ə, n.

a springless Russian wagon.
[Russ.]

telemark

tel'i-märk, n.

a sudden turn on the outer ski,
first practised at *Telemark* in
Norway.
v.i. to execute a telemark.

telesm

tel'ezm, n.

a talisman.
adjs. **telesmat'ic, -al.**

adv. **telesmaťically.**

[Gr. *telesma*.]

telestic

ti-les'tik, adj.

relating to the mysteries.

[Gr. *telestikos* — Gr. *teleein*, to fulfil, consummate, initiate, perform — *telos*, end, rite, etc.]

telestich

tel-es'tik, tel'es-tik, n.

a poem or block of words whose final letters spell a name or word.

[Gr. *telos*, end, *stichos*, row.]

telson

tel'sən, n.

the hindermost part of a crustacean or arachnid.

[Gr. *telson*, a headland in ploughing; cf. *telos*, end.]

temse, tems

tems, temz, n.

a sieve.

v.t. to sift.

[O.E. *temesian*, to sift; cf. Du. *tems*.]

tenace

ten'ās, -is, n.

the combination in one hand of the cards next above and next below the other side's best in the suit.

[Sp. *tenaza*, pincers.]

tenaculum

te-nak'ū-ləm, n.

a surgical hook or forceps for picking up blood-vessels.

[L. *tenāculum*, holder, pincers.]

tenaille

te-nāl', (*fort.*) n.

an outwork in the main ditch in front of the curtain.

n. **tenaillon** (*te-nal'yən*) a work to strengthen the side of a small ravelin. — Also **tenail'.**

[Fr., — L. *tenāculum*, pincers — *tenēre*, to hold.]

tenné

ten'ā, (*her.*) n.

an orange-brown tincture. — Also adj.

[Obs. Fr.]

tenrec

ten'rek, **tanrec** *tan'rek*, ns.

a large Madagascan insectivore (*Centetes*).

[Malagasy *t(r)àndraka*.]

tenson

ten'sn, n.

a competition in verse between two troubadours before a court of love: a subdivision of the chanson so composed. — Also **ten'zon.**

[Fr., — L. *tēnsiō, -ōnis*, a struggle.]

teocalli

tā, tē-ō-kal'(y)i, n.

a Mexican pyramid temple.

[Nahuatl, — *teotl*, god, *calli*, house.]

tepefy

tep'i-fī, v.t. and v.i.

to make or become tepid.

[L. *tepefacĕre — tepēre*, to be tepid, *facĕre*, to make.]

terai

ter-ī', n.

a wide-brimmed double-crowned ventilated hat, first worn in the *Terai* (Taрái), India.

teraph

ter'əf, n.

in ancient Jewish religion and divination, an image of some sort — pl. **ter'aphim** (also used as sing.).

[Heb.]

teras

ter'əs, (*med.*) n.

a monstrosity: — pl. **ter'ata**.

n. **ter'atism** a monster: an abnormal person or animal, esp. as a foetus.

adj. **teratogenic** (*ter-ə-tō-jen'ik*) producing monsters: causing abnormal growth (in a foetus).

ns. **terat'ogen** an agent that raises the incidence of congenital malformations; **teratogeny** (*-toj'i-ni*) the production of monsters.

adjs. **ter'atoid** monstrous; **teratolog'ic, -al**.

ns. **teratol'ogist; teratol'ogy** the study of malformations or abnormal growths, animal or vegetable: a tale of marvels; **teratō'ma** a tumour, containing tissue from all three germ-layers: — pl. **teratō'mata**.

adj. **teratō'matous**.

[Gr. *teras, -atos*, a monster.]

tercio

tûr'si-ō, -shi-ō (*Scott* **tertia**), (*hist.*) n.

an infantry regiment, orig. Spanish: — pl. **ter'cios**.

[Sp.]

terefa(h)

tə-rā-fä', -rā', adj.

not ritually clean, not kosher.

[Heb. *tāraph*, to tear.]

terek

ter'ek, n.

a sandpiper (*Xenus cinereus*) found at the river *Terek* (Russia) and elsewhere (also **Terek sandpiper**).

terete

tə-rēt', ter'ēt, (*biol.*) adj.
smooth and cylindrical.
[L. *terēs, terĕtis*, smooth, *terĕre*,
to rub.]

terrella

ter-el'ə, n.
a magnetic model of the earth.
[A mod. dim. of L. *terra*, the
earth.]

terret, territ

ter'it, n.
a swivel-ring: a ring for
fastening a chain to: a ring or
loop through which driving reins
pass. — Also **torr'et, turr'et.**
[O.Fr. *toret*, dim. of *tor, tour*, a
round.]

teru-tero

ter'ōō-ter'ō, n.
the Cayenne lapwing: — pl.
ter'u-ter'os.

teston

tes'tən, n.
a name for various coins, orig.
bearing a king's or duke's head:
a Henry VIII shilling: later a
sixpence.
n. **testoon'** a Portuguese or
Italian teston.
[Obs. Fr. *teston*, Port. *testão*, It.
testone — It. *testa*, head.]

testrill

(*Shak.*), **testril** *tes'tril*, n.
a sixpence.

tetronal

tet'rən-əl, n.
a hypnotic and sedative drug
rarely used because of its high
toxicity.

tetter

tet'ər, (*Shak.*) n.
a skin eruption.
v.t. to affect with a tetter.
adj. **tett'erous** (*Shak.*).
[O.E. *teter.*]

tettix

tet'iks, n.
a cicada: an ornament for the
hair of that shape (*Gr. ant.*).
[Gr.]

tewit, tewhit

tē'(h)wit (*Scot.* **teuchat**
tūhh'ət), (*dial.*) ns.
a lapwing.
[Imit.]

thairm

thārm, (*Scot.*) n.
an intestine: catgut, a musical
string.
[O.E. *tharm, thearm.*]

thalweg

täl'vähh, -veg, n.

the longitudinal profile of the bottom of a river-bed.

[Ger., — *Thal* (now *Tal*), valley, *Weg*, way.]

thar

t'här, tär, n.

properly the serow: by confusion applied to the tahr.

[Nepali (Indic language of Nepal) *thār*.]

theave

thēv, (*dial.*) n.

a young ewe, esp. of the first year.

thenar

thē'när, n.

the palm: the ball of the thumb: the sole. — Also adj.

[Gr. *thĕnăr, -ăros*.]

theow

thā'ow, (*O.E. hist.*) n.

a slave.

[O.E. *thēow*.]

theriac

thē'ri-ak, **theriaca** *thē-rī'ə-kə*, (*arch.*) ns.

an antidote to venomous bites, etc.

adj. **thērī'acal**.

[Gr. *thēriakē* — *thērion*, a wild beast.]

thesmothete

thes'mō-thēt, n.

a law-giver, esp. one of the six junior archons in ancient Athens.

[Gr. *thesmothetēs* — *thesmos*, law, *thetēs*, a placer, setter.]

thete

thēt, (*Gr. hist.*) n.

orig. a serf: a poor freeman in Athens under Solon's constitution.

[Gr. *thēs, thētos*.]

thiasus

thī'ə-səs, n.

a company or troop of worshippers, esp. a Bacchic rout.

[Gr. *thiasos*.]

thible

thib'l, thīb'l, **thivel** *thiv'l, thīv'l*, (*Northern*) ns.

a porridge-stick.

[Origin unknown.]

thig

thig, (*Scot.*) v.i.

to beg: to live on alms.
v.t. to beg: to get by begging: — pa.t. and pa.p. **thigg'it**.
ns. **thigg'er; thigg'ing**.
thigging and sorning extortionate begging and sponging.

[O.N. *thiggja*; cf. O.E. *thicgan*, to take.]

thirdborough

thûrd′bər-ə, (*hist.*) n.

an under-constable.

[Supposed to be from O.E. *frithborh,* a surety for peace .]

thlipsis

thlip′sis, n.

constriction: compression.

[Gr. *thlīpsis* — *thlībein,* to press.]

thrave

thrāv, **threave** *thrēv,* (*dial.*) ns.

two stooks of (usu.) twelve sheaves each: two dozen: a good number.

[Scand.; cf. Icel. *threfi,* Dan. *trave.*]

thremmatology

threm-ə-tol′ə-ji, n.

the science of breeding domestic animals and plants.

[Gr. *thremma, -atos,* a nurseling, *logos,* discourse.]

thwaite

thwāt, n.

a piece of reclaimed land — common in place names.

[O.N. *thveit.*]

thylacine

thī′lə-sēn, -sīn, -sin, n.

the so-called Tasmanian wolf.

[Gr. *thȳlakos,* pouch.]

tical

ti-käl′, tik′l, n.

an obsolete Siamese silver coin, about equal to a rupee, now replaced by the baht: a unit of weight.

[Port. *tical.*]

ticca

tik′ə, (*Ind.*) adj.

hired.

[Hind. *thīkā,* hire.]

tickey, ticky

tik′i, (*S.Afr.*) n.

a former S. Afr. coin, a threepenny-bit: now used of a decimal coin of small denomination.

[Origin uncertain.]

tiffany

tif′ə-ni, n.

a silk-like gauze.

adj. of tiffany: transparent.

[Gr. *theophaneia,* theophany, or *diaphaneia,* transparency.]

tige

tēzh, n.

the shaft of a column.

[Fr., — L. *tībia,* a pipe.]

tigon

tī′gon, n.

the offspring of a tiger and a lioness. — Also **tíg′lon.**

[*tiger, lion.*]

tika

tē'kə, n.

a red mark on the forehead of Hindu women, formerly of religious significance but now counted as a beauty spot. [Hind.]

tiki

tik'ē, n.

an image, often in the form of a small greenstone ornament, representing an ancestor—in some Polynesian cultures, worn as an amulet. [Maori.]

til

til, tēl, n.

sesame. — Also **teel**. **til'-oil; til'-seed**. [Hind. *til* — Sans. *tila*.]

tilbury

til'bər-i, n.

a kind of gig, for two. [Said to be so named from its first maker.]

timariot

ti-mä'ri-ot, (*hist.*) n.

a Turkish feudal militiaman. [Fr., — Turk. *timār*.]

timbrel

tim'brəl, n.

an ancient Oriental tabor or tambourine.

adj. **tim'brel'd** (*Milt.*) sung to the timbrel.

[O.Fr. *timbre* — L. *tympanum*, drum.]

timenoguy

tim'ən-og-i, n.

a rope stretched from place to place in a ship, esp. one to prevent the fore-sheet fouling (*naut.*): a makeshift: a what's-its-name. [Origin obscure.]

tinamou

tin'ə-mōō, n.

a South American partridge-like bird (*Tinamus*) of or akin to the Ratitae. [Fr., — Galibi (Indian language of Fr. Guiana) *tinamu*.]

tincal

ting'kəl, n.

crude borax. [Malay *tingkal*.]

tinchel

tin'hhyəl, ting'kəl, n.

a circle of men who close in round a herd of deer. [Gael. *timchioll*, a circuit.]

tindal

tin'dəl, n.

a petty-officer of lascars.

[Malayalam *tandal.*]

tipper

tip'ər, n.

a kind of ale — from Thomas *Tipper*, who brewed it in Sussex.

tirasse

ti-ras', n.

a pedal-coupler in an organ.

tirrivee, tirrivie

tir'i-vi, or *-vē', (Scot.) n.*

a tantrum or fit of passion: a commotion.

titi, tee-tee

tē'tē, n.

a small South American monkey (*Callicebus*).

titoki

ti-tok'i, tē', n.

a New Zealand tree with reddish paniculate flowers.

[Maori.]

tityre-tu

tit-, tīt-i-ri-tōō', -tū', n.

a member of a 17th-century fraternity of aristocratic hooligans.

[Opening words of Virgil's first eclogue, *Tītyre tū,* Tityrus, thou (lying under the spreading beech), conjectured to indicate the class that had beech trees and leisure to lie under them.]

toby

tō'bi, n.

the road (*thieves' slang*): robbery on the road: a stop-cock in a gas- or water-main under the road (*Scot.*): the cover protecting it (*Scot.*):

high toby highway robbery on horseback; **low toby** footpad robbery.

[Shelta *tōbar.*]

tocher

tohh'ər, (Scot.) n.

a dowry.

v.t. to dower.

adj. **toch'erless.**

n. **toch'er-good** property given as tocher.

[Ir. *tochar,* Gael. *tochradh.*]

toco

tō'kō, (slang) n.

punishment: — pl. **tō'cos.** — Also **tō'kō:** — pl. **tō'kos.**

[Origin uncertain; Gr. *tokos,* interest, and Hindi *thōkō* — *thoknā,* to thrash, have been suggested.]

togue

tōg, n.

the Great Lake char (or trout), a gigantic salmonid of North America.

[From Indian name.]

toheroa

tō-ə-rō'ə, n.

an edible shellfish found at low tide buried in sandy beaches.

[Maori.]

toho

tō-hō', interj.

a call to pointers to stop: — pl. **tohos'**.

tohu bohu

tō'hōō bō'hōō,

chaos.

[Heb. *thōhū wa-bhōhū*, emptiness and desolation (Gen. i. 2).]

toise

toiz, n.

an old French lineal measure = 6·395 feet (very nearly 2 metres).

[Fr., — L. *tendĕre, tēnsum*, to stretch.]

toiseach, toisech

tō'shəhh (*hist.*), n.

an ancient Celtic noble below a mormaor.

[Gael.]

tola

tō'lə, n.

an Indian unit of weight=180 grains troy (11·66 grammes).

[Hind., — Sans. *tulā*, weight.]

tolt

tōlt, n.

an old English writ removing a court-baron cause to a county court.

[A.Fr. *tolte* — L.L. *tolta* — L. *tollĕre*, to take away.]

tomalley

to-mal'i, n.

American lobster fat ('liver'), eaten as a delicacy: extended to tamal.

[Said to be Carib.]

toman

tō-män', n.

a myriad, or ten thousand: a former Persian gold coin worth 10000 dinars.

[Pers. *tumān*.]

tombac, tombak

tom'bak, n.

an alloy of copper with a little zinc: an alloy of copper and arsenic.

[Fr. *tombac* — Malay *tambaga*, copper.]

tomboc

tom'bok, n.

a Javanese long-handled weapon.

tombolo

tom'bə-lō, n.

a bar of sand or gravel connecting an island with another or with the mainland: — pl. **tom'bolos.**

[It.]

tomium

tō'mi-əm, n.

the cutting edge of a bird's bill. adj. **tō'mial.**

[Latinised from Gr. *tomeion*, a knife-edge — *temnein*, to cut.]

tonnag

tō'nag, n.

a shawl with a shaped neck and side fastening.

[Gael.]

toparch

top'ärk, n.

the ruler of a district. n. **top'archy** a toparch's territory.

[Gr. *toparchēs* — *topos*, a place, *archein*, to rule.]

tophus

tō'fəs, n.

a gouty deposit: — pl. **tō'phi** (*-fī*).

adj. **tophā'ceous.**

[L. *tōphus*, *tōfus*, porous stone, tufa.]

toran(a)

tōr', *tör'ən(-ə)*, ns.

in India, a type of arched gateway: also a garland of flowers or leaves hung between two points.

[Hind.]

torchon

tör-shō̃, n. (Fr.)

a duster or dish-cloth: (in full **torchon lace**) peasants' bobbin lace of loose texture and geometrical design, or a machine-made imitation: **(torchon paper)** a rough paper for water-colour drawing.

[Fr., — *torcher*, to wipe.]

torcular

tör'kū-lər, n.

a tourniquet.

[L. *torcular*, *-āris*, a wine-press, oil-press.]

toreutic

tör-ū'tik, *-ōō'*, adj.

of chased or embossed metal-work. n.sing. **toreu'tics** artistic work in metal.

[Gr. *toreutikos*, *-ē*, *-on* — *toreuein*, to bore.]

torgoch

tör'gohh, n.

the red-bellied char.

[W.]

torii

tör'ē-ē, n.

a Japanese Shinto temple gateway.

[Jap.]

torsel

tör'sl, n.

a plate in a brick wall to support the end of a beam. — Also **tassel.**

[L. *taxillus,* a die, It. *tassello,* Fr. *tasseau.*]

torsk

törsk, n.

a North Atlantic fish (*Brosmius brosme*) of the cod family, with long single dorsal fin.

[Sw., Norw., Dan. *torsk* — O.N. *thorskr*; cf. Ger. *Dorsch,* haddock.]

touraco

tōō'rə-kō, or *-kō',* n.

an African bird (*Turacus*) of the plantain-eater family, with a horny shield on the forehead and remarkable pigments in its feathers: — pl. **touracos.**

[Supposed to be a W. African name.]

tozie

tōz'i, (*Scott*) n.

a shawl made from a goat's inner coat.

trachelate

trak'ə-lāt, adj.

having a neck.

[Gr. *trachēlos,* neck.]

tracklement

trak'l-mənt, (*dial.*) n.

a condiment, accompaniment, etc.

[Ety. uncertain.]

tragelaph

trag', traj'i-laf, n.

a fabulous animal, part goat, part stag: a harnessed antelope (**Tragelaphus** *-el'ə-fəs*). adj. **tragel'aphine.**

[Gr. *tragelaphos* — *tragos,* a goat, *elaphos,* a deer.]

tragopan

trag'ō-pan, n.

a brilliant Asiatic horned pheasant.

[Gr. *tragopān,* hornbill — *tragos,* goat, *Pān,* the god Pan.]

tralaticious, tralatitious

tral-ə-tish'əs, adj.

transmitted: traditional: handed on, second-hand.

[L. *trālātīcius* — *trānslātum,* serving as supine to *trānsferre.*]

trangam

trang'gəm, n.

a trumpery gimcrack.

[Origin unknown.]

transenna

tran-sen'ə, n.

a screen enclosing a shrine.

[L. *trānsenna*.]

tranter

trant'ər, (*dial.*) n.

a hawker: a carrier.

v.t. and v.i. **trant**

(back-formation) to hawk.

[Cf. L.L. *trāvetārius*.]

trass

tras, n.

an earthy volcanic tuff used as a hydraulic cement. — Also **tarras', terras'**.

[Du. *tras*.]

treague

trēg, (*Spens.*) n.

a truce.

[L.L. *tregua, treuga* — Goth. *triggwa*, treaty.]

trebuchet

treb'ū-shet, trā-bü-shā', n.

a mediaeval military engine for launching stones, etc.

[O.Fr.]

tregetour

trej'ə-tər, n.

a juggler (*obs.*): a trickster: a deceiver.

[O.Fr. *tresgetour — tresgeter —* L. *trāns, jactāre*, to throw.]

trehala

tri-hä'lə, n.

Turkish manna, a sweet substance got from the cocoons of a type of beetle.

[Turk. *tīqālah*.]

trémie, tremie

trā-mē, trem'i, n.

a hopper-like device for laying concrete under water.

[Fr., hopper — L. *trimodia*, a three-peck measure.]

tret

tret, n.

an allowance to purchasers of 4lb. on every 104 lb. for waste.

[Poss. A.Fr. *tret*, pull, turn of the scale or Fr. *traite*, transport, both — *traire*, to draw — L. *trahĕre, tractum*.]

trevally

tri-val'i, n.

an Australian horse-mackerel (Caranx) of various species.

[Prob. a modification of **cavally**.]

tribade
trib'ad, n.

a woman homosexual.
adj. **tribad'ic.**
ns. **trib'adism, trib'ady**
lesbian masturbation simulating heterosexual intercourse in the missionary position.
[Fr. through L. *tribas, -adis* — Gr. *tribas, -ados* — *tribein*, to rub.]

tribble
trib'l, n.

a horizontal frame with wires stretched across it for drying paper.

tricerion
trī-sē'ri-on, (*Greek Church*) n.

a three-branched candlestick.
[Late Gr., — Gr. *kēros*, wax.]

tridarn
trē'därn, n.

a Welsh dresser having three tiers or stages.
[Welsh.]

tringle
tring'gl, n.

a curtain-rod.
[Fr.]

triones
trī-ō'nēz, n.pl.

the seven stars of the Plough.
[L. *triōnēs*, plough-oxen.]

tripsis
trip'sis, n.

pulverisation: shampooing: massage.
[Gr. *trīpsis* — *trībein*, to rub.]

tripudium
trī-pū'di-əm, tri-pōōd'i-ōōm, n.

an ancient Roman religious dance in triple time, or dance generally: divination from the hopping of birds feeding, or from the dropping of scraps from their bills.
adj. **tripu'diary.**
v.i. **tripu'diate** to dance for joy: to exult: to stamp.
n. **tripudiā'tion.**
[L. *trĭpŭdium*, prob. from *trēs*, three, *pēs, pedis*, foot.]

trisula
tri-sōō'lə, n.

the trident of Siva. — Also **trisul'.**
[Sans. *triśūla*.]

troat
trōt, v.i.

to bellow, as a buck. — Also n.
[O.Fr. *trout, trut,* interj. used to urge on animals.]

trommel

trom'əl, n.

a revolving cylindrical sieve for cleaning or sizing minerals.
[Ger. *Trommel*, drum.]

tron

tron, **trone** *trōn,* (chiefly *Scot.*) ns.

a public weighing machine, used also as a place of punishment as by nailing the ear: the market-place: a system of weights used at the tron.
[O.Fr. *trone* — L. *trŭtina* — Gr. *trȳtanē*, a pair of scales.]

troolie, troelie, troely

trōō'li, n.

the bussu palm: its leaf.
[Tupí *tururi*.]

troparion

trop-ār'i-on, or *-ar',* (*Greek Church*) n.

a stanza or short hymn: — pl. **tropar'ia.**
[Dim. of Gr. *tropos,* trope.]

troupial, troopial

trōō'pi-əl, n.

a bird (*Icterus icterus*) famous for its song: any bird of the Icteridae.
[Fr. *troupiale* — *troupe,* troop.]

trucage, truquage

trü-käzh, (Fr.) n.

faking of works of art.
n. **truqueur** (*trü-kœr*) a faker of works of art.

truchman

truch'mən, (*obs.*) n.

an interpreter: — pl. **truch'men** or **truchmans.**
[Ar. *turjamān.*]

trumeau

trōō-mō', n.

a piece of wall or pillar between two openings: — pl. **trumeaux** (*-mōz'*).
[Fr.]

tsamba

tsam'bə, n.

a Tibetan barley dish.
[Tibetan.]

tsunami

tsōō-nä'mē, n.

a very swiftly travelling sea wave that attains great height.
[Jap. *tsu,* harbour, *nami,* wave.]

tuart, tooart

tōō'ərt, **tewart** *tū', ns.*

a strong-timbered Eucalyptus (*E. gomphocephala*).
[Australian Aboriginal.]

tuchun

tōō-chün', dōō-jün', n.

a Chinese military governor.

[Chin.]

tuckahoe

tuk'ə-hō, n.

an edible but tasteless underground fungus of the southern United States: the edible rootstock of several American aroids: an inhabitant of eastern Virginia.

[From Algonquian.]

tucutuco

tōō-kōō-tōō'kō, **tucotuco** *tōō-kō-tōō'kō,* ns.

a South American rodent of mole-like habits: — pl. **-cos.**

[From its cry.]

tulchan

tulhh'ən, n.

a calf's skin set beside a cow to make her give milk freely. **tulchan bishop** (*Scot. hist.*) a titular bishop appointed to transmit most of the revenues of a diocese to the nobles (1572).

[Gael. *tul(a)chan,* a hillock.]

tule

tōō'lā, n.

a large American bulrush (Scirpus).

[Sp., — Nahuatl *tollin.*]

tulwar

tul'wär, n.

an Indian sabre.

[Hind. *talwār.*]

tupik

tū'pik, **tupek** *-pek,* ns.

an Eskimo skin tent.

[Eskimo.]

tuque

tūk, n.

a Canadian cap made by tucking in one tapered end of a long cylindrical bag, closed at both ends.

[Fr. *toque.*]

turbary

tûr'bə-ri, n.

the right to take peat from another's ground: a place where peat is dug.

[L.L. *turbāria* — *turba,* turf; of Gmc. origin .]

turbit

tûr'bit, n.

a domestic pigeon having white body, coloured wings, and short beak.

[Ety. dub.]

turion

tū'ri-ən, n.

an underground bud, growing upward into a new stem.

[L. *turiō, -ōnis,* a shoot.]

turlough

tûr'lohh, (*Ir.*) n.

a pond dry in summer.

[Ir. *turloch*.]

turm

(*Milt.* **turme**), *tûrm*, n.

a troop.

[L. *turma*.]

turndun

tûrn'dun, **tundun** *tun'*, ns.

an Australian bull-roarer.

[Aboriginal.]

tusche

tōōsh, n.

a substance used in lithography for drawing the design which then does not take up the printing medium.

[Ger. *tuschen*, to touch up (with paint, etc.).]

tuskar, tusker

tus'kər, **twiscar** *twis'kər*, (*Orkney* and *Shetland*) ns.

a peat-spade.

[O.N. *torfskeri* — *torf*, turf, *skera*, to cut.]

tutenag

tū'ti-nag, n.

an alloy of zinc, copper, etc.: (*loosely*) zinc.

[Marathi *tuttināg*.]

tutiorism

tū'ti-ər-izm, n.

in R.C. moral theology, the doctrine that in a case of doubt between right and wrong one should take the safer course, i.e. the one in verbal accordance with the law.

n. and adj. **tū'tiorist.**

[L. *tūtior*, *-ōris*, safer, comp. of *tūtus*, safe.]

twaite

twāt, n.

one of the British species of shad. — Also **twaite shad.**

[Origin unknown.]

twankay

twang'kā, n.

a kind of green tea: gin (*slang*).

[*Tong-ke* or Tun-chi in China.]

twibill

twī'bil, n.

a double-headed axe.

[O.E. *twibill*.]

twitten

twit'n, (*dial.*) n.

a narrow lane between two walls or hedges. — Also **twitt'ing.**

[Perh. related to L.G. *twiete*, alley, lane.]

tye

tī, n.

an inclined trough for washing
ore.

v.t. to wash in a tye.

[O.E. *tēag*, case, chest.]

tymp

timp, n.

the plate of a blast-furnace
opening.

tystie

tī'sti, (*dial.*) n.

the black guillemot.

[Scand.; cf. O.N. *theist*.]

tzimmes

tsi'mis, n.

a sweetened stew or casserole
of vegetables, fruit and
sometimes meat: — pl.
tzimm'es.

[Yiddish.]

U

udo

ōō'dō, n.

a Japanese species of Aralia with edible shoots: — pl. **u'dos.**

[Jap.]

ule, hule

ōō'lā, n.

a Central American rubber tree (*Castilloa*): its crude rubber.

[Sp. *hule* — Nahuatl *ulli*.]

ulema

ōō'li-mə, n.

the body of professional theologians, expounders of the law, in a Muslim country: a member of such a body.

[Ar. '*ulema*, pl. of '*ālim*, learned.]

uliginous

ū-lij'i-nəs, adj.

slimy: oozy: swampy: growing in swampy places.

[L. *ūlīginōsus* — *ūlīgō*, *-inis*, moisture.]

ulitis

ū-lī'tis, n.

inflammation of the gums.

[Gr. *oula*, gums, *-itis*.]

ulosis

ū-lō'sis, n.

the formation of a scar.

[Gr. *oulōsis* — *oulē*, a scar.]

ultion

ul'shən, n.

revenge: avengement.

[L. *ultiō*, *-ōnis*.]

ultroneous

ul-trō'ni-əs, adj.

spontaneous, voluntary.
adv. **ultrō'neously.**
n. **ultrō'neousness.**

[L. *ultrōneus* — *ultrō*, spontaneously.]

umbles

um'blz, n.pl.

entrails (liver, heart, etc.), esp. of a deer. — Also **hum'bles, num'bles.**
n. **um'ble-pie'** also **hum'ble-pie', num'ble-pie'** a pie made from the umbles of a deer.

[O.Fr. *nombles,* from *lomble,*
loin — L. *lumbulus,* dim. of
lumbus, loin.]

umbrette

um-bret', n.

the hammerhead (*Scopus
umbretta*), a brown African bird
akin to the storks, remarkable
for its huge nest. — Also
um′bre (*-bər*), **umber-bird.**

[Fr. *ombrette* — *ombre,* umber.]

umbriere

um′bri-ēr, (*Spens.*) n.

a visor. — Also **um′brere,
um′bril, um′brel.**

[O.Fr. *ombriere, ombrel,*
shade.]

umiak, oomia(c)k, oomiac

ōō′mi-ak, ōōm′yak, n.

an open skin boat, manned by
women.

[Eskimo.]

unalist

ū′nəl-ist, n.

a holder of one benefice.

[L. *ūnus,* one.]

unau

ū′nö, ōō′now, n.

the two-toed sloth.

[Fr., from Tupí.]

unberufen

ōōn-bə-rōōf′ən, (Ger.) adj.

not called for — used as an
exclamation to avert the ill-luck
that may possibly follow an
over-confident or boastful
statement.

uncus

ung′kəs, n.

a hook or hook-like process: —
pl. **unci** (*un′sī*).
adjs. **unc′ate** hooked;
unciform (*un′si-förm*)
hook-shaped; **un′cinate, -d**
unciform: hooked at the end.
n. **uncī′nus** a hooklet: a
marginal tooth of a mollusc's
radula: a hooked chaeta in
annelids: — pl. **uncī′nī.**

[L. *uncus* and *uncinus,* hook.]

undern

un′dərn, (*obs.*) n.

the third hour, about nine in the
morning: terce: the forenoon:
the afternoon or early evening:
a light meal.
n. **un′derntime** (*Spens.*
un′dertime) the time of the
midday meal.

[O.E. *undern.*]

urachus

ū′rə-kəs, n.

a ligament connecting the
bladder with the umbilicus.

[Gr. *ourachos,* the fetal
structure from which it is
formed.]

urd

ûrd, n.

an Indian plant of the bean family (*Phaseolus mungo*), or its edible blackish seed. — Also **urd bean, black gram**.

[Hindi.]

uredo

ū-rē'dō, n.

rust in plants: a rust-fungus in its summer stage (also **ure'do-stage**): — pl. **uredines** (*ū-rē'di-nēz*).

n.pl. **Uredinā'lēs** the Uredineae.

adj. **uredine** (*ū'ri-dīn*).

n.pl. **Uredineae** (*ū-ri-din'i-ē*) the rust-fungi, an order of parasitic Basidiomycetes.

adj. **uredin'ial** (*U.S.*).

ns. **uredin'iospore**, **urē'diospore** (*U.S.*) a uredospore; **uredin'ium**, **urē'dium** (*U.S.*) a uredosorus: —both pl. **-ia**.

adj. **urē'dinous**.

ns. **urēdoso'rus** (*-sö'*, *-sō'*) a pustule containing uredospores; **urē'dospore** a spore produced by rust-fungi in the uredo-stage.

[L. *ūrēdō, -inis*, blight — *ūrĕre*, to burn.]

urent

ū'rənt, adj.

burning, stinging.

[L. *ūrēns, -entis*, pr.p. of *ūrĕre*, to burn.]

urinant

ū'rin-ənt, (*her.*) adj.

diving, head downward.

n. **ū'rinātor** a diver.

[L. *ūrīnārī*, to plunge.]

urite

ū'rīt, n.

an abdominal segment.

[Gr. *ourā*, a tail.]

urman

ōōr-män', n.

(swampy) pine forest.

[Russ., — Tatar *ūrmān*.]

urson

ûr'sən, n.

the Canadian porcupine.

[Fr. *ourson*, dim. of *ours* — L. *ursus*, bear.]

urubu

ōō-rōō-bōō', n.

a S. American vulture.

[Tupí *urubú*.]

urus

ū'rəs, n.

the aurochs.

urva

ûr'və, n.

the crab-eating mongoose of south-eastern Asia.

[Nepali.]

usucapion

ū-zū-kā'pi-ən, **usucaption**
-kap'shən, (*Rom. law*) ns.
the acquisition of property by
long possession and enjoyment.
n. **usucā'pient** one who
claims or holds by usucapion.
v.t. **ū'sucapt** (*-kapt*) to acquire
so.
adj. **usucapt'ible.**
[L. *ūsūcapĕre* — *ūsus*, use,
capĕre, *captum*, to take.]

utis

ū'tis, (*Shak.*) n.
clamour, din.
[M.E. *ūthēs*, hue and cry, app.
— O.E. *ūt*, out, *hæs*, hest.]

uvarovite

ōō-vä'rō-vīt, n.
a green lime-chrome garnet.
[After Count S. S. *Uvarov*,
Russian minister of education.]

V

vakass
vä′käs, n.
an Armenian ephod.

vakil, vakeel
vä-kēl′, n.
an Indian agent, representative,
or pleader.
[Hind., — Ar. *vakīl*.]

valgus
val′gəs, adj.
bow-legged: of a deviation from
the longitudinal alignment of the
body in which the distal part of
the deformity turns away from
the midline (*med.*). — Also
val′gous (*rare*).
n. the condition of being
bow-legged: (for *tālipēs valgus*)
out-turned club-foot.
[L., bow-legged.]

vali
vä-lē′, n.
a governor, esp. of a vilayet.
[Turk.]

vallecula
va-lek′ū-lə, n.
a groove or furrow: — pl.
vallec′ulae (*-lē*).
adjs. **vallec′ular,**

vallec′ulate.
[L.L. dim. of L. *vallis*, valley.]

valonia, vallonia, valonea
və-lō′ni-ə, n.
a tanning material, acorns of a
Levantine oak (valonia oak,
Quercus aegilops) or similar
species.
[It. *vallonea* — Gr. *balanos,* an
acorn.]

vamplate
vam′plāt, n.
a guard for the hand on a lance.
[A.Fr. *van-* for *avant*, before,
plate, plate.]

vang
vang, n.
a guy-rope to steady a gaff.
[A form of **fang.**]

vapulate
vap′ū-lāt, v.t.
to flog.
v.i. to be flogged.
n. **vapūlā′tion** a flogging.
[L. *vāpulāre, -ātum*, to be
flogged.]

vara

vä′rä, n.

a Spanish-American linear measure, varying from 33 to 43 inches (*c.* 84–110 cm).

[See **vare.**]

varan

var′ən, n.

a monitor lizard.

n. **Var′anus** the monitor genus, constituting the family **Varanidae** (*-an′*).

[Ar. *waran.*]

vare

vār, n.

a vara: a wand of authority.

[Sp. *vara,* a rod — L. *vāra,* a trestle, forked stick — *vārus,* crooked.]

varec, varech

var′ek, n.

kelp: wrack.

[Fr.; of Scand. origin.]

vareuse

vä-rœz′, (*southern U.S.*) n.

a kind of loose jacket.

[Fr.]

vargueño

vär-gān′yō, n.

a cabinet or desk of a kind made at *Vargas* (Bargas) near Toledo: — pl. **vargue′ños.**

varicella

var-i-sel′ə, n.

chickenpox.

adjs. **varicell′ar; varicell′oid** resembling varicella; **varicell′ous** pertaining to varicella.

[Irreg. dim. of **variola.**]

varna

vûr′nə, vär′nə, n.

any of the four great Hindu castes.

[Sans., class.]

vartabed

vär′tə-bed, n.

a member of an Armenian order of clergy.

[Armenian *vartabet.*]

varus

vā′rəs, adj. (*med.*)

of a deviation from the longitudinal alignment of the body in which the distal part of the deformity turns towards the midline.

n. (for *tālipēs vārus*) in-turned club-foot.

[L. *vārus,* bent, knock-kneed.]

varve

värv, (*geol.*) n.

a seasonal layer of clay deposited in still water, of service in fixing Ice Age chronology.

adjs. **varve(d)** stratified in distinct layers of annual deposit. [Sw. *varv*, layer.]

vavasour

vav'ə-sōōr, **valvassor** *val'və-sör*, ns.

one who held his lands of a tenant in chief.

n. **vav'asory** the tenure or the lands of a vavasour.

[O.Fr., app. — L.L. *vassus vassōrum*, vassal of vassals — *vassus*, vassal.]

vedalia

vi-dā'li-ə, n.

an orig. Australian ladybird, *Rodolia cardinalis*, introduced elsewhere to control insect pests.

veery

vēr'i, n.

the tawny thrush of North America.

[Prob. imit.]

vega

vā'gə, n.

a low fertile plain: a tobacco-field (*Cuba*).

[Sp.]

veilleuse

vā-yœz', n.

a shaded night-lamp.

[Fr., — *veiller*, to watch.]

velatura

vel-ə-tōō'rə, n.

a method of glazing a painting by rubbing with the hand.

[It.]

velitation

vel-i-tā'shən, n.

a skirmish.

[L. *vēlitātiō, -ōnis* — *vēles, -itis*, a light-armed soldier.]

vell

vel, n.

the fourth stomach of a calf, used in making rennet.

[Origin unknown.]

vellicate

vel'i-kāt, v.t. and v.i.

to twitch.

n. **vellicā'tion.**

[L. *vellicāre, -ātum*, to pluck.]

vellon

ve-lyōn', n.

billon: old Spanish copper money.

[Sp. *vellon* — Fr. *billon*.]

velskoen

fel'skōōn, (*S.Afr.*) n.

a shoe made of rawhide.

[Du. *vel*, skin, *schoen*, shoe.]

venatic, -al

vi-nat'ik, -əl, adjs.

pertaining to hunting.

adv. **venat'ically.**

ns. **venation** (*vi-nā'shən; rare*)
hunting: a hunt; **venā'tor** a
huntsman, hunter.

adj. **venatorial** (*ven-ə-tō'ri-əl,
-tö'*).

[L. *vēnārī*, to hunt, *vēnātiō*,
hunting, *vēnātor*, a hunter.]

venefic, -al

vi-nef'ik, -əl, **veneficious**
ven-i-fish'əs, **veneficous**
vi-nef'i-kəs, adjs.

acting by poison or potions or
by sorcery.

advs. **venef'ically,
venefic'(i)ously.**

[L. *venēficus — venēnum*,
poison, *facĕre*, to do.]

ventail,

(*Spens.*) **ventayle, ventaile,**
ven'tāl, n.

in mediaeval armour, the part of
a helmet protecting the lower
part of the face.

[Fr. *ventail*, O.Fr. *ventaille*; ety.
confused; ultimately from L.
ventus, wind.]

verecund

ver'i-kund, adj.

modest.

[L. *verēcundus*.]

verquere

vər-k(w)ēr', n.

an obsolete form of
backgammon. — (*Scott*)
verquire'.

[Du. *verkeeren*, to turn round, to
play at backgammon.]

versute

vər-sūt', adj.

crafty, wily.

[L. *versūtus*.]

vervel

vûr'vl, **varvel** *vär'*, ns.

a ring for a hawk's jess.

adjs. **ver'velled, var'velled.**

[Fr. *vervelle*.]

vervet

vûr'vit, n.

an African guenon monkey.

[Fr.]

vetiver

vet'i-vər, n.

cuscus roots.

vettura

vet-tōō'rə, n.

a carriage, cab, or car.

n. **vetturino** (*-rē'nō*) its driver or
proprietor: — pl. **vetturi'ni**
(*-nē*).

[It., — L. *vectūra*, a carrying —
vehĕre, to convey.]

vibrissa

vī-bris'ə, n.

a tactile bristle, as a cat's whisker: a vaneless rictal feather: a bristle, hair, as in the nostril: — pl. **vibriss'ae** (-*ē*).

[L., a hair in the nostril.]

victorine

vik-tə-rēn', n.

a fur tippet with long ends: a variety of peach.

[Woman's name.]

vidame

vē-däm', n.

in French feudal jurisprudence, the deputy of a bishop in temporal affairs: a minor noble.

[Fr., — L.L. *vicedominus.*]

viduous

vid'ū-əs, adj.

widowed: empty.

n. **vid'ūage** widowhood: widows collectively.

adj. **vid'ūal.**

n. **vidū'ity** widowhood.

[L. *vidua*, a widow, *viduus*, deprived, bereaved.]

vigia

vi-jē'ə (Sp. *vi-hhē'ä*), n.

a danger warning on a chart.

[Sp. *vigía*, look-out — L. *vigilia.*]

vihara

vē-hä'rə, n.

a Buddhist or Jain precinct, temple, or monastery.

[Sans. *vihāra.*]

vihuela

vi-wā'lə, n.

an old Spanish musical instrument, akin to the guitar.

[Sp.]

vilayet

vil-ä'yet, n.

a Turkish province.

[Turk. *vilāyet* — Ar. *welāyeh.*]

vimana

vi-män'ə, n.

the central shrine of an Indian temple with pyramidal roof: a temple gate: a heavenly chariot, chariot of the gods.

[Sans. *vimāna*, lit. a marking out.]

vimineous

vim-in'i-əs, adj.

with long flexible shoots.

[L. *vīmineus* — *vīmen, -inis*, osier, switch.]

vina

vē'nə, n.

an Indian stringed instrument with fretted finger-board over two gourds.

[Sans. *vīṇā.*]

319

vinew

vin'ū, v.t. and v.i.

to make or become mouldy.
n. mouldiness.

adj. **vin'ewed** mouldy: musty.

[O.E. *fynegian*, to mould —
fynig, mouldy — *fyne*, mould.]

virement

vē-rə-mã, *vīr'mənt*, n.

authorised transference of a
surplus to balance a deficit
under another head: authorised
redirection of funds for one
purpose to a more urgent
occasion.

[Fr.]

virgate

vûr'gāt, adj.

rodlike: twiggy.
n. an old land measure,
commonly 30 acres.

[L. *virga*, rod.]

viscacha

vis-kä'chə, n.

a S. American burrowing rodent
of heavy build. — Also
**vizca'cha, bisca'cha,
bizca'cha.**

n. **viscachera** (*-chā'rə*) a
settlement of viscachas.

[Sp., — Quechua *huiscacha*.]

visite

vi-zēt', n.

a woman's light short cloak
worn in the mid 19th century.

[Fr.]

visne

vē'ni, (*law*) n.

a venue.

[O.Fr. *visné*, neighbourhood —
L. *vīcīnus*, neighbour.]

vison

vī'sən, n.

the American mink.

[Fr.; origin unknown.]

vitellus

vi-, *vī-tel'əs*, n.

the yolk of an egg: — pl.
vitell'ī.

adj. **vit'ellary** pertaining to the
vitellus: yellow like the yolk of
an egg.
n. **vitell'icle** a yolk-sac.
adj. **vitelligenous** (*-ij'*)
producing yolk.
ns. **vitell'in** a phosphoprotein
present in yolks of eggs;
vitell'ine a vitellus.
adj. vitellary.

[L., a yolk; a transferred use of
vitellus — *vitulus*, a calf.]

vitiligo

vit-i-lī'gō, *-ə-lē'gō*, n.

a skin abnormality in which
irregular patches of the skin

lose colour and turn white.

[L. *vitilīgo*, a skin eruption.]

vitrain

vit′rān, n.

a separable constituent of bright coal, of vitreous appearance.

[L. *vitrum*, glass, and suff. -*ain*.]

vivda

viv′dä, vev′dä, n.

in Shetland, meat hung and dried without salt. — Also **vif′da.**

[Perh. O.N. *vöthvi*, muscle.]

vivers

vē′vərz, (*Scot.*) n.pl.

food, eatables.

[Fr. *vivres* — L. *vīvĕre*, to live.]

vives

vīvz, n.sing.

a disease of horses, swelling of the submaxillary glands.

[O.Fr. *avives, vives* — Sp. *avivas* — Ar. *addhība* — *al*, the, *dhība*, she-wolf.]

vizsla

viz′lə, vizh′lə, n.

a Hungarian breed of hunting dog with smooth red or rust-coloured coat.

[*Vizsla*, a town in Hungary.]

vlei

flā, n.

low-lying ground where a shallow lake forms in the wet season (*Afrik.*): a swamp (local *U.S.*). — Also **vly.**

[Dial. Du., — Du. *wallei*, valley.]

voar

vōr, vör, n.

in Orkney and Shetland, spring, seed-time.

[O.N. *vār*, spring.]

voe

vō, n.

in Orkney and Shetland, a bay, creek.

[O.N. *vāgr*, a creek.]

vogie

vō′gi, (*Scot.*) adj.

vain: merry.

[Origin obscure.]

voivode

voi′vōd, **vaivode** *vā′vōd*, ns.

orig., the leader of an army: later, in south-east Europe, the title of the head of an administrative division: in Moldavia and Walachia, the former title of the princes: in Turkey, an inferior administrative official. ns. **voi′vodeship, vai′vodeship.**

[Russ. *voevoda* (Serb. *vojvoda*, Pol. *wojewoda*), a general.]

vola

vō'lə, n.

the hollow of the hand or foot:
— pl. **volae** (*vō'lē*).
adj. **vo'lar** pertaining to the
palm or to the sole.

[L.]

volost

vō'lost, n.

a division for local government
in Russia (*hist.*): a soviet of a
rural district.

[Russ. *volost.*]

volucrine

vol'ū-krin, -krīn, adj.

pertaining to birds, bird-like.

[L. *volucris*, a bird — *volāre*, to
fly.]

vomer

vō'mər, n.

a bone of the skull in most
vertebrates — in man, a thin flat
bone, shaped like a wedge or
ploughshare, forming part of the
middle partition of the nose.
adj. **vomerine** (*vō'* or *vo'*).
vo'mero- used in composition,
as **vomeronas'al**, pertaining
to the vomer and the nasal
cavity.

[L. *vōmer*, a ploughshare.]

vorpal

vör'pəl, adj.

a nonsense word coined by
Lewis Carroll to describe a
sword, now used to mean
sharp-edged.

voteen

vō-tēn', (Ir.) n.

a devotee.

vou(l)ge

voōzh, n.

a weapon carried by
foot-soldiers in the 14th century,
having a blade fixed on a long
staff.

[Fr.]

vraic

vrāk, n.

a Channel Islands name for
seaweed, used for fuel and
manure.
ns. **vraick'er** a gatherer of
vraic; **vraick'ing** the gathering
of vraic.

[Dial. Fr.; see **varec.**]

vug

vug, n.

a Cornish miner's name for a
cavity in a rock, usu. lined with
crystals.
adj. **vugg'y.**

vulsella

vul-sel'ə, n.

a forceps with toothed or
clawed blades: — pl.
vulsell'ae (-ē). — Also
vulsell'um: — pl. -**a.**

[L.]

W

wadmal

wäd' or *wud'məl*, (*hist.*) n.

a thick or coarse woollen cloth, woven esp. in Orkney and Shetland. — Also **wad'maal**, **wad'mol(l)**.

[O.N. *vathmāl* — *vāth*, cloth, *māl*, measure.]

wadset

wod'set, (*Scot.*) n.

a mortgage: something pledged or pawned. — Also **wadsett**.

v.t. to mortgage: to pawn.

n. **wad'setter** mortgagee.

wagenboom

vä'gən-bōm, -bōōm, **waboom** (*Afrik.*) *vä'bōōm*, ns.

a S. African tree (*Protea grandiflora*) whose wood is used in making wagon wheels.

[Du., wagon-tree.]

wagmoire

wag'moir, (*Spens.*) n.

a quagmire.

wahine

wä-hē'ne, n.

a Maori woman.

[Maori.]

wakiki

wä'kē-kē, n.

shell money.

[Melanesian.]

waler

wä'lər, n.

in India, a horse imported from New South *Wales*, or from Australia generally.

wallaroo

wol-ə-rōō', n.

a large kangaroo (*Macropus robustus*). — Also known as **euro**.

[Aboriginal *wolarū*.]

wallwort

wöl'wərt, n.

dwarf elder (also called Danewort, Dane's blood, etc.), a plant with an offensive smell and taste.

[O.E. *wealhwyrt, wǣlwyrt* — *wealh*, a foreigner, or (prob. orig., from the belief that it grew on battlefields) *wǣl*, slaughter, and *wyrt*, a root, a plant.]

walty

wol'ti, (*naut.*) adj.
inclined to lean or roll over.
[Obs. adj. *walt*, unsteady (—
O.E. *wealt*, found only in
unwealt, steady), and suff. -*y*.]

wampee

wom-pē', n.
an edible Asiatic fruit
(*Clausena*; family Rutaceae)
about the size of a large grape,
with a hard yellow rind.
[Chin. *hwang-pī*, lit. yellow
skin.]

wampish

wom'pish, (*Scott*) v.t.
to brandish, flourish, wave
about. — Also v.i.
[Origin uncertain.]

wamus

wöm'əs, wom'əs, (*U.S.*) n.
a kind of cardigan, or a strong
jacket, buttoned at neck and
wrists. — Also **wamm'us,
wamp'us.**
[Du. *wammes* — O.Fr.
wambais, a military tunic orig.
worn under armour.]

wanderoo

won-də-rōō', n.
usu. applied to the lion-tailed
macaque, a native of the
Malabar coast of India: properly,
a langur of Sri Lanka.
[Sinhalese *wanderu*, monkey.]

wang

wang, (*obs.*) n.
the cheek: a wang-tooth.
wang'-tooth a molar.
[O.E. *wange.*]

wanigan

won'i-gən, n.
in a lumber camp, a chest for
supplies, or a kind of houseboat
for loggers and their supplies:
also the pay-office. — Also
wan'gan, wan'gun.
[Algonquian.]

wanty

won'ti, n.
a belt used to secure a load on
a pack-horse's back (*obs.*): the
belly-band of a shaft-horse
(*dial.*): a short rope, esp. one
used for binding hay on a cart
(*dial.*).

wanze

wonz, (*obs.*) v.i.
to decrease, waste away.
[O.E. *wansian.*]

wapentake

wop'n-tāk, (esp. *hist.*) n.
a name given in Yorkshire and
certain other shires to a
territorial division of the county
similar to the *hundred* of
southern counties.
[Late O.E. *wǽpen(ge)tæc*,
O.N. *vāpnatak*, lit.

weapon-taking, assent at a meeting being signified by brandishing a weapon.]

wapiti

wop'i-ti, n.

a species (*Cervus canadensis*) of deer of large size, native to N. America.

[Algonquian.]

wapper

wop'ər, (*dial.*) v.i.

to blink: to move tremulously.
adj. **wapp'er-eyed** blinking.
n. **wapp'er-jaw** a projecting under-jaw.
adj. **wapp'er-jawed.**

[Cf. Du. *wapperen,* to oscillate.]

warby

wör'bi, (*Austr. coll.*) adj.

worn-out, decrepit, unattractive: unwell, unsteady.

[Poss. from Eng. dial. *warbie,* a maggot.]

warrigal

wor'i-gal, wor'ə-gl, n.

the Australian wild dog, the dingo: a wild Australian horse.
adj. wild, savage. — Also
warr'agal, warr'agle, warr'agul.

[Aboriginal.]

wase

wāz, (*dial.*) n.

a wisp of hay, straw, etc.: a pad on the head to ease the pressure of a burden.

[Gmc. word; perh. Scand.]

wastel

wos'tl, **was'tel-bread** (*-bred*), (*obs.*) ns.

bread made from the finest of the flour.

[O.Fr. *wastel,* a variant of *guastel, gastel* (Fr. *gâteau,* cake); of Gmc. origin.]

watchet

woch'it, (*arch.*) n.

a pale blue: a material of this colour: an angling fly.
adj. pale blue.

[O.Fr. *wachet,* perh. orig. a material.]

wavey, wavy

wā'vi, n.

the snow-goose.

[Cree.]

wayzgoose, wase-goose

wāz'gōōs, n.

a printers' annual dinner or picnic. — Earlier **way'goose.**

[Origin obscure.]

wedeln

vā′dəln, (also with *cap.*) n.

a style of downhill skiing in which the skis, kept parallel and close together, are swivelled rapidly from side to side.
n.pl. such swivelling movements.
v.i. (also with *cap.*) to execute wedeln on a downhill run.
[Ger., orig. to wag one's tail.]

weem

wēm, (*Scot.*) n.
a subterranean dwelling.
[Early Gael. *uaim*, cavern.]

weka

we′kə, n.
any of the flightless rails (Ocydromus) of New Zealand.
[Maori, imit.]

whangam

(h)wang′gam, (*Goldsmith*) n.
an imaginary animal.

whare

(h)wor′i, hwär′ā, fär′ā, (*New Zealand*) n.
a house.
[Maori.]

wheeple

(h)wē′pl, (*Scot.*) v.i.
to make a long drawn-out cry such as that of the curlew: to whistle feebly. — Also v.t. and n.
[Imit.]

whippletree

(h)wip′l-trē, n.
the cross-piece of a carriage, plough, etc., which is made so as to swing on a pivot and to which the traces of a harnessed animal are fixed (often used in conjunction with a doubletree).
[From **whip.**]

whitling

(h)wit′ling, n.
a kind of trout, probably a young bull-trout.

whittaw

(h)wit′ö, (*dial.*) n.
a saddler. — Also **whitt′awer.**

wigan

wig′ən, n.
a stiff canvas-like fabric for stiffening garments: a plain grey cloth for boot-linings, etc.
[*Wigan*, the town.]

williwaw

wil′i-wö, n.
a gust of cold wind blowing seawards from a mountainous coast, e.g. in the Straits of Magellan: a sudden squall (also *fig.*).
[Origin uncertain.]

willy-willy

wil'i-wil'i, (*Austr.*) n.

a cyclone.

[Aboriginal.]

windle

win'dl, n.

an appliance for winding yarn.
— Also (*Scot.*) **winn'le.**

wintle

win'tl, (*Scot.*) v.i.

to stagger.

n. a stagger.

[Flem. *windtelen — winden*, to
wind.]

wisent

wē'zənt, vē', n.

another name for the European
bison.

[Ger.]

wishtonwish

wish'tən-wish, n.

the N. American prairie-dog: the
whip-poor-will (*Fenimore
Cooper*).

[Amer. Ind.]

witloof

wit'lōf, n.

a kind of chicory with large
leaves.

[Du., lit. white leaves.]

witwall

wit'wöl, (*dial.*) n.

the green woodpecker, or the
greater spotted woodpecker.

[Cf. Ger. *Wittewal, Wiedewall*.]

wobbegong

wob'i-gong, n.

a carpet shark.

[Aboriginal.]

wonga-wonga

wong'(g)ə-wong'(g)ə, n.

the large Australian white-faced
pigeon (also **wong'a**): any of
several varieties of hardy
evergreen climbing vine of the
family *Bignoniaceae*.

[Aboriginal.]

woodie

wōōd'i, -ē, (*Scot.*) n.

the gallows.

woold

wōōld, v.t.

to wind a rope or chain round.

adj. **woold'ed.**

ns. **woold'er** a stick used in
woolding a mast or yard: a pin
in a ropemaker's top;
woold'ing.

[Du. *woelen*; Ger. (*be*)*wuhlen*.]

woomera

wōōm'ər-ə, **womera** *wom'*,
woomerang *wōōm'ər-ang*, ns.

a throwing-stick.

[Aboriginal.]

wootz

wōōts, n.

steel made in India, from ancient times, by fusing iron with carbonaceous matter.

[For *wook* — Kanarese *ukku*, steel.]

worral, worrel

wor'əl, n.

a monitor lizard.

[Ar. *waral*, lizard.]

worricow, worrycow, wirricow

wur'i-kow, (*Scot.*) n.

a hobgoblin: the devil: anything frightful or even only grotesque.

[**worry** (vb.), and *cow*, a hobgoblin.]

wortle

wûr'tl, n.

a perforated plate through which wire, tubing, is drawn to make it thinner. — Also **whirtle**.

[Ety. uncertain.]

woubit

wōō'bit, n. (usu. **hairy woubit**)

a hairy caterpillar, esp. one of a tiger-moth: applied derogatorily to a person, often implying smallness and shabbiness. — Also **woo'but, ou'bit, oo'bit**.

[M.E. *wolbode, wolbede*; prob.

— *wol*, wool; meaning of second element unknown.]

wourali, woorali

wōō-rä'li, **woora'ra** (-*rä'rə*), **oura'li, oura'ri** (-*rä'ri*), **ura'li** (*ōō*-), **ura'ri** ns.

the plant yielding curare.

[Carib. variants of *kurari*.]

wowf

wowf, (*Scot.*) adj.

crazy.

[Origin unknown.]

wow-wow, wou-wou

wow'-wow, n.

the name for two types of gibbon found in Indonesia, the *silver gibbon* of Java and the *agile gibbon* of Sumatra.

[Imit. of its cry.]

wroath

rōth, (*Shak.*) n.

misfortune.

wurley

wûr'lē, (*Austr.*) n.

an Aborigine's hut, traditionally made of branches, bark, leaves and plaited grass: a nest, esp. a rat's nest: — pl. **wur'leys** or **wur'lies**.

[Aboriginal.]

wyandotte

wī'an-dot, n.

a useful breed of the domestic fowl, of American origin.

[From the N. American tribe so called.]

X

xebec

zē'bek, n.

a small three-masted vessel much used by the former corsairs of Algiers.

[Fr. *chebec,* influenced by Sp. form; perh. from Turkish or Arabic.]

xerafin, xeraphim

sher'ə-fēn, -fēm, (Port.) ns.

a silver coin of Goa.

xoanon

zō'ə-non, n.

a primitive statue, said to be fallen from heaven, orig. of wood, later overlaid with ivory and gold.

[Gr. *xoanon* — *xeein,* to carve.]

xyster

zis'tər, n.

a surgeon's instrument for scraping bones.

[Gr. *xystēr,* a graving tool.]

xystus

zis'təs, (ant.) n.

a covered portico used by athletes for their exercises: an open colonnade: a tree-planted walk. — Also **xyst, xys'tos.**

[L., — Gr. *xystos* or *-on,* perh. orig. a cleared or raked place — *xyein,* to scrape; cf. **xyster.**]

Y

yabby, yabbie
yab'i, (Austr.) n.
a small freshwater crayfish, often used as bait.
[Aboriginal.]

yacca
yak'ə, n.
either of two evergreens (Podocarpus) of the West Indies, or their wood.
[Sp. *yaca,* from Taino.]

yagger
yag'ər, (Scot.) n.
a pedlar.

yakhdan
yak'dän, n.
a box used for carrying ice, strapped on to the back of an animal.
[Pers. *yakh,* ice, *dān,* box.]

yakka
yak'ə, (Austr.) n.
hard toil. — Also **yacker, yakker.**
[Aboriginal (Queensland) word.]

yale
yāl, n.
a fabulous beast, depicted in heraldry, resembling a horse with tusks, horns and an elephant's tail.
[L. *ealē.*]

yamen
yä'men, n.
the offices and residence of a mandarin.
[Chin.]

yapok, yapock
yap'ək, n.
the S. American amphibious opossum (*Chironectes minimus*), which feeds on shrimps, etc.
[From river *Oyapok,* in French Guiana.]

yapp
yap, n.
a limp leather binding in which the cover overlaps the edges of the book.
[*Yapp,* a bookseller.]

yardang

yär'däng, n.

a ridge formed by wind erosion from sand, silt, etc., usually lying parallel to the prevailing wind direction.

[Turk. abl. of *yar*, steep bank, precipice.]

yarpha, yarfa

yär'fə, n.

peaty soil in Shetland: clayey, sandy, or fibrous peat: a peat-bog.

[O.N. *jörfi*, gravel.]

yatag(h)an

yat'ə-gan, n.

a long Turkish dagger, without guard, usu. curved.

[Turk. *yātāghan*.]

yaud

yöd, yäd, (*Scot.*) n.

a mare: an old mare: an old horse generally.

[O.N. *jalda*.]

yauld, yald

yöld, yäld, (*Scot.*) adjs.

active, nimble, strong.

[Ety. unknown.]

yaup

yöp, (*Scot.*) adj.

hungry.

[O.E. *gēap*, shrewd.]

yaupon

yö'pən, n.

a bushy evergreen shrub of the holly genus, native to the S.E. coasts of the U.S., its leaves yielding the medicinal 'black drink' of the Indians. — Also **yapon** (*yö'*), **yupon** (*yōō'*).

[Amer. Indian.]

yean

yēn, (*arch.* and *dial.*) v.t. and v.i.

esp. of a sheep, to bring forth (young).

n. **yean'ling** a lamb or a kid. — Also adj.

[O.E. *ge-, eanian*, to bring forth; *ēacen*, increased, pregnant.]

yegg

yeg, (*U.S.*) n.

a burglar, esp. a burglar of safes. — Also **yegg'man**.

[Poss. the name of an American safe-breaker.]

yeld

yeld, **yell** *yel*, (*Scot.*) adjs.

barren: not giving milk: unproductive.

[Late O.E. *gelde*.]

yelt

yelt, (*dial.*) n.

a young sow.

[O.E. *gilte* — M.L.G. *gelte*, a spayed sow.]

yex

yeks, (*dial.*) v.i.

to hiccup, belch, spit.

n. a hiccup, etc. — Also **yesk**.

[O.E. *geocsian,* to sob.]

yite

yīt, (*dial.*) n.

the yellow-hammer.

[Origin obscure.]

ylang-ylang

ē'lang-ē'lang, n.

a tree (*Canangium odoratum*) of the Malay Archipelago and Peninsula, the Philippines, etc., or an essence (also **ylang-ylang oil**) distilled from its flowers.

[Tagálog.]

ylem

ī'ləm, n.

the prime substance whence according to some theories, the elements are sprung.

[O.Fr. *ilem* — L. *hȳlem,* accus. of *hȳlē* — Gr. *hȳlē,* matter.]

ynambu

ē-näm-bōō', n.

a very large tinamou.

[Port. *inambu*; of Tupí origin, related to **tinamou**.]

yojan

yō'jan, **yojana** *yō'ja-nə,* ns.

an Indian measure of distance, usu. about five miles.

[Hind. *yojan* — Sans. *yojana,* (distance covered in one) yoking.]

yoldring

yōld'ring, n.

a yellow-hammer.

[Variant of dial. *yowlring* — O.E. *geolu.*]

yu

yü, ū, n.

precious jade (nephrite or jadeite). — Also **yu'-stone**.

[Chin. *yü, yü-shih.*]

yuan

yü-än, n.

the monetary unit of the People's Republic of China: — pl. **yuan**.

[Chin. *yüan.*]

yucker

yuk'ər, n.

the American flicker or golden-winged woodpecker.

[Imit. of its note.]

yuft

yuft, n.

Russia leather.

[Russ. *yuft.*]

yuga

yōō′gə, n.

one of the Hindu ages of the world. — Also **yug.**

[Sans.]

yuke

yōōk, **yuck** *yuk* (*dial.*) vs.i.

to itch.

ns. itching: the itch. — Also **youk, yeuk, euk, ewk.**

adjs. **yuk′y, yuck′y** itchy.

[Same as **itch;** prob. influenced by the M.Du. form, *jeuken.*]

yulan

yōō′lan, n.

a Chinese magnolia, with large white flowers.

[Chin.]

Z

zabeta
za-bē'ta, (Ar.) n.
a stated tariff.

zabra
zä'brä, (*hist.*) n.
a small vessel on the Spanish coast.
[Sp.]

zack
zak, (*Austr. slang*) n.
formerly a sixpenny, now a five-cent, piece.

zakuska
zä-kōōs'ka, n.
an hors-d'œuvre: a snack: — pl. **zakuski** (*-kē*).
[Russ.]

zamarra, zamarro
thä-mär'ä, -ō, (Sp.) ns.
a shepherd's sheepskin coat: — pls. **-s**.

zambo
zam'bō, n.
the offspring of a Negro man and an American Indian woman: anyone of mixed Negro and Indian blood: — pl.

zam'bos.
[Sp.]

zambomba
thäm-bom'bä, n.
a simple Spanish musical instrument, made by stretching a piece of parchment over a wide-mouthed jar and inserting a stick in it, sounded by rubbing the stick with the fingers.
[Sp.]

zamouse
za-mōōs', n.
the short-horned buffalo of West Africa.
[Ar. *jāmūs.*]

zampogna
tsam-pō'nyä, n.
the Italian bagpipe.
[It.]

zanella
zə-nel'ə, n.
a mixed twilled fabric for covering umbrellas.
[Origin uncertain.]

zanja

thäng'hhä, n.

an irrigating canal.
n. **zanjero** (*-hhā'rō*) one who superintends the distribution of water in irrigation canals: — pl. **zanje'ros**.
[Sp.]

zanze

zän'ze, n.

an African musical instrument.
[Ar. *sanj*, castanets, cymbals.]

zaptieh

zap'ti-e, n.

a Turkish policeman. — Also **zap'tiah, zab'tieh.**
[From Turk.]

zareba

zə-rē'bä, n.

in the Sudan, a stockade, thorn-hedge, etc., against wild animals or enemies: a fortified camp generally. — Also **zaree'ba, zari'ba, zere'ba, zeri'ba.**
[Ar. *zarībah*, pen or enclosure for cattle.]

zarf

zärf, n.

an ornamental holder for a hot coffee-cup. — Also **zurf.**
[Ar. *zarf*, a vessel.]

zastruga

zas-trōō'gä, n.

one of a series of long parallel snow-ridges on open wind-swept regions of snow. — Also **sastru'ga:** — pl. **-gi** (*-gē*).
[Russ.]

zebub

zē'bub, n.

the zimb.
[Ar. (dial.) *zubāb*, a fly.]

zein

zē'in, n.

a protein found in Indian corn.

zel

zel, n.

a form of Oriental cymbal.
[Turk. *zīl*.]

zelotypia

zel-ō-tip'i-ə, n.

jealousy: morbid zeal in the prosecution of any project or cause.
[Gr. *zēlotypiā*, jealousy — *zēlos*, zeal, *typtein*, to strike.]

zendik

zen'dik, n.

an unbeliever in revealed religion in the East: one who practises magic.
[Ar. *zendīq*.]

zerda

zûr'də, n.

a fennec.

[Ar. *zardawa*.]

zetetic

zē-tet'ik, adj.

proceeding by inquiry.

n. a search, investigation: a seeker, the name taken by some of the Pyrrhonists.

[Gr. *zētētikos* — *zēteein*, to seek.]

zibet

zib'it, n.

an Asiatic civet.

[It. *zibetto* — Ar. *zabād*.]

ziffius

zif'i-əs, (*Spens.*) n.

a sea-monster, perh. a swordfish.

ziganka

zi-gang'kə, n.

a Russian country-dance: the music for such, usu. quick, with a drone bass.

[Russ. *tsyganka*, a gypsy woman.]

zillah, zila

zil'a, n.

an administrative district in India.

[Ar. *dila* (in Hindi pronunciation, *zila*), a rib, thence a side, a district.]

zimb

zimb, n.

an Ethiopian dipterous insect, like the tsetse, hurtful to cattle.

[Amharic, a fly.]

zimbi

zim'bi, n.

a kind of cowrie used as money.

[Port. *zimbo*; of African origin.]

zimocca

zi-mok'ə, n.

a type of bath-sponge.

[Mod. L.]

zingel

tsing'əl, zing'əl, n.

a fish of the perch family, found in the Danube.

[Ger.]

zinke

tsing'kə, n.

an old wind instrument like the cornet.

[Ger.]

zizel

ziz'əl, n.

the ground-squirrel.

[Ger. *Ziesel*.]

zoiatria

zō-i-at′ri-ə, zō-ī-ə-trī′ə, n.,
zoiatrics *zō-i-at′riks*, n.sing.
veterinary surgery.

[Gr. *zōion*, an animal, *iātreiā*,
healing.]

zoism

zō′izm, n.

the doctrine that life originates
from a specific vital principle.
n. **zō′ist** one who maintains
this theory.

[Gr. *zōē*, life.]

zonda

son′də, n.

a dry, hot, and dusty wind
blowing from the Andes across
the Argentine pampas, during
July and August.

[Sp.; perh. from Amer. Indian.]

zoozoo

zōō′zōō, (*dial.*) n.

the wood-pigeon.

[From the sound made by it.]

zopilote

sō-pi-lō′te, n.

one of the smaller American
vultures — the turkey-buzzard,
or the urubu.

[Mex. Sp.]

zoppo

tsop′pō, (*mus.*) adj.

with syncopation.

[It.]

zorro

sor′ō, n.

a S. American fox or fox-like
wild dog: — pl. **zorr′os**.
ns. **zoril, zorille** (*zor′il, -il′*) an
African skunk-like musteline
animal (*Zorilla*); **zorillo**
(*sor-ē′yō, zor-il′ō*) a S. American
skunk: — pl. **zorill′os; zorino**
(*zor-ēn′ō*) a euphemism for
skunk fur used to make
garments: — pl. **zorin′os**.

[Sp. *zorro, zorra*, fox, *zorilla* (Fr.
zorille) skunk.]

zoster

zos′tər, n.

an ancient Greek waist-belt for
men: herpes zoster or shingles.

[Gr. *zōstēr*, a girdle.]

zucchetto

tsōō-ket′ō, n.

the skullcap of an ecclesiastic,
covering the tonsure: — pl.
zucchett′os. — Also
zuchett′a, -o (pl. -os).

[It. dim. of *zucca*, a gourd.]

zufolo

tsōō′fō-lō, n.

a small flute or flageolet used in
training singing-birds. — Also

339

zuff'olo: — pl. **zuf(f)'oli** (-ē).
[It.]

zugzwang
tsōōhh'tsväng, n.
in chess, a blockade position in which any move is disadvantageous to the blockaded player.
[Ger.]

zumbooruk
zum'bōō-ruk or, -bōō', n.
a small cannon mounted on a swivel, carried on the back of a camel. — Also **zum'booruck, zom'boruk, zam'boorak.**
[Hind. zambūrak; from Pers.]

zupa
zū'pə, n.
a confederation of village communities governed by a **zū'pan,** in the early history of Serbia, etc.
[Serbian.]

zuz
zōōz, n.
a silver coin of ancient Palestine.
[Heb.]

zwitterion
tsvit'ər-ī-ən, n.
an ion carrying both a positive and a negative charge.
[Ger. Zwitter, a hybrid, and **ion.**]

zymome
zī'mōm, n.
an old name for the part of gluten insoluble in alcohol.
[Gr. zȳmōma, a fermented mixture.]

zymurgy
zī'mûr-ji, n.
the department of technological chemistry that treats of wine-making, brewing, distilling, and similar processes involving fermentation.
[Gr. zȳmē, leaven, ergon, work.]

zythum
zī'thəm, n.
a kind of beer made by the ancient Egyptians — much commended by Diodorus Siculus, a writer of the first century B.C.
[Gr. zȳthos.]

FOR THE BEST IN PAPERBACKS, LOOK FOR THE 🐧

In every corner of the world, on every subject under the sun, Penguin represents quality and variety – the very best in publishing today.

For complete information about books available from Penguin – including Puffins, Penguin Classics and Arkana – and how to order them, write to us at the appropriate address below. Please note that for copyright reasons the selection of books varies from country to country.

In the United Kingdom: Please write to *Dept JC, Penguin Books Ltd, FREEPOST, West Drayton, Middlesex, UB7 0BR.*

If you have any difficulty in obtaining a title, please send your order with the correct money, plus ten per cent for postage and packaging, to *PO Box No 11, West Drayton, Middlesex*

In the United States: Please write to *Dept BA, Penguin, 299 Murray Hill Parkway, East Rutherford, New Jersey 07073*

In Canada: Please write to *Penguin Books Canada Ltd, 2801 John Street, Markham, Ontario L3R 1B4*

In Australia: Please write to the *Marketing Department, Penguin Books Australia Ltd, P.O. Box 257, Ringwood, Victoria 3134*

In New Zealand: Please write to the *Marketing Department, Penguin Books (NZ) Ltd, Private Bag, Takapuna, Auckland 9*

In India: Please write to *Penguin Overseas Ltd, 706 Eros Apartments, 56 Nehru Place, New Delhi, 110019*

In the Netherlands: Please write to *Penguin Books Netherlands B.V., Postbus 3507, NL–1001 AH, Amsterdam*

In West Germany: Please write to *Penguin Books Ltd, Friedrichstrasse 10–12, D–6000 Frankfurt/Main 1*

In Spain: Please write to *Alhambra Longman S.A., Fernandez de la Hoz 9, E–28010 Madrid*

In Italy: Please write to *Penguin Italia s.r.l., Via Como 4, I-20096 Pioltello (Milano)*

In France: Please write to *Penguin France S.A., 17 rue Lejeune, F-31000 Toulouse*

In Japan: Please write to *Longman Penguin Japan Co Ltd, Yamaguchi Building, 2–12–9 Kanda Jimbocho, Chiyoda-Ku, Tokyo 101*